GIVE YOUR CHILD A FUTURE

GIVE YOUR CHILD A FUTURE

John V. Gilmore and Eunice C. Gilmore

Prentice-Hall, Inc., Englewood Cliffs, New Jersey 07632

Give Your Child a Future
by John V. Gilmore and Eunice C. Gilmore
© 1982 by John V. Gilmore

Address inquiries to Prentice-Hall, Inc.
Englewood Cliffs, N.J. 07632
Printed in the United States of America
Prentice-Hall International, Inc., London
Prentice-Hall of Australia, Pty. Ltd., Sydney
Prentice-Hall Canada Inc. Toronto
Prentice-Hall of India Private Ltd., New Delhi
Prentice-Hall of Japan, Inc., Tokyo
Prentice-Hall of Southeast Asia Pte. Ltd., Singapore
Whitehall Books Limited, Wellington, New Zealand
10 9 8 7 6 5 4 3 2 1

ISBN 0-13-356964-0

ISBN 0-13-356956-X {PBK}

Library of Congress Cataloging in Publication Data

GILMORE, JOHN V.
    Give your child a future.
    Includes bibliographical references and index.
    1. Child rearing.   2. Children—Attitudes.   3. Self-
respect.   4. Academic achievement.   I. Gilmore, Eunice C.
II. Title.
HQ755.8.G53   649'.1   82-5373
ISBN 0-13-356964-0   AACR2
ISBN 0-13-356956-X (pbk.)

DEDICATED TO OUR CHILDREN

CONTENTS

"Productive love always implies a syndrome of attitudes; that of *care, responsibility, respect* and *knowledge.*"

Erich Fromm

PREFACE

In 1932, just out of college and facing the Great Depression, I secured a modest job teaching high school students in a small rural community amid the rolling hills of western Pennsylvania. I taught a little of everything, learning as much as did my pupils. Typically, the quality of their performance varied considerably. A few were my best, the vast majority only average students. In those days, if someone did poorly, it was considered to be either his own fault or the result of the currently popular notion of "individual differences" (in other words, the inheritance factor). Beyond that, no one really inquired.

With that five-year teaching stint I began nearly five decades of continuous involvement, in various capacities, on the educational scene. Throughout these years I have grappled with the question, "Why do some children succeed in school while others don't?"

In the late 1930s, in the process of meeting state requirements for certification as a school psychologist, I took a graduate course in the teaching of remedial reading. At that time, it was believed that improving reading would improve school grades. For several years I taught courses in the improvement of reading skills at various educational levels all the way from junior high school to graduate school. The results, in terms of actual gains in academic grades, were less than convincing. There was no real evidence that students who had taken the courses had any better grades than those who had not.

As my teaching duties brought me into contact with university students, the nagging question remained. If reading skill by itself was not significant, what really accounted for differences in academic success?

In 1944, I married Eunice Crocker, and she has been a partner and coworker in all my professional activities since that time.

Following World War II there was considerable investigation of the factors underlying normal personality development. I became especially intrigued with Abraham Maslow's studies of self-actualizing persons and his insistence that if psychologists were to make a major contribution to mental health, they should study the characteristics of outstanding individuals, the "champions" in various fields of endeavor.

In 1950, I was fortunate to be able to test Dr. Maslow's

suggestion in a study of the personality traits, parent-child relationships, and achievement levels of freshmen at Massachusetts Institute of Technology. My investigation found that the quality of students' answers on five items out of a 130-item sentence completion test ("At home we. . . .," "Father. . . .," "Mother. . . .," "One's parents. . . .," and "My family. . . .") could significantly predict the level of their academic grades at the end of the first semester. Here was statistical evidence, at least for this particular M.I.T. class, that one valid factor in their academic success was their perception of parents and family life.

The attempt to predict academic grades on the basis of the Freudian defense mechanisms was unsuccessful, indicating that although the importance of parents in psychoanalytic theory was validated by our research, our findings had revealed a different kind of parent-child relationship than psychoanalysts were finding in their patients. Freud was concerned with mental illness; he did not study productive people. The average M.I.T. student is an active, coping individual—not a defensive one. As a result of what we had learned, we proceeded to study the parental backgrounds of productive young people.

I then composed another sentence completion test comprised of significant items selected from the original instrument used at M.I.T. Over the next twenty years, graduate students at both doctoral and master's degree levels used this test, together with other measures, in studying student populations of all ages and from all educational and socioeconomic backgrounds. The results of these investigations corroborated the findings of the M.I.T. research: positive parent-child relationships were found to be associated with high achievement, poor ones with low achievement.

In private clinical practice during the 1950s, I specialized in adolescent academic problems. Finding it difficult to give meaningful help to my young clients directly, I began to talk with their parents. When the latter followed my advice to become more accepting and supportive with their teenagers, the grades of the latter usually improved perceptibly.

Although parents were helped by my recommendations, they expressed a need for more concrete practical suggestions to help them improve their parenting skills. The frequent comment was, "Don't tell me just to love my child. Tell me how to do it!" In response to these requests I composed *Suggestions for Parents*. This small booklet listed brief and specific *Do* and *Don't* guidelines designed to help parents improve relationships with their children, aiming to improve the latter's academic and social behavior. It has been used for the past fifteen years—largely in the New England area—by schools, organizations, and individual parents from all educational and socioeconomic backgrounds.

However, the precise dynamics involved in the relationship between parental attitudes and children's functioning remained unclear. The launching of Sputnik by the Soviet Union in 1957 precipitated a flood of investigations examining the nonintellectual factors involved in academic achievement. For a time the factor of "motivation" commanded considerable attention. This term appeared to differentiate levels of human accomplishment since it identified a willingness to work as an observable characteristic; yet it served chiefly to describe a symptom rather than explaining the actual cause of a need to achieve.

In 1964 I organized a graduate program at Boston University of Education that trained students in the Department of Counselor Education to become parent educators. During an eight-year period these trainees, using the *Suggestions* booklet and other materials, instructed approximately 500 parent pairs from diverse economic and educational levels.

The chief aim was enhancement of the child's self-esteem and improvement of his academic achievement. Every training program featured the use of experimental (trained) and control (untrained) parent groups. The children themselves were not involved.

To measure the effectiveness of the parental instruction, the children's grade averages at the end of the school year during which their parents received training were compared with their averages at the end of the previous year. Their grades were also compared with those of children in a control group, whose parents had not been trained.

During this eight-year period, approximately 80 percent of the children in the trained families significantly improved their academic records at the end of the school year in contrast to the children in the control groups. According to their parents' testimony, they also became happier, more skilled socially, more responsible, and even physically healthier. These studies included children from the first through the twelfth grades. Some follow-up studies conducted two and three years later indicated that these children maintained high grades, in some cases very high, as long as their parents continued to apply the child-rearing practices in which they had been instructed.

While supervising this research at Boston University, I surveyed the psychological and educational literature in the fields of academic achievement, scientific and artistic creativity, and leadership. Extensive reading in these three areas led progressively to one conclusion: All outstanding students, scholars, scientists, artists, and leaders have as their common distinguishing trait a desire to contribute to the welfare of society.

Other characteristics of such individuals emerged. As a group they possessed a sense of identity, excellent coping skills, and an attitude of social responsibility. Moreover, it became increasingly clear that these traits had been nurtured and developed within their family backgrounds.

The term self-esteem (roughly synonymous with self-confidence, self-image, etc.) was chosen as the preferred term to describe the predominant personality difference between high and low achievers in the three areas of scholarship, creativity, and leadership.

The following works have had particular influence on my thinking:

—The 1960 follow-up survey of Terman's Gifted Group (selected in 1922), which found that the more successful members had higher self-esteem as adults than the less successful, and that the greatest difference between the two groups was the parental encouragement during childhood of initiative, independence, and school achievement of the successful group;

—Otto Fenichel's *Psychoanalytic Theory of Neurosis* (1945), which brilliantly postulated the theoretical beginnings of self-esteem in the feeding experiences of infancy;

—The investigations of Rosenberg (1965) and Coopersmith (1967), which focused attention on the important role of parents in determining the level of self-esteem in both adolescent and elementary school populations;

—Laboratory experiments at the University of Pennsylvania under Aronfreed (1968), which demonstrated scientifically that feelings of empathy could be established in children by three simple "expressive cues": a smile, an affectionate word, and a hug.

We chose the term "productive" to describe the lives and accomplishments of outstanding individuals. If achievement is dependent on parent-child relationships, the labels "brilliant" and "gifted" (implying the influence of inheritance) are not suitable for application to the current method of identifying achievement in terms of output.

The result of this investigation was a textbook, *The Productive Personality* (San Francisco: Albion Publishing Company, 1974), which is a forerunner of our present book.

These discoveries have formed the basis of a parent training program which has continued, as time and money have permitted, throughout the past decade. In Wellesley, a suburb of Boston, I have taught small groups of parents without interruption under the auspices of the public schools. In 1978 questionnaires were distributed to all Wellesley families who had taken the courses during the preceding eight years. Ninety-four percent of the responding couples indicated that they were continuing to find the suggestions helpful in improving and sustaining the quality of their family life. They reported consistently high levels of both academic and social functioning in at least one of their children.

The program has also operated successfully in a different setting. In the fall of 1976 it was inaugurated in Mount Airy, North Carolina, an isolated rural-industrial community of 15,000 in the extreme northwest portion of the state. When questionnaires were distributed at the end of the first year, 75 percent of the responding couples reported that "all" of their children had improved substantially in schoolwork as a result of the parent training. Even more heartening was the revelation that 95 percent of the target children (those previously identified as underachievers) were functioning at an improved level.

A well-designed, audited research project conducted in North Carolina in 1979 under David Long has validated our hypothesis that the "magic triad" (the hug, the smile, and the affectionate word) increases children's self-esteem. Long also found that self-esteem was significantly related to improved academic achievement.

A recent doctoral thesis ("The Differential Effects of a Gilmore Self-Esteem and a S.T.E.P. Parent Counseling Approach for Low Achieving Latency Age Children" by Peter Esters, Boston University School of Education, 1980) found that our approach has improved children's self-esteem more effectively than the Dinkmeyer-McKay S.T.E.P. program (which combines the approaches to parent training of Rudolph Dreikurs and Thomas Gordon).

In view of the data accumulated from these studies, we felt that the information should be made available to parents. Writing a book for parents is an awesome responsibility; fathers and mothers have a right to expect that any manual for their use should meet the following requirements:

1. The recommendations should be based on a sound, accepted theory of personality development that deals with early parent-child relationships. We agree with Dr. Daniel Offer that "psychoanalytic theory comes the closest of all the theories to ex-

plain the integration of the physiological, intellectual, and psycho-social areas of child development." However, before this approach is recommended to parents, it should be validated.

2. The approach should deal with underlying causes rather than symptoms. (Increasing a child's self-esteem, for example, may solve a number of related problems such as learning difficulties, social adjustment, and even health ailments.)

3. The recommendations should be based on research and their effectiveness tested.

4. They should be simple, clear, direct, and easy to apply.

5. They should be suitable for use by parents of any educational or socioeconomic status.

6. The program should focus on developing the child's competencies and goals, hence preparing him for life's challenges and, incidentally, further enhancing his self-image.

7. The recommendations must also contribute to the parents' own self-esteem if they are to adopt them permanently. Nothing will encourage parents more than their child's scholastic success.

Give Your Child a Future attempts to meet all these requirements.

I wish to express utmost gratitude to my talented wife and co-author Eunice for her numerous contributions and editorial expertise. My special appreciation is also extended to David H. Long for his countless helpful and specific suggestions and his utmost devotion to the parent training program from its inception. Acknowledgement is also made to Phyllis Stock, Margaret Miner, and the editorial staff of Prentice-Hall for considerable editorial assistance throughout many months of the manuscript's preparation. The members of my training classes at the Gilmore Institute have likewise been very helpful.

We are deeply indebted to Frank Goble, president of the Thomas Jefferson Research Center, 1143 North Lake Avenue, Pasadena, California, for his steadfast interest and his enthusiastic commitment to bring this program to the attention of as many parents as possible. The Jefferson Center has assumed responsibility for the publicizing the program nationwide.

John V. Gilmore
Wellesley Hills, Massachusetts

GIVE YOUR CHILD A FUTURE

PARENTS, THE FIRST INFLUENCE

"The future holds little promise today for men and women who are not independent and interested in learning."

Joan Beck

A MESSAGE TO PARENTS

"What does the future hold for my child?"

It is never too soon to ask this question—which carries with it a flood of other questions—but we must ask it differently. How will my child cope with the future, adapt confidently and easily to the changed circumstances of the world thirty years hence? How will he or she retain a sense of long-range objectives? How will our future adults balance the myriad (and often, conflicting) demands of marriage, parental roles, and vocational obligations? How will they retain gentleness and compassion amid the pressures of the twenty-first century?

"How can my child do better in school?"

The key to tomorrow is the educational preparation of today. If you are conscientious parents you have probably asked this second question. You sense that your boys and girls can always do better, in or out of school. All of us, in fact, are capable of doing better.

"How can we be better parents?"

Man's character is his fate—so said the ancient philosopher.

1

Yet we need not be fatalists. Our children's future is in our hands now.

This book is addressed to you who are concerned with all of these questions. Its central focus is your children's self-esteem, the way they feel about themselves. It emphasizes your role as the chief source of that self-esteem from the time of their birth. It also demonstrates the close relationship between self-esteem and intellectual competence, healthy social development, physical and psychological well-being, and aspirations for future accomplishment. In brief, it is concerned with productive personality functioning.

Today's world is complex, technocratic, increasingly interdependent, and changing rapidly. It desperately needs competent, informed, and productive citizens and leaders to help solve its problems. There is a growing demand for people with highly specialized skills in all areas of human activity. By the turn of the century, children currently in grade school will be facing the tremendous challenges of a society that is quite different from ours today.

But more is needed than mere competence. Our sons and daughters will have to be broadly educated, alert, interested, and compassionately involved with the needs of others. They must be both competent and caring, able to perform their own jobs well and also capable of living in love and harmony with others. Moreover, if they become parents themselves, they must raise children who will continue to contribute to their own families, their neighborhoods, and the larger community.

Sigmund Freud summarized it well some years ago. He said that the healthy human being must be capable of two functions: *He or she must be able to love and to work.*

The task of nurturing children so they develop into such adults consumes many years. From the time they are infants, you are their first, most important, and most influential teachers. According to numerous authorities, you will lay the educational foundations of their lives before they even enter first grade.[1]

At about age six your youngsters step on the first rung of the long ladder of formal education. School represents their entry into a different and more competitive world. In school their teachers are not related to them or emotionally involved with them. From now on your children's progress will be evaluated and measured against that of their contemporaries. Their school accomplishments henceforth will be reflected in a permanent record representing not only their scholastic skills but also their ability to cope with and solve other kinds of problems. Periodically they will be subjected to standardized tests which place them on a statistical curve in relation to other girls and boys of similar age.

Why is formal schooling considered important? And what do we expect of our schools? There are two answers to these important questions.

First, school is expected to provide your child with systematic training in the development of intellectual skills. Reading, writing, logical thinking, and quantitative reasoning are indispensable for whatever trade, profession, or means of livelihood the child may later choose. Second, school should supply the child with knowledge and understanding of the surrounding world—its past, present, and future needs—to help him or her become a contributing citizen.

Schools cannot accomplish these vital tasks alone. Admittedly, some fulfill their functions better than others. In all cases, however, you as parents are key members of the educational team. You play two special roles in your children's development: you transmit a unique cultural heritage from your generation to theirs; and you provide them with steadfast, constant, and lasting emotional support. In addition, you should provide the schools with cooperation and support to help them attain their objectives.

But, you say, "Our children are no longer infants. They are already part-way through school. They're not doing very well, either. The teachers say they're just 'average.' What are we supposed to do now? There's too much water over the dam already. We're discouraged!"

The answer to this is loud and clear. *It is not too late at any age to bring about constructive change in your child's development.*

If teachers tell you that your child is "just average," don't be satisfied with their judgment. It is not enough these days to be an average child. By far the largest group of students in our schools today are those who could, with proper support, be doing better than they are. These young people are often overlooked because they appear to present no problem to teachers or administrators.

No one really knows the maximum level of a human being's ability. And no one has the right to refer to any individual as having average ability or to dismiss him as "doing his best." If you are really serious about your children's futures, it is within your power to raise the level of their present accomplishment, provided you are willing to apply—conscientiously, patiently, and persistently—a few tested psychological principles.

In addition to scholastic achievement, you probably also

desire other things for your sons and daughters. You want them to become socially competent and responsible, able to get along well with others. You also hope they will acquire other skills, in music or athletics, for example.

If you sincerely desire the best possible development for your children, you will gain immeasurably from applying the suggestions contained in this book.

What is first required of almost all parents whose children are faltering is a fundamental change in attitude. Criticism must be replaced with approval and support. Coldness and indifference must give way to empathy, warmth, interest, caring, firm expectations, and above all, long-range goals for your youngsters. You will need much patience and persistence. Results do not come immediately, but over a period of time you will begin to note small improvements. Your child may show unexpected thoughtfulness, or bickering with a brother or sister may lessen. Eventually, a commendable spelling or arithmetic paper comes home and the child's pride in accomplishment begins to surface. The change you have brought about in your youngster's psychological environment brings about a change in his or her performance.

A few additional comments about our approach should be noted.

● It is positive, developmental, and preventive rather than treatment for a particular problem.

● It provides you with background information on the normal course of children's personality development.

● Although suitable for use by parents of all age groups including adolescents, it is most appropriate for those whose youngsters are in elementary and early junior high school.

● This is not a "cookbook." There is no list of "recipes" to cover all situations and events. However, basic guidelines are defined in the simple Do's and Don't's at the end of each chapter. Specific applications are left to you, since you are most closely involved with your child.

● Our approach is not particularly concerned with raising your children's IQ, although their verbal ability should be enhanced as you improve their psychological and learning environments. This improvement may later show up in their performance on IQ tests.

Finally, this approach offers you two unexpected benefits. First, you will find that your efforts to express more affection and interest toward your children will not only heighten their own self-esteem but will also make it easier for you to fashion a warmer relationship with your youngsters. Second, as your children respond with improved functioning in various areas of life, including schoolwork, you will be encouraged to continue your efforts. In short, you will find that the process of changing fundamental attitudes is self-reinforcing.

It is to you who are willing to work for a brighter, more productive future for your children and for yourselves that this book is offered. You need much help in your demanding task.

WHO IS PRODUCTIVE?

We define a productive person as an individual who, through some expression of himself, contributes to those around him.[2] He can be a child as well as an adult.

We are inclined to think of productive adults only in terms of unusual contributions such as those of Beethoven, Shakespeare, Einstein, or Churchill. However, thousands of less well-known persons can be called productive. There is the dedicated worker in almost any field. There is the devoted parent. There is the responsible, achieving student contributing skills and energy to school activities.

Children function at different levels of productivity. Let us examine a typical adolescent population.

The highly productive students have certain attributes:

They have a sense of identity. They are comfortable with themselves; they know who they are and where they are going.

They are socially responsible and empathic toward others. They adhere to high moral and ethical principles.

They solve problems well. Efficient and independent, they organize details effectively, concentrate on difficult tasks for long periods of time. In brief, they know how to get things done.

Their life is oriented toward long-range goals. They are hopeful and optimistic as they progress toward their goals.

Students of low productivity are quite different:

They are often uncertain about their own identity and self-esteem.

They tend to be unreliable and confused in their social values.

They are dependent on their peers for support and attention.

They have weak coping skills and their work habits are poor. They may be impulsive and distractible.

They are easily discouraged and confront future challenges with despondency.[3]

Between these two extremes is a very large group of young people whose members are difficult to identify. They are neither highly productive nor suffering from serious academic or social problems. In effect they display a mixture of some personality strengths and some weaknesses.

They are not entirely sure of their identity. They tend to be somewhat self-conscious and to draw attention to themselves by dress and mannerisms.

Socially, they are oriented toward peers, although they are less peer-dependent than the unproductive group.

Their academic records fall within a broadly average range. Their coping skills are not seriously impaired but neither are they particularly effective.

They tend to live largely in the present, with long-range goals still rather poorly defined.

PRODUCTIVITY AND SELF-ESTEEM

Productive and unproductive individuals differ greatly in one critical characteristic: self-esteem. Productive children feel good about themselves because they are psychologically secure. Unproductive children are unhappy with themselves because they are unsure of the support of those around them.

Studies indicate that all individuals, of any age, must have high self-esteem if they are to cope effectively with the demands of the educational, social, and economic worlds. Imbedded in children's self-esteem is their sense of hope for the future. Those close to them must therefore give them continual assurance that their efforts will be recognized and rewarded.

The primary source of children's self-esteem is their parents' love. Youngsters must have absolute confidence that their fathers and mothers believe in, support, and deeply care about them. Without this confidence they will suffer from a prevailing sense of defeat and hopelessness that is characterized by a "What's the use?" attitude. If there is nothing to hope for, there is no reason to care, and hence no reason to take action.[4]

Self-esteem must be fostered from the time of birth. It requires constant renewal and reinforcement as long as the individual lives. It is enhanced by praise and acceptance and is lowered by criticism and expressed disapproval. It exists when parents, from their children's earliest years, have provided them affection, warmth, and support and have praised them as persons as well as for their accomplishments.

PRODUCTIVE AND UNPRODUCTIVE FAMILIES

What distinguishes the home life of a highly productive, successful child from that of an underachiever or school dropout?

Research has identified the following factors typically present in highly productive families:[5]

There is usually a stable marriage in which the parents are mutually supportive of each other.

Maturity, good emotional health, and responsibility characterize both marriage partners.

There is agreement between spouses on basic values, ethical principles, and family goals.

The family is closely knit; communication is warm and spontaneous.

Father and mother play equally prominent and supportive roles.

Affection and encouragement are continually expressed toward all family members.

An interest in education and constant encouragement of all educational endeavors are evident.

The family as a unit has excellent coping skills.

Discipline and effective family organization arise from essentially democratic principles. Discipline is consistent and fair.

Firm parental expectations of children's accomplishments direct youngsters toward realistic long-range goals.

The homes of unproductive children present a different picture. Children with learning problems, children who are not socially responsible, and children who suffer from identity confusion, drug use, or psychosomatic complaints usually come from homes with such characteristics as these:[6]

Husband and wife tend to function not as teammates but as rivals or opponents.

The parents may be immature and insecure themselves.

They often disagree on major and minor issues.

They tend to be unempathic, cold, and critical.

The father is apt to be weak in leadership and unconcerned about his children's success in school.

Parents may be autocratic and inclined to use physical punishment as a means of discipline.

Parents typically emphasize obedience, conformity, and social relationships with peers as their priorities.

The family seems satisfied with short-term goals.

It is such homes that produce children with low self-esteem, poorly developed intellectual skills, and limited productivity.

THE ROLES OF MOTHER AND FATHER

Fathers and mothers play both separate and joint roles in rearing their families. Traditionally these roles have been differentiated. Mother's chief responsibility was to give physical care and affection to the children and to maintain an orderly household. Father's primary task was to provide economic security. These roles have rapidly been changing.

Over half of all mothers of school-aged children are now employed outside the home. Many work at full-time jobs throughout the year; some hold important professional positions; some work in a variety of part-time but nevertheless demanding jobs.

Such mothers—particularly those working full-time and without household help—face enormous stresses. The demands of the job, tight schedules, household chores, the difficulty of finding adequate care for the children, and most of all, the responsibilities of truly effective parenting all take a physical and emotional toll.

In these circumstances, one fact is obvious. *Father can no longer assume that his role in the family is merely that of a provider.*

Just how parents share the duties and responsibilities of a loving and productive family life will depend on career or professional obligations of each spouse as well as many other factors unique to their situation. Although conscientious husband–wife teams attempt to divide all tasks evenly, such as household maintenance and shopping trips, it is usually impossible to avoid having the mother more involved with domestic concerns than the father. Whatever the schedule, though, children's needs should be given priority. Parents must arrange their time to ensure that one or the other is available for storytelling, bedtime routines, helping with number facts, trips to the orthodontist, transportation to music lessons (and appreciation of the young student's efforts), Little League baseball games, friends' birthday parties—an endless list.

Fathers and mothers should make a point of spending time alone with their individual children so that they can become acquainted with the special skills, expressed interests, styles of coping, and special preferences of each. Current research seems to indicate that children's verbal ability is related to the mother's warmth, communication, encouragement, and early intellectual stimulation, although this finding may be subject to modification depending on the special interests and professional orientation of each spouse.[7] Development of analytic and quantitative thinking appears to come from the father. The father's presence, concern, and nurturance have been found to be related to high achievement in children of both sexes.[8]

Parenting is a demanding, 24-hour-a-day, seven-day-a-week job, especially for the adult who is confined more closely to home during the early childhood years. It is desirable for each parent to have a regular change of routine. If both are working, this can be extremely difficult to arrange; nevertheless it is very helpful. Perhaps there can be "time off" on Saturdays for one spouse, with the other taking temporary charge of the household. After a long, hard week on the job, Mom may need to hightail it to the tennis court for a morning while Dad takes over dishes, laundry, home chores, and children. He and the children can do these jobs together, and there will be much friendly chatter between him and his offspring as well as a chance to catch up with serious events in each other's lives. Weather permitting, Mom can reciprocate by letting her husband get away for an occasional Saturday afternoon round of golf or a chance to catch up on personal errands. Each parent's need for a regular change of routine is best provided by the other spouse, who in turn will relish the opportunity of additional friendly companionship with the growing youngsters.

There is encouraging evidence that the general perception of the father's role is changing. Many of our younger men are deeply involved with their wives in the entire pregnancy and delivery experience, to the tremendous enrichment of the lives they share with each other and with their offspring. There are rich rewards for all men who, perhaps unlike their own fathers, are taking the time and energy for specific caretaking and emotional involvement with their youngsters.

THE SINGLE PARENT

In countless homes today one adult, whether widowed, separated, or divorced, is obliged to play a dual parental role. It is a most difficult assignment. Nevertheless, thousands of mothers (and fathers) are attempting to shoulder this enormous responsibility alone.

It is difficult for one adult alone to supply the diverse experience and constant support that two can give. In addition, the single parent lacks the regular backup help available to married partners.

Yet it is well within the reach of a single parent to rear a productive child. Many are doing an outstanding job of it. The task is easier when certain conditions exist. Some of these consist of the individual's own assets and strengths; others are found in the environment.

> *Personal assets.* The most effective single parent is a strong, stable, and levelheaded individual who clearly understands the requirements of good parenting. Determination, commitment, imagination, and resourcefulness are also needed. And it helps if the single parent enjoyed good parental models in his or her own background.

> *Education, training, and job status.* The single parent who is equipped to work in a relatively secure and meaningful occupation is usually happier and more supportive than one who is not. He or she derives a sense of pride, self-esteem, and fulfillment from work outside the home, and this feeling provides a source of strength within the family.

> *Flexible working hours and/or a part-time work schedule.* Flexible working hours and/or, if possible, part-time work are

ideal for the single parent. Part-time work is less draining on one's time, energy, and emotional resources. The children are provided with the security of the parent's presence in the home.

Grandparents. Grandparents who live nearby and are in good health are likely to be sympathetic, understanding, and supportive baby-sitters and surrogate parents. They have a special stake in the children's optimum development.

Other adults. An unmarried aunt or uncle, a kind neighbor or friend, or another single parent in similar circumstances are other possible sources of regular or emergency assistance. Any levelheaded, sympathetic adult can serve as a regular sounding board in the discussion of problems.

Groups and organizations. A church or synagogue can offer the occasional help of its professional staff. Wisely led organizations of single parents can be another resource, provided they are more than mere dating bureaus.

A sex-role model for children in the one-parent home. Children who are growing up in a one-parent home should have opportunities for some form of companionship with adults of the opposite sex. Big brother or big sister organizations may be able to help. Failing this, someone in the extended family can play this supportive role.

Child-care facilities. Currently, a small but growing number of business and educational institutions are providing day-care facilities for children of employees, administrative staffers, and university faculty and students.[9] Some have instituted a voucher system by which employees are provided the means of financing care of their children in private, qualified facilities. The demand for improved and far more widely available day care is a public concern of the utmost urgency.

If one or more of these supports are available to a single parent, the task of rearing productive children will be easier. Without any of them, the parent faces a very difficult task.

There is nothing new about single parenthood. A century or more ago death from disease, accident, shipwreck, war, or childbirth resulted in many widows and widowers. Children in these homes nevertheless grew and flourished under the loving care and guidance of the surviving parent or other adults, often under conditions of economic deprivation and hardship. In fact, sometimes it is easier for one devoted and single-minded parent to raise productive children alone than in the company of an uncaring, selfish, and uncooperative spouse. The emotionally divorced couple who are continuously at war with one another provide at best a poor environment for the development of their offspring.

It is beyond the scope of this book to deal with the many issues surrounding the single parent's situation today. Currently counsel is available from a wide variety of sources. However, the advice in this book is certainly applicable to the single-parent family.

In the last analysis, success at the parenting job rests upon qualities within the individual: self-confidence, steadfast devotion to the children, and persistent determination.

BUILDING A PRODUCTIVE CHILD: A PRESCRIPTION

The prescription for rearing productive children is simple though demanding:

● Provide them from an early age with a warmly affectionate and accepting environment.

● Stimulate their curiosity about the world around them.

● Foster their acquisition of basic learning skills in every way possible.

● Maintain high expectations for their future development and achievement.

● Finally, give them lifelong reinforcement, praise, and encouragement.

The result? Children, and later adults, equipped to cope with the demands of school and society.

The following chapters contain suggestions to help parents attain these objectives.

2

SEVEN CHILDREN

In this and the next chapter we will describe the lives, personalities, and backgrounds of seven children. The characters and situations that emerge are essentially composites based on individual children with whom we have worked as well as on material drawn from various studies on similar children in similar families. For convenience, we will place all the children in the same school system at the same time, although one came from a different state and they were not all contemporaries.

The sources of these composites are numerous. For the past 25 years we have observed and studied children's personalities, social characteristics, and coping skills as well as a great variety of family backgrounds and parent–child interactions that have produced different outcomes in children's lives—some more successful than others. Our information has come from acquaintances, professional colleagues, graduate students in training to be parent educators, interviews with several hundred private clients, and close study of the professional literature. A further source has been our empirical study several years ago of M.I.T. students achieving at three different levels; the study examined their personality traits and attitudes toward parents.[1]

The distinguishing characteristics of each of the following young people are typical of their real-life counterparts, some highly productive and others less so. As was pointed out in the previous chapter, high achievers have certain common personality and coping traits while average and low achievers have others.

We will introduce these seven youngsters in two groups. Five are described as functioning at various levels of productivity. The remaining two are children of parents who, under the guidance of our educational program, made some fundamental changes in their attitudes and child-rearing practices which in turn wrought changes in their youngsters' lives and prospects.

DIFFERENT LEVELS OF PRODUCTIVITY

Steve, a Successful Senior

Seventeen-year-old Steve is vice-president of his class, a member of the student council, and an honor-roll student carrying a full load of college preparatory courses, including two at the advanced-placement level. Steve is also on the varsity tennis team and in the woodwind section of the high school orchestra. His leadership of the youth group at his church consumes some of his time on weekends. For the past two summers he has worked with underprivileged boys in a nearby fresh air camp and plans to return to the same job during the coming season. An essay he wrote for a local contest received first prize for its thoughtful and mature grasp of pressing social problems. Steve has a wide circle of friends—both boys and girls—and a couple of special buddies. He dates occasionally but doesn't get involved. He is always on the go, full of energy, enthusiastic, alert, and eager to tackle problems. He is also widely respected by teachers, fellow students, and friends. Steve seems to have everything going for him. He has just been accepted by three of the top colleges in the country. After graduation, he plans to attend law school and possibly enter government work.

Steve is the second boy in a family of two boys and one girl. His older brother, a sophomore at a large university, and his ninth-grade sister are both able students who have numerous outside interests and have also enjoyed some leadership positions in school. Both parents are college graduates; his father is progressing upward in a large insurance firm and his mother is chief librarian at the high school.

Ned, an Easygoing Junior

Ned is coasting along in a somewhat happy-go-lucky fashion at the end of his junior year of high school. The guidance office records show that his mental ability is well above average, but his grades hover in the C to C-minus range and he is on the verge of flunking French. After school Ned can be found with his gang in the school parking lot or the local hangout. He comes home at irregular and unpredictable hours. He works about fifteen hours a week at the local gas station. At home the tube and his electric guitar occupy much of his time. He's not much of a reader although he occasionally looks through *Sports Illustrated*. In the fourth and fifth grades he had special help every week at the school reading center.

Ned often spends weekends at a friend's house, where there is beer at hand and usually no adults around on Saturday evening. Apart from his guitar and his friends, Ned has few interests, little concern about developing any special skills, and virtually no vocational goals. When his parents attempt to limit his nights out, he complains about not having enough "fun." He missed the deadline for registering for the Scholastic Aptitude Test and is not certain that he wants any more education after high school.

Ned's father left college at the end of his freshman year and went to work. Now he's treasurer of a small manufacturing company located in a neighboring town. Prior to her marriage his mother was trained as a secretary; she is now office manager in the local electric company. Ned's older sister, who attended junior college for one year, is married and living away from home. The parents bowl regularly on Friday evenings with their league and are faithful members of a weekly bridge club. His father also directs the Community Fund drive each year.

Mary, an Ambitious Sophomore
Tenth-grade Mary has been immersed in scientific pursuits for the past several years. A consistent honor-roll student, she is healthy, energetic, and busy with a few committees and projects in which she is interested. Mary's special love is her research project in biology, to which she has devoted every spare moment for the past few months and which she is about to present at the high school science fair (her teacher considers this project outstanding). She plans to continue her involvement in the sciences, enter a premedical program in college, and then attend medical school. Mary has many friends of both sexes, although she is still a little shy about dating. Because her parents have other children to support and educate, Mary will need substantial scholarship help for college. She works fifteen hours a week at the local supermarket and full-time during vacations.

Mary is the third child in a family of four. One older brother is in college on a scholarship, the other an honor student in the twelfth grade. Her younger sister is doing well in the sixth grade. Mary's parents finished high school. Her father is employed as manager of a local hardware store in which her mother works part-time.

Bert, an Average Sixth-Grader

Bert's schoolwork leaves something to be desired. On tests of general ability he ranks in the upper 20 percent of his class, yet his teacher complains that he gets his assignments in late and seems to need a good deal of help. A slow reader, he views book reports and special research projects with some distaste. Though he's fairly good at arithmetic, his papers are somewhat spotty.

Bert is good-natured, fun-loving, and popular on the playground. He's always available for touch football after school. At home he tends to gravitate to his favorite TV programs (often at the expense of completing his homework properly) and needs frequent reminders to do his share of household chores.

Bert is the youngest of three children. His older sister is a sophomore in a four-year liberal arts college, and an older brother is a junior in high school. His father, an accountant, is an active member of the town's finance committee. His mother, who works for a local real estate firm, participates in the activities of the Women's Guild at the church. Both enjoy a fairly active social life. They are pleasant people with an easygoing attitude toward academic matters, school included.

Jill, a Fourth-Grade Dynamo

Fourth-grade Jill seems to be perpetually in motion. Schoolwork comes easily to her; she gets it done fast (and correctly, too). Jill is enthusiastic about her numerous after-school activities: Girl Scouts, chorus, softball. Once a week or so she lugs home an armful of library books and is well on the way to becoming an omnivorous reader. Jill is popular on the school playground; she seems to be adept at organizing impromptu games and helping to arbitrate minor disputes. People wonder where she gets her energy and general competence, her ability to be "good at everything."

Jill is the middle child in a family of five—two boys and three girls. Her father, who never finished high school, is a clerk in the local post office. He's active in the Baptist church, where he also serves as part-time custodian. Jill's mother, a licensed practical nurse, works at a nearby nursing home. Her oldest brother is attending engineering school on a full scholarship from the United Negro College Fund. Her second oldest brother is a good sixth-grade student and her younger sisters are doing well in the lower grades.

TWO LIVES THAT WERE CHANGED

Sometimes parent education can make a big difference in a child's life. Here are Dan and Adam.

Dan, a Determined Ninth Grader

Although he is now an excellent student, Dan was not always as successful as he is today. A creative and independent thinker and a class leader, he is also on the freshman football team. Carpentry is his special hobby and he's worked hard at remodeling his parents' basement. Dan wants to become an architect.

Dan is the youngest of four children. His sister, a college graduate, now works for a well-known magazine and his two older brothers are in college. His sister and one of his brothers were voted the outstanding students of their respective graduating classes. Both parents are college graduates. His father is a businessman and his mother is interested in community affairs.

Dan's scholastic record in elementary school was mediocre and somewhat inconsistent. In grade four, for example, he earned an A in social studies because he liked it, but averaged a "gentleman's C" in everything else. At this time he was somewhat impulsive and careless in his homework (particularly arithmetic), a bit restless and inattentive in class, slightly above average in height and weight, somewhat self-conscious, and troubled with mild hay fever during the summer. He liked having a good time with his friends and was too attached to the television set for his own good. He was what might be called just an average child.

At the beginning of his fifth-grade year Dan's parents, sensing that he might not become as successful as his older sister and brothers, were concerned about his development. They joined one of our courses, which was then being offered at Dan's elementary school. During the course they took a good look at his situation and came to realize that, quite unintentionally, they were taking their youngest child somewhat for granted. They began to give Dan the same kind of attention, support, and encouragement that their three older children had received. In particular, Dan's father began to spend more time with him. The results were quickly evident. Dan became more attentive in class, more interested in schoolwork, more confident. He completed a long outside report and his teacher praised him for doing an excellent job. By year's end he had attained a B average. In sixth grade he was elected president of his class and his grades improved still further. In junior high school he played on the soccer team and maintained a high honor-roll average. His hay fever gradually subsided. Dan began to think about going to college. He has continued to make excellent progress ever since.

Adam, a Thriving Ten-Year-Old

Adam is also doing well in school. He has made particular improvement during the past year and is now getting A's and B's in all his fourth-grade subjects. Popular with his friends, Adam likes to engage in impromptu wrestling and football after school. He belongs to the local Boy Scout group and sings in the children's choir at church. His 11-year-old sister and 7-year-old brother are also doing well. Adam has recently decided that he is going to work very hard from now on. He likes arithmetic and wants to become an engineer. His sister, also good at math, wants to go into computer science.

At the time we first heard of Adam's case, his mother had been recently divorced. A high school graduate, she was supporting her family by working as a floor supervisor in a local textile plant. The family lived in a two-bedroom apartment in a federal housing project. The children seldom saw or heard from their father. The family's resources were tight; they had to watch every penny.

During the first three grades Adam experienced some difficulties in school. Both before and during the separation and divorce of his parents there were many problems in his home. But Adam's mother, an intelligent, conscientious woman, was determined that her children would become successful students. During Adam's third-grade year she joined one of our courses, and since then she has devoted all her spare time and energy to her children, with outstanding results. Adam's schoolwork and that of his sister and brother have improved markedly. All three are now happy, working hard, and doing well.

COMPARISONS

These seven students attend the same school system. Steve, Mary, Ned, and Dan often pass each other in the high school corridors; they have been taught by some of the same teachers. Bert, Jill, and Adam are in the same elementary school; their parents sometimes meet at PTA meetings or occasionally on the street.

IQ scores of these seven children do not differ markedly. There are, however, differences in their performance. Steve, Mary, Dan, Adam, and Jill emerge as creative, happy, healthy, and productive individuals. Bert is a typical C student whose family has somewhat limited expectations for his future development and performance. Ned has a variety of problems, some of which are not being recognized by his family.

These young people differ from one another in three areas of personality functioning: (1) their perception of themselves (their self-image or self-concept), (2) their competence in solving problems (which is reflected in their performance of tasks in and out of school), and (3) their attitudes toward others (their sense of social responsibility).

What causes these differences? Why are some students more secure in self-image, more competent and achieving in school, and happier?

The causes of these differences lie with the parents and the atmosphere in the homes. Our next task, then, is to study the values, concerns, and goals that distinguish the parents of highly successful young people like Steve, Mary, Dan, Adam, and Jill from those that characterize the less successful families of Bert and Ned. These differences will be discussed in the next chapter.

SEVEN FAMILIES

This chapter consists of anecdotes from the family lives of the children introduced in Chapter Two. The situations and conversations are based on events which we have observed directly as professionals (and as parents ourselves) as well as on events reported by other professional observers and by parents in our classes.

We will focus on the almost universally problematic issues of television viewing, homework, discipline, money management, dating, and other social activities. The ways that these families cope with these issues reflect a characteristic variety of parental attitudes toward school achievement, the acquisition of special skills, and views of their children's potential roles in the future. They reveal different styles of parent–child communication and interaction and the results that arise from these differences.

In the following pages we will imagine ourselves as observing various domestic scenes. The situations are consistent with what we know about children and families functioning at different levels of productivity. Like the children themselves, both families and scenes have many counterparts in real life.

A VISIT TO THE HOMES

Communication

It's suppertime at Steve's house. His father has just come in from work. "Dad's home!" shouts Steve to his sister. The two of them take turns chatting with Dad about the school day. The chemistry test wasn't too bad, the basketball game went well. Ned's father, on the other hand, claims he's too tired to talk when he gets home. Stretching out in his big chair in the television room, he yawns, "I'll listen to you after I've had a drink and seen the news."

Sometimes Steve's father has to work evenings and he doesn't get home for dinner. But he always telephones. He gets a big kick out of talking with his children when he's all alone in the office. Ned's father sometimes works evenings, too. He thinks calling home is a nice idea but usually he's "too busy."

Adam's mother tries to write a letter to each of her three children every week. Her little handwritten notes are not models of good grammar or punctuation, but they are warm, sincere, and full of appreciation of her children and their accomplishments. The children cherish these notes. Adam carries his around in his coat pocket for days.

Bert's father, whose office associate sometimes drops a line to his youngsters, thinks letter writing is a little silly. "Bert's too young to get letters from his father. My father never wrote to me until I was in the Army. Anyhow, why should I write him when I see him every day?"

The Marriage Relationship
Dan comes home from school one afternoon to find his mother unwrapping some roses. A note from his father says, "Happy Birthday to me!" Puzzled, Dan asks his mother why Dad sends her flowers every year when it isn't either of their birthdays. Mother explains. "Dad always says he was 'born' the day he met me, and this is his way of celebrating. Isn't he thoughtful? It means a lot to both of us."

Bert, a sixth-grade pal of Jill's older brother, has spent the afternoon at her house. While there he heard Jill's father tell her mother that he loved her. At supper he describes this scene at home, confronting his Daddy with "I never hear you tell Mom that. Why?" "Well," replies Dad, a little sheepishly, "I've told your Mother I loved her. I'm not the sort of person who can keep repeating it."

Enjoyment of Family Leisure
Dan's familiy, all avid hikers and campers, often backpack on trails for four or five days at a time. His mother says they love the experience of getting away together in the out-of-doors. Ned's father dislikes hiking, sees no point in it.

In Mary's family "eating out" is viewed as a special treat, especially when it becomes each child's turn to go out alone with Mom or Dad. To Ned's query as they are leaving school together on a

Friday afternoon, Mary proudly responds, "Tonight I have a dinner date with Daddy." "Aw, gee!" exclaims Ned. "I wish my father would take me out to dinner. He never does anything like that. Sometimes when he and my mother go out for dinner they ask me if I want to come along. I always say 'No' because if I go, I don't have anyone to talk to."

Adam's mother cannot afford to take her children out to dinner at restaurants, but on weekends she and the children often pack a picnic lunch and go on a little outing in the park.

Leaving school on Friday afternoon, Ned and Steve are discussing weekend plans. Ned proposes that they take in a movie that evening. Steve, explaining that he's not free, says, "This is the night we have our special family dinner. We never make any other plans that night. Mom gets out the candles. I'm going home to make the dessert. See you Monday!" Ned recalls rather ruefully that his mother once had candles on the dinner table. At the end of the meal his father had said, "I hope you don't have any more candles. I want to see what I'm eating."

Encouragement of Reading
From the time Steve, Mary, and Jill were toddlers they were read to regularly at bedtime (Mary's mother remembers reading *Winnie the Pooh* until they knew it by heart). All three of these children knew their alphabet by the time they were three or four years old, and they could pick out and identify many printed words before they entered first grade. All, according to their parents, are now avid readers. Word games are also popular in these families. Jill tells her friends how much she enjoys beating her mother at Scrabble.

Ned's mother is annoyed that he seems so indifferent to reading. She has recently commented that they didn't teach him to read before he went to school. ("We heard it might cause trouble in the first grade.") She might have added that when Ned was a little fellow, she and her husband didn't get around to reading to him very often. They have been telling Ned for years that he should read something besides the sports page. They're also trying to get him to read *Time* magazine but he doesn't seem to be interested. "Oh, well!" sighs his mother. "I've always heard that boys don't read as much as girls anyway—isn't that right?"

Parental Attitudes Toward Schoolwork
While Bert is playing with Jill's older brother at Jill's house, he catches sight of the refrigerator door in the kitchen. It's a somewhat chaotic mass of papers. Jill explains that it serves as a bulletin

board: "Mom puts up our tests and the things we do at school so everybody in the family can see." Bert goes home and asks his Mom if she'll do the same for him. A little doubtful of the effect on her neat kitchen, Mom says, "Can't you find some other place for them?"

Ned and Steve are comparing marks on recent tests. Steve is disappointed with his B minus in chemistry. He tells Ned that he's talked the matter over with his father, who has reassured him by saying, "That's all right, Steve. I'm sure the next test will go better." Ned, having just received a B minus in biology, reacts bitterly. "Here I got a B minus for once, and I was hoping my father would say something nice about it. He didn't say a word." Ned feels his Dad never praises him for anything. "I guess I never do anything good as far as he's concerned!"

Ninth-grade Dan, upset by an unusually low grade he's received on a history quiz, has discussed the matter at home. His Dad felt the situation serious enough to warrant a talk with the teacher. The teacher explained that grades on that quiz had been low for all the students. Feeling partly to blame, she had already decided not to count them in the final averages. Dan was reassured by this explanation and especially by his father's support and concern.

Although Ned's school grades are generally mediocre and, in the case of French, close to outright failure, his father refuses to become involved. "I'm not going to fight Ned's battles for him. It's up to him to go talk with the teacher. I told him to come to me with his math but he never does. Well, it's *his* problem. Sometime he's going to have to stand on his own feet and he'd better begin right now."

The night before a big biology test Mary asks if Mom will listen to her go over her notes. Mother says, "Of course, dear. When would you like to do it?" On another evening Ned asks his Dad where he can get information for a report on Roosevelt's Four Freedoms. Dad replies curtly, "Why don't you look them up in the encyclopedia yourself?"

Adam's mother realizes she must keep in close touch with his schoolwork. She enjoys meeting frequently with his teacher. It means a lot to Adam to know his mother cares so much about his work at school.

Events at School
The annual science fair is very important. Mary's father and mother are always on hand to view her exhibit, which often wins a prize. Dan's father invariably attends the ninth-grade football game so he can cheer his son on at right halfback. Jill's mother tries to be in the

audience whenever the elementary school chorus presents a little program.

Ned does not participate in either athletics or music. Once he was in the gym show, but his parents didn't attend because it was their regular evening for bowling.

Nonacademic Skills

Steve, now on the high school tennis team, has fond memories of learning the game in past years: hitting balls with a small-sized racket as they were tossed to him in the driveway, rallying with Mom or Dad on an unused public court as a 6-year-old, attending his first tennis classes at age nine. Now he receives considerable coaching on the high school team and often beats his Dad.

Ned's father wishes he were more of an athlete. "I wanted to teach him how to play tennis when he was little but he was always out playing with his friends."

Dan's father taught him how to play chess when he was ten. Over the years they have enjoyed the game on vacations and holidays. Dan has developed a considerable amount of skill, and he usually wins handily over his Dad.

Bert's father would like to teach Bert how to play chess, but somehow they never seem to get around to it.

Steve's mother, reminiscing about early musical activities in their home, recalls how she would put *Stars and Stripes Forever* on the record player and let 3-year-old Stevie beat time lustily on a small drum. There was always a lot of singing in the home, especially when the children were little. When Steve was eight, he enjoyed a year of piano lessons, and a year later he began study of the clarinet.

In Ned's house there has been little interest in music. When he was nine, they started him on piano lessons. His mother says, "He said he wanted to take lessons but we told him if he didn't practice we weren't going to pay for them." About a month later Ned had lost interest in practicing and the lessons were discontinued.

Attitudes Toward the Future

Mary's parents, neither of whom went to college, have encouraged all their children to get as much education and training as possible so they can make a real contribution to society when they grow up. Mary's interest has always been science. She can remember that from the time she was a little girl, she would search for interesting rocks, plants, and bugs which she brought home for her numerous collections. She also recalls the day trips her family made to the science museum in the neighboring city, the library books on scientific subjects she brought home, the stories she read about people—especially women—in scientific careers, the do-it-yourself projects she worked on in the basement, and especially the fact that her parents were *always* interested. "Mary plans to be a doctor," says her father.

Ned's father tells his friends that Ned can be anything he wants to be and they'll support him in his choice of work. "But," he adds, "It's up to him. He'll have to pay for some of his training." Though now in his junior year, Ned has no idea what he wants to do after school. He hasn't taken the Scholastic Aptitude Test. His father doesn't know whether he plans to attend college but hopes that by the end of the semester, or during his senior year, he'll come to some decision. "I told him to go to the guidance department and get some help." Ned is obviously just drifting at present.

When Bert is asked what he would like to be when he grows up, he says he hasn't the slightest idea. He's more concerned with having fun at the present time.

Attitudes Toward Money

Steve's father maintains that unless it's absolutely necessary, students shouldn't work at paid jobs on school days. These are years when they should be focusing their energies on compiling a good academic record, developing various skills, and contributing to school and community life. Steve is saving his summer earnings at a fresh air camp for general college expenses. He takes an occasional weekend baby-sitting job. He's learned to manage his monthly allowance carefully. If special financial problems arise, he and his parents talk them over.

Mary's situation is somewhat different. Her father says, "All four of our youngsters are ambitious and plan to go to college. They know they'll have to help." Mary's older brother is already in college on a scholarship. The three older children (including Mary) all work part-time and are banking everything they can. This, of course, means some sacrifices. Mary has had to give up basketball and working for the school magazine this year. Her homework and her job at the supermarket are all she can handle.

Ned works about fifteen hours a week at the local gas station. His parents don't know exactly how much he earns or how he spends it. His father, who hasn't given him an allowance since seventh grade, says, "He's supposed to earn his spending money." Ned has always had a paper route or some other small job. He and his parents seldom talk about money. His mother thinks he's saving to buy a car his senior year. His Dad, who has always encouraged him to work, says, "There's nothing like the experience of earning money."

Finances are handled carefully in Jill's family. She says her parents give her a small allowance each week. They've agreed what it is to cover and she can't ask for any more until the next weekend. Bert's story is a bit different. Although his father is a professional accountant, money is handled rather casually at home. Bert gets no regular allowance. His mother gives him a quarter when he asks for money and his father slips him a dollar bill sometimes. It's fairly obvious that Bert isn't getting much training in money management.

Organization of Family Activities

There are five busy people in Steve's household. In order to coordinate their lives and schedules to some degree, they've resorted to a weekly family council meeting. The children take an active part in these sessions: they make suggestions on how to keep things running smoothly; they formulate rules and, more importantly, help to enforce them. During the school year the meetings are quite regular and the agenda is usually full. Household chores, special commitments for the coming week, transportation problems, possible conflicts of schedules, even next summer's vacation plans are all reviewed regularly. Steve's parents are pleased with the way the council operates. His mother says, "We find we aren't nearly as bossy during the rest of the week."

Ned's father once thought of having family meetings, but he didn't work very hard at it. Recently he called a meeting for a certain Sunday evening. The two children were not enthusiastic about it. They were sure he would spend the meeting lecturing them. Ned's older sister knew something about Roberts Rules of Order and she devised, with her brother, a plan to sabotage the affair: after their father called the meeting to order, Ned made a motion to adjourn and his sister seconded it, and that was the end of the meeting. Their father was so disgusted with them that he never tried it again.

Television

"About six years ago," says Mary's mother, "we talked the whole TV situation over. It hasn't really been any problem since." The children decided they just didn't have time to watch during the week.

Although exceptions were to be made for certain special programs, the children are usually too busy to watch them. By common agreement, Sunday television viewing was eliminated because it was interfering with family conversations and projects.

Bert's mother admits that television is a headache in their house. However, she has had little or no success in controlling the problem. Last year Bert was told he could watch after he had "finished" his homework. It seemed that he always managed to get through his last assignment in time for his favorite program. When his parents were out, the set usually stayed on all evening. The arrival of final school grades at the end of the year precipitated a family scene. Yet, despite his parents' objections, Bert has wheedled them into permitting him to continue last year's arrangement.

Social Life

Adam loves to go to Boy Scouts. He enjoys singing in the children's choir on Sundays. He plays sandlot football with his buddies.

"We've never worried about our children's social life," says Dan's mother. Dan is busy with football practice all fall, and the Student Council activities and his church youth group take up the rest of his spare time. Dan knows a lot of people but he has time for only a few special friends. His parents know them, chat on the phone when they call, and occasionally run into them downtown. For the most part, Dan seems to enjoy being with his family.

Ned's parents have a different attitude. His mother says, "His father feels that friends are important in the business world and Ned should know how to cultivate them." Ned goes out Friday and Saturday evenings with his gang. Sometimes they congregate at someone's house; at other times they just sit in a car with beer and cigarettes. Ned's parents, who know little about the other boys or their families, worry about the gang's possible use of marijuana and other drugs. But they think Ned needs his "social life."

Community Affairs

Nearly every year someone asks Steve's father if he will run for the school board or the city council. His reply has always been, "When my youngest child is a junior in college, I'll consider it." Until then he feels he can't take time and energy either from his family or his company, his two essential responsibilities for the present. His first obligation to the community is to develop as fine a family as possible. The fathers and mothers of Mary and Dan receive similar requests, but they too limit themselves to short-term assignments such as temporary committees. They are glad to help but are careful not to become too involved in major, time-consuming responsibilities.

Ned's father, on the other hand, has directed the Community Fund for the last three years and has recently agreed to chair a committee that is planning a new community center. Bert's father spends considerable time on work for the town finance committee.

CONCLUSION

There are obviously some contrasts in the life-styles of these seven families, and some of the children are more successful than others. Let us examine some fundamental differences in the atmosphere of the various homes and in the attitudes and values of the parents concerning education.

The Productive Families

The families of Steve, Mary, Dan, and Jill have basic strengths and general traits of good emotional health that have already been mentioned in Chapter One: strong and stable marriages, shared values, warmth of communication, affectionate and supportive relations with their children, and aspirations toward high future goals. Although Adam's mother is forced to rear her family alone, she is bravely providing her youngsters with a similar environment.

In these families there is also specific evidence of a steadfast parental commitment to the children's intellectual and educational development. This is illustrated by such practices as the following:

● The parents devoted considerable time to their children's informal preschool education, thus giving them the basis of the learning skills that are necessary for high performance in school.

● Both mothers and fathers, no matter how busy, follow their children's daily school progress with keen interest and support. The fathers keep in constant touch, sometimes by phone or letter.

● The parents are attentive to homework needs. They are willing, when asked, to lend a hand with assignments, although they do not do the children's work for them.

● They keep in touch with their children's teachers, especially in the early grades.

● They are quietly alert to the presence of any school-related problems which may call for special parental intervention.

● They faithfully attend extracurricular school functions in which their youngsters are involved.

● They encourage the development of nonacademic skills.

● They do not overemphasize social life either for their children or for themselves.

The Less Productive Families

In the homes of Bert and Ned life is reasonably stable and comfortable. There is nothing seriously wrong in either household. But something is lacking that is clearly present in the productive homes. Bert and Ned do not seem to feel from their parents the same degree of concern, warmth, support, and especially, a sense of firm expectation of accomplishment.

Bert's situation is typical of that of many average sixth graders. He lives pretty much in the present, enjoys his friends, views school with a somewhat casual attitude, has no particular idea about what he will eventually do with his life. His father and mother are capable and well-intentioned people but a little lacking in sensitivity to their son's emotional needs and without genuine concern for his school achievement. The fact that Bert's father views the letter-writing custom with skepticism, doesn't take the trouble to sit down with him and learn the game of chess, fails to give him sound training in money management, and apparently spends considerable time on his professional and community activities shows that his priorities are somewhat skewed. Bert's mother is more concerned about the appearance of her neat kitchen than about Bert's need for a little recognition; she has failed to control his television viewing effectively; and she and her husband seem relatively indifferent to the importance of his schoolwork. Bert apparently sees little overt evidence of caring affection between his parents although everything goes smoothly on the surface and the couple enjoy a pleasant and active social life.

Ned's life is similar to Bert's but his prospects of future accomplishment are dimmer; for better or worse he's already well down the educational road and drifting through the crucial junior year of high school. His father, possibly because his own experience of higher education was unsatisfactory, is taking little interest in his son's school progress. He's either too tired or too busy to talk over daily happenings or to offer occasional help with small problems. He withholds praise even when Ned's efforts occasionally produce a creditable grade. He takes little or no interest in Ned's development of nonacademic skills or participation in extracurricular events. His mother laments the fact that he doesn't read but no foundation of interest in reading was laid in Ned's preschool years. As in Bert's home, such issues as TV viewing and money management are handled very casually. There is virtually no discussion of Ned's future plans; everything is being left up to him. The parents' attitude may be characterized in one word: indifference.

These pictures of family life are real; we have known many counterparts. In every public or private high school graduating class in this country there are a small number (perhaps 3 to 5 percent) of outstanding young people whose accomplishments have been nurtured in productive homes. This is a significant number when you consider what these young people can do for society in subsequent years. At the other end of the scale there are countless numbers of children whose motivation toward academic accomplishment, for one reason or another, is less than it should be.

Many parents who have enjoyed the benefits of college education and professional training themselves resemble the families of Steve, Dan, and other such productive youngsters. They are ambitious—possibly unrealistically ambitious—for their children's academic attainments. If at times their demands and pressures seem ineffective, they still provide the vitally necessary emotional support that their children will always need in order to sustain their efforts.

The fact that concerned and supportive child rearing does not depend on the social class or academic background of the parents is illustrated by some of the families described above. Jill and Adam come from modest homes; Mary's family is obliged to live frugally. Income, race, and the parents' own schooling don't seem to matter.

On the other hand, inadequate parenting can characterize any socioeconomic group. A professionally successful couple whose attitude toward their offspring is casual and somewhat uncaring consign them to the custody of private schools and summer camps. A struggling household of five or six children with an overworked mother and a husband in an unrewarding and poorly paid job is troubled with chronic conflict, tension, and serious achievement problems among the youngsters. However, there need be no barrier to good parenting because of economic or social circumstances.

Let us return to Bert and Ned. It is not too late to help them achieve at a higher level. It is still possible for both sets of parents to create more warmth, acceptance, and sense of support and caring in their homes. In such an environment Bert and Ned will certainly function more productively than they do at present. In the chapters that follow are some suggestions that have been of help to fathers and mothers whose children are experiencing similar difficulties.

PARENTAL LOVE, THE SOURCE OF CHILDREN'S SELF-ESTEEM

"Why should anyone have to tell me how to love my child? Don't I do it already?"

Nearly all of us can profit from a little thought on this subject.

What is affection? How is it expressed? Why is it so vital to our success as parents? Why is it always important, whether a child is two, ten, eighteen, or even thirty-five?

Affection and love are the lifeblood of emotional growth. To give love to our children is to nourish them as we nourish their bodies with food. With affection and love we build their self-esteem, their sense of uniqueness, their very identity as persons. All the productive children whom we met in Chapters Two and Three have received continual emotional support from their parents.

We are really talking about the *art of giving affection*. Giving is the essence of a creative human relationship. By giving another individual affection, we give recognition and support, acknowledge his or her significance and worth as a human being.

When we give affection, we are giving something of ourselves. The persons who are most able to give affection are those who have previously received (and are receiving) it in generous abundance. This means that if we were loved and cherished by our own fathers and mothers and if our own marriage is happy and stable, it will be easier for us to love and treasure our children. But even if one's own childhood was less than happy, it is still quite possible to become a good parent.

Families are bound closely together for many years, and day after day, in innumerable ways, parents interact and communicate with their children. Through hundreds of daily interactions, even the most trivial and casual ones, we communicate all kinds of emotions.

These interactions should be positive and supportive. Nevertheless, they may also be negative, humiliating, and destructive.

In order to express affection and love to others, we must first empathize with them. Empathy, "feeling with" (or, even more literally, feeling "into") another person, means the experience of genuinely understanding and sharing that individual's position and point of view in his or her particular situation of the moment.

Successful parents are, above all, empathic persons. They *care* about and are quick to respond to their children's feelings. The toddler who has just bumped his head on the table leg needs a kiss "to make it well." The 6-year-old who is apprehensive of that first day in a new school wants Mummy to walk to the bus with her. The shy seventh-grader facing the first school party or the young football player before the big game of the season need another kind of special reassurance. When the high school senior faces an important college entrance test or awaits the fateful day of admission to (or rejection from) his or her choice of college, someone loving must be nearby. Loneliness, humiliation, apprehension, embarrassment, disappointment—all these arouse the need for comfort and support. At stake is the child's most precious possession, self-esteem.

THE PSYCHOLOGICAL BASIS OF SELF-ESTEEM

The process of showing affection and building self-esteem in a child begins when you form an empathic relationship with your newborn baby. Tiny infants are wholly dependent on two satisfactions: having their hunger pangs relieved and being held comfortably in someone's arms. They soon associate feeding with the security of being held and loved by the empathic and supportive person who gives them nourishment. After feeding they feel supremely content.

This sense of total satisfaction is akin to high self-esteem. All is right with the child's little world.

Otto Fenichel, a disciple of Freud, has described this situation well. When the infant experiences the emotional security of being physically fed and psychologically "safe," he senses one very important fact. He is dependent on others for both physical and psychological gratification. Although the child does not realize it, his self-esteem needs will *always* be present.

In a brilliant analogy between physical and psychological nourishment, Fenichel writes:

Every token of love from the more powerful adult . . . has the same effect as the supply of milk had on the infant. The small child loses self-esteem when he loses love and attains it when he regains love. That is what makes children educable. *They need supplies of affection so badly that they are ready to renounce other satisfactions if rewards of affection are promised or if withdrawal of affection is threatened.*[1]

These words contain the lifelong challenge of creative parenthood. *To rear productive children, we must be prepared to give them the constant love that feeds self-esteem.*

This love must be unconditional. And it must be expressed as long as we live.

EXPRESSING AFFECTION IN EVERYDAY LIFE

Affection and love are communicated in different ways: through physical closeness, facial expression or bodily gesture, the spoken word (even, when appropriate, an understanding silence), and written communication. During the 1960's it was scientifically demonstrated that an adult can promote empathy in children in three ways: by smiling, by showing verbal approval through a "pleased and excited tone of voice," and by a hug.[2]

A smile, an affectionate word, and a hug. They form what we call the "Magic Triad," which is the foundation of effective parenting.

Physical Contact

Embracing, cuddling, kissing, and touching are all part and parcel of warm, intimate family life. Physical closeness is essential to survival in the earliest months of a baby's development. Infants left for long periods of time in orphanages and institutions with little loving attention become apathetic and sickly and may even die.

During their first two years it is impossible to hug or cuddle children too much. Frequent and loving physical closeness remains important for many, many years for all members of a family.

The word *hugging* originates partly in the Old Norse word "hugga," meaning to comfort or console. Most of us associate hugging with pleasant memories of jumping into a favorite uncle's arms, embracing our teammates after the big football victory, or meeting old classmates at a school reunion. Hugging can, however, be more than a spontaneous expression of joy, as shown in the following incident:

The pretty china plate slips from little John's hands and crashes in pieces on the floor. Sobbing, John brings Mother to view the sad remains. Mother understands. She merely puts her arms around John and holds him tightly. No one has to say a word.

The physical embrace is a resource in moments of grief, terror, loss, and helplessness, as well as ardent love and devotion. Support and reassurance can be conveyed by almost any kind of physical touching:

Seven-year-old Sally has fallen off her bike and broken her leg. She is on a stretcher waiting to be wheeled into the operating room. Daddy is there with her, holding her hand. Sally is apprehensive, but when the anesthesia mask goes over her face she will be a brave girl.

When our children are young, it is easy to indulge them with physical affection. Babies and little children are cute and appealing. As they grow into noisy grade-school youngsters and later into sometimes moody adolescents, it is more difficult to be openly expressive and loving toward them. It's a pity that some of us find it inappropriate to be outwardly affectionate with our older children. In every teenager there is something of the little child's unspoken need for reassurance and support, however reluctantly it might be admitted.

Fortunately, there is growing recognition that children of all ages need physical affection. The recent bumper stickers—"Did you hug your child today?"—are part of an encouraging trend. The bear hug, the pat on the back, the arm over the shoulder, a gentle touch—all of these convey a sense of caring and all are appropriate among persons of any age.

In the workaday world touching is formalized in the handshake that signifies welcome, recognition, respect, congratulations, or commitment to an agreement. But within the family itself, more intimate, informal forms of physical contact are always appropriate and always needed.

Facial Expression and Body Language

The smile, the loving glance, the nod of approval, and the meaningful wink are all means of expressing empathy and support. They tell others that we like them, understand how they are feeling, approve of what they are doing, and want to encourage them to continue their efforts. *The smile is especially significant; its power to increase another's self-esteem cannot be overestimated.* A frown, on the other hand, means rejection and criticism. Without a word being spoken, moods can be vividly transmitted through the expression of the face.

Body language—a movement of the head or hand, even so trivial a gesture as a shrug of the shoulders—is also tremendously powerful in conveying feelings. Rejection or indifference can be felt in the smallest bodily movement of an individual, or even in posture and attitude:

Eighteen-month-old Teddy hasn't quite learned to say when he needs to go to the bathroom. He toddles over to his mother, who is sitting at the desk looking over the mail. Mother is preoccupied: the bill for repairing the transmission on the car has come and it's much bigger than she expected. Teddy, still unable to verbalize his need of the moment, pulls on Mother's skirt but can't attract her attention. Against this temporary wall of indifference he reacts with dismay and, a few moments later, with the inevitable accident.

A parent who is preoccupied can, often quite unintentionally, depress the morale of a small child. In the above situation words of explanation might help if the child were old enough to understand and use them. Instead there is a momentary welling up of unspoken bewilderment and hurt. Physical gesture, or any form of body language, is indeed a powerful means of communication, for good or ill.

The Spoken Word

As soon as youngsters begin to talk, words become the essential means of communication. Carefully chosen and gently spoken, words can convey appreciation, approval, praise, understanding, encouragement, reassurance, consolation, and sympathy.

A great many well-intentioned parents fail to give their children enough verbal support. Two false notions seem to prevail. The first is that praise and approval are somehow not good for children, may make them conceited and unrealistic about their abilities. The second is that it is hypocritical and insincere to lavish praise on a child.

Two principles should be kept in mind:

Praise does not spoil children. It meets their basic needs. The best way to spoil children is *not* to praise them. If they seldom receive an appreciative compliment, they are bound to feel chronically insecure and anxious. They will grow up craving approval in any form they can get it. They are likely to engage in undesirable attention-getting behavior (clowning, for example) in inappropriate circumstances.

Children should be praised for what they are, not merely for what they do. Some writers have recommended that you praise only the task and not the child who has performed it.[3] Praising a child only for good performance of a job is insufficient for one reason: the praise is qualified. It can be withdrawn at any time. The child wonders, "What will happen if I don't do as well next time?" Even when your praise focuses specifically on task performance, the child must *always* feel that he or she is also appreciated as a person:

"You're a wonderful girl, Jeanie. What a great job you did washing the car!"

Growing up is a struggle. The compliments from the outside world are not always forthcoming. You, as parents, are the principal source from which they must come. Don't be afraid to use them! With a little effort you can cultivate the habit of seeking daily opportunities to utter the positive, loving, supportive words that can make a world of difference in a child's (or an adult's) morale.

Complimenting is an art that can be cultivated. It is *not* empty flattery. It has been pointed out by Jack Denton Scott that a true compliment is distinguished by a number of characteristics. It is sincere. It is specific and appropriate to the occasion. It enhances the recipient's sense of dignity and importance. It is effectively timed. Above all, it is thoughtful.[4]

Don't be too concerned, however, about the "sincerity" of a compliment. When the compliment comes from the heart, and you really want to make someone feel better, your remark will be sincere. You can always find something to praise if you look for it.

The issue is simple kindness. Keep this rule in mind: *If my words or actions are kind, they are right; if they are not kind, they are wrong.*

Sometimes it is difficult to find just the right words to express praise. We tend to regard children's activities from an adult's point of view. It's important to look at a given task or behavior through a small child's eyes. If, for example, you want to compliment 3-year-old Susie's table manners, remember that to her there are a great many components: napkin in lap, taking small mouthfuls, eating her meat and vegetables, staying at the table, talking in turn, not feeding the dog. It's hard for her to remember all this. Try to be specific rather than general in your remarks. "I like the way you use your fork now, Susie" is better than "I like the way you eat your dinner." Say to a 10-year-old who has helped with supper, "I like the way you fixed the salad!" or, to the lad who has cleaned the garage, "My, it was so great to see all the tools neat for a change!"

It is also very important to make appreciative comments about personal appearance. Your teenage daughter (and your son, too!) love to hear, "You look great this morning!" Even the simple exclamation "What a great boy/girl!" can do untold wonders for any child's morale.

In communicating with our children it helps, above all, to use imagination. Specifically, try to remember to talk with them as you would with an adult. With our peers we use common courtesy. We guard our language with certain amenities. We try to be pleasant even if we must be businesslike. Simply remembering to talk with our sons and daughters as if we were talking with adults improves communication with them enormously.

Many well-meaning parents fall into certain habits of communication that are far more destructive to their children's morale than they realize. In particular, they should guard against the following:

Criticism. Many of us have the mistaken idea that the best way to train a child is through the use of criticism. Criticism of any kind inevitably lowers the self-image. Sidney Simon has pointed out that we are usually unaware of how much we ourselves have been damaged in the past by a multitude of small putdowns. A child may not openly react to a critical remark but it always leaves some sort of scar.

Thousands of children, in Simon's words, are wounded by parents' well-intentioned but negative comments.[5] Harsh, impatient, and deflating remarks ("Don't do that." "What did I tell you?" "Now you listen to me!" "Aren't you ever going to grow up?" "What you're doing makes me feel bad!") do untold damage.

Beware also of the negative message that is conveyed by so-called "constructive" criticism. All criticism is destructive. Your children will still feel hurt if you preface your remarks by saying, "I'm telling you this for your own good" or some similar comment.

All children have to be directed, helped, and taught—but there are less damaging methods than outright criticism and evaluation, particularly in front of others. What we are really trying to provide for our youngsters is guidance—quiet, gentle, if necessary private instruction concerning some aspect of their behavior. If something has gone amiss, we try to learn the facts. We find out what happened; we ask a child if he or she knew the action was wrong; we explain why it was wrong; we arrange an appropriate penalty. And we can do all of this without humiliating the child unnecessarily. Such matters are aspects of effective discipline, which is discussed in Chapter Seven. If you reward good behavior with praise, you will have little need to criticize.

Correcting children's errors of grammar or pronunciation. It is understandable that conscientious parents want their children to develop good speech habits. However, remember that it may take them years to learn to speak clearly, expressively, and correctly. Good English is learned gradually in school and from listening to people who speak well. It is better not to be habitually critical of minor grammatical errors (use of "good" instead of "well," "me" instead of "I," etc.) or occasional mispronunciations of unfamiliar words. When we tactlessly interrupt children who are trying to tell us something of importance to them at that moment for the mere purpose of correcting such errors, we damage them: we lower their self-esteem; we make them feel that we are not really listening to what they are saying; we inhibit their spontaneity and creativity.

Sixth-grade Betsy's well-intentioned mother, who has habitually corrected her daughter's grammar and pronunciation, learns from her teacher that Betsy's written compositions are curiously "stilted and uncreative." Small wonder!

Inconsistent (sometimes called "double-bind") communication. Double-bind communication occurs when the speaker's words convey mixed signals and feelings. A positive comment is shortly followed by a negative one. A critical and deflating remark destroys the value of a previous compliment:

A harassed mother explodes to her youngsters: "The trouble with you children is you have too much done for you!" A few minutes later, feeling guilty, she says softly, "Well, when can I take you downtown?"

Teenage Sally comes into the kitchen. Her mother says, "Have some of this new batch of cookies?" After Sally has eaten two or three with relish, she hears this comment: "My! You're getting heavy, aren't you?"

When a parent vacillates between praise and criticism, enthusiasm and indifference, solicitude and neglect, indulgence and sternness, rigidity and permissiveness, the result is a mixed and contradictory message that throws the child into a state of confusion.

Teasing. Though seemingly an innocent practice, teasing can actually be very cruel. Some parents, for want of better communicative skills, have the unfortunate habit of teasing or poking fun at their children. Tickling is in the same category; when carried to extremes it can actually exhaust the victim. Research workers have found that some mothers will talk to their infant girls but are more likely to tickle their baby boys. It is wise to refrain from both teasing and tickling. And don't permit your children to tease or ridicule each other!

Playing the martyr. Don't say, or even imply, "Look what I'm doing for you." You accomplish nothing by such a statement, and your children are likely to feel that they are an unwanted burden. Remember that no child ever asked to be born!

Quarrels between spouses in the children's presence. Don't quarrel openly before your children. Occasional minor disagreements are probably not harmful in an otherwise secure family, provided they are discussed calmly. Continual bickering is another matter: the children are bound to feel rejected, alienated, or—worse still—forced to take sides with one of the parents. If a child is aware that he is the center of an argument between his father and mother, he is bound to feel guilty.

The Art of Empathic Listening

A crucial element in all good verbal communication is the art of listening.[6] Unfortunately, this skill is possessed by relatively few persons.

A good listener waits until the speaker is finished before commenting or asking questions. He or she also has the ability to detect the feeling behind the words and the hidden meaning in what the speaker is really saying. These skills are routinely taught to professional interviewers, counselors, and therapists. Parents need them, too!

Always give your full attention to children when they wish to talk with you, especially if they appear anxious and preoccupied. If they are small, kneel or sit down next to them. Let them share their experiences with you freely. Give them smiling reassurance. Your responsiveness will help them in turn to become responsive to others. Don't ask too many questions. Let them do the talking. And don't interrupt!

When, as occasionally happens, it seems necessary for a child to get something off his chest, let him express his annoyance to you in words. Don't be too concerned about his talking back. A small child's "Mama, I don't like you!" should be no cause for alarm. If he can't express his irritation in words, it may be repressed or displaced onto someone or something else. He may hit his brother or sister, kick the dog or develop a stomachache.

Children have special need of an accepting listener when they come home from the long day at school. They can hardly wait to tell about the day's accomplishments as well as the stresses of the classroom. A teacher's criticism, a difficult test, or slights from peers can leave a child very unhappy. An understanding father or mother needs to say little in response. By listening attentively, he or she conveys the support that enables the child to look beyond the day's events with renewed confidence and courage.

The Written Word

Julie dear, I'm so glad you let me read your theme last evening. It was a great job. You're learning to plan your ideas and find just the right words to say what you mean. You certainly deserve the good mark Mrs. Smith gave you!

I'll be thinking of you during the math test this morning.

All my love to a wonderful girl,
Dad

Julie finds this letter under her bedroom door when she gets up. It raises her spirits all during the hard day at school.

Most of us correspond somewhat regularly with relatives and friends who live at a distance. Seldom, however, does it occur to us that the members of our household—our own children or spouse—might like a letter or note from us. We see these individuals day in and day out. Why should we sit down and *write* to them?

A handwritten letter (or even a short note) is valuable for four reasons:

Like a hug or handclasp, it is a form of intimate personal contact.

It is a form of giving; the writer has expended time and effort for the reader's special benefit.

It is more permanent than spoken words. Unlike a conversation, it can impart its message again and again since it can be reread once, twenty, or a hundred times—perhaps kept for years.

Finally, a letter has great psychological power. If affectionate and appreciative, it can bring the reader encouragement and happiness. If negative or critical, its effect can be devastating. In either case, it can greatly influence the quality of a relationship between two individuals.

In these days of instant communication by telephone, radio, and television, letter writing has become something of a lost art. Many beautiful letters written in past centuries are now recognized as classics: those of the apostle Paul to the early Christian churches; the loving correspondence between Elizabeth Barrett and Robert Browning; the warmly intimate, humorous, and affectionate letters from President Theodore Roosevelt to his children; and many others. Luckily, we need not be such accomplished authors. For our children, our words carry special power and significance. Fathers and mothers are a young child's world and they remain uniquely important throughout the growing-up years.

In homes where parents begin to write letters on a regular basis, they note changes in the family atmosphere. The children are appreciative, whether they show their feelings directly or not. The letters are often kept and reread. Not uncommonly, there is less tension in the household, and brothers and sisters begin to show more affection toward one another.

Letters do *not* need to be long. Short sunshine notes of only a few lines are immensely successful and they take but moments to write:

Dear Bobby, You're a great boy, and a great speller! Loads of love, Mom

Jane, dear. Thanks so much for helping with the dishes last night. Love you! Dad

Third-grade Bobby finds his note in his lunchbox at school. Dad's words of affection, left on his little daughter's bureau, send her off to school with a spring in her step. The day is brightened for both children.

Such notes can be put in all sorts of places: in a lunchbox, in a textbook, on a pillow, in a shirt pocket, on the dashboard of the car, in a gym bag. Let the notes, if possible, be discovered when you're not around. Your children will be pleased and touched when they find them.[7]

Letters can, of course, be somewhat longer and more formal. But regardless of how much you write, three elements can be included to great effect, as in Dad's letter to Julie:

Some approving reference to a specific act or accomplishment on the child's part that you have recently noted.

Some sort of compliment to the child as a total person.

An affectionate expression of love at the conclusion, in which you are not afraid to use superlatives!

Don't be concerned about making such a letter polished in style. Write in longhand. Once you've begun the practice, you should try to continue it, for children quickly begin to look forward to such communications.

Letters that arrive through the mail have a special importance, particularly for the older child, who looks for the canceled stamp. When a parent is away, even briefly, a letter makes the separation easier. A child as young as two years will beam when Mother reads him a colorful card that his Daddy has left before departing on a business trip:

Daddy is on a trip. Daddy will be home soon. I love you.

By the time Daddy returns, the card is usually wrinkled and worn from contact with warm little hands.

Letters to preschool children also provide an excellent opportunity for building a sight vocabulary. If the writer prints and uses short words and phrases repeatedly, a 4-year-old can begin to decipher them with help. However, development of reading skill should not be the primary purpose of letter writing; using a letter only as an instructional tool will defeat its purpose.

The letter-writing habit can become contagious. When, as frequently happens, we find our youngsters' own sunshine notes to us in strategic places around the house, we can feel justifiably pleased:

Dear Dad,
I found your letter under the door when I got up this morning. You don't know what it did for me. I was worried sick about the algebra test.

You know English is my best subject and I'm glad you liked my theme. But the math!

The test wasn't too bad, after all. I guess I was thinking about what you wrote. Anyhow, it got me through.

Love, Julie

In expressing their love for us on paper, our children are also beginning to develop a highly refined and civilized style of shared intimacy that can become a lifelong source of pleasure. Moreover, the spontaneous enjoyment of writing such notes is a valuable step toward increasing one's skill in the act of writing itself. Thousands of today's educators bemoan the pathetic incompetence of young people's written work. Any way in which parents can encourage the sheer enjoyment of informal note and letter writing can help to improve this situation.

FAMILY GAMES

Certain games can particularly successful in encouraging children's self-confidence, especially in large families. The three that follow give everyone concerned some attention and support, and they are fun.

"The Best Thing That I Did Today" requires little or no preparation. Individual family members take turns describing to the others, usually at supper, their best accomplishment of the day. Preferably each person stands up, is given the floor, and is allotted sufficient time to tell the full story to an attentive audience. The story may or may not relate to school or work, but it should involve a genuine achievement: the 5-year-old tied her new shoes all alone; Jack got 100 in spelling; Sue passed behind-the-wheel training; Mom closed a real estate sale; Dad's journal article was accepted for publication.

After each speech, everyone applauds. The potential for enhancing the self-esteem of each speaker is obvious.

"The Best Thing That I Did Today" is particularly successful with young children. It not only provides each youngster with recognition but also implicitly emphasizes the importance of good task performance in any field and at any age.

"What I Like Best About My Family" is another supper-table game. Each individual describes what he or she likes best about the family. Parents are likely to be surprised by the number, diversity, and enthusiasm of the comments: "I like it when we all rake leaves in the fall," "I like it when we go to Grandma's for Thanksgiving," "I

like the way we all sang in the car coming home from the picnic last night." This is the time to remember treasured family customs, such as the rituals of the Christmas season (the special candy and cookie making, the caroling, trimming the tree with the faded paper chains lovingly resurrected each year).

This game helps everyone to feel that the family is special. This is *our* family. There is no other family quite like it in the world. We like to do special things together. Other families like to do other things, but we're proud to be the way we are.

Parents may learn as much from this game as their children. They will find that each person puts an individual value on family activities. Learning that what seems relatively inconsequential to an adult is very significant for a young child can be a most enlightening and also humbling experience. A child's sense of family consists of his or her store of such memories which can never be taken away.

A third and slightly more competitive game is *"King or Queen for a Week."* Its basic object is to reward the family member who, in the entire group's opinion, has contributed most to the general welfare or happiness in the home during the preceding week. A wide-mouthed container or jar large enough to hold a number of small folded pieces of paper is placed in a central location in the house. During the week this is to receive a number of little sunshine notes from one family member to another. Each note will refer to some act of kindness on the recipient's part which the writer feels has contributed to someone else's happiness:

> From thirteen-year-old Johnny to Mom: "I like the way we talked when I came home from school yesterday."

> From nine-year-old Beth to Daddy: "Thanks for taking my kitty to the vet and being so nice to her."

> From four-year-old Patsy (with Daddy's help) to her big brother: "I liked it when you played catch with me."

> Or, to Mother: "You kissed me when I fell off my bike, and I felt better."

Each individual agrees to write and place in the jar at least two such anecdotes about each other family member. Naturally some persons will receive more notes than others. At the week's end, the notes are taken from the jar, read aloud to the assembled family, and counted.

Two scores are possible. The person receiving the largest

number of appreciative notes becomes King or Queen for a week. The person who wrote the most notes becomes Prince or Princess for a week. If desired, an appropriate reward can be offered for these distinctions—perhaps a favorite dessert or some special privilege.

This game fascinates children when it is first played. After trying it two or three times, it's wise to take a break from it temporarily to preserve the players' enthusiasm. You also need to provide some leadership by reminding the participants to write their notes of appreciation during the week rather than waiting to stuff the jar hastily at the last minute.

The benefits of the game are numerous. It discourages the formation of family alignments and petty rivalries because each individual is required to think about every other person in positive terms; it teaches family members not to take each other for granted; it also recognizes and therefore encourages acts of generosity, consideration, and thoughtfulness that are the basis of all productive social living.

CONCLUSION

Self-esteem is the foundation of productive personality development. It is fragile, easily destroyed, and in need of constant renewal. Throughout your children's lives, and especially during their years at home, your aim should be to communicate constant affection and support to them. The means are utterly simple: a smile, a loving spoken or written word, and a hug.

Not everyone will find it easy to follow these suggestions. The childhood backgrounds of some fathers and mothers have been stressful, conflicted, and emotionally deprived. Without having personally experienced loving, tender, supportive care from their own parents, these persons lack effective models for expressing affection to their youngsters, verbal or otherwise. Others may be afraid to let themselves go in expressing their feelings. A third group find it difficult to view their children positively, to see any qualities that they feel they can praise or approve.

Such persons are usually uncomfortable and inadequate in the parental role. Having unresolved problems and little self-esteem, they can unwittingly deprive their own youngsters of the necessary psychological support. These parents can profit from professional help. Such counsel may never succeed in solving all the adult's problems but it may indirectly benefit the children. Good parenting is tremendously rewarding, but at times it can be emotionally draining even for persons in the best of mental health.

Through the various practices described in this chapter, you have limitless opportunities for expressing to your children affection, pride, understanding, sympathy, encouragement, and recognition. You can be continually alert to the dangers of making even well-intentioned critical remarks. You can avoid comments that bear a subtle message of rejection (correcting grammatical errors, double-bind communication, teasing, playing the martyr, or bickering with your spouse). You can search ceaselessly to enhance the beauty and potential of even the short, fleeting moments of human contact that are available in today's fast tempo of living. In so doing you assure your sons and daughters of your total and continuing concern for them. With this knowledge they can function without a crushing burden of anxiety; their self-esteem is secure.

Finally, remember the great importance of exchanging expressions of affection with your spouse. Your children need the reassurance of seeing this loving interaction between you, for you are, quite literally, their world. What is more, they need to be able to view you as models of the husband–wife relationship which they themselves will one day enter.

SPECIFIC SUGGESTIONS

Do:

Do make the "Magic Triad" (the hug, the smile, and the loving word) a part of daily life with your children and your mate.

Do remember that warm physical contact is important for all ages, especially for infants and young children.

Do be conscious of the special importance of your smile and the power of even small physical gestures.

Do search continually for the right (i.e., kind, positive, and loving) words to say to your child.

Do listen empathically to your children!

Do write loving and supportive notes and letters to all members of your family.

Don't:

Don't let a day in your child's life go by without in some way letting her or him know of your love.

Don't use criticism or other negative and destructive forms of communication.

Don't quarrel openly with your spouse.

5

PARENTAL LOVE, THE SOURCE OF A SENSE OF IDENTITY

"Who am I?"
"Where am I going?"
"What's the meaning of my life?"

There is little doubt that identity, or some concept akin to it, is a vital aspect of personality development. In a broad sense, identity is the sum of all the parts of the individual; it denotes a oneness or wholeness.[1]

When we speak of persons with a sense of identity, we usually mean individuals who—irrespective of age—have certain unique characteristics. Such persons are consistent, predictable, and always the same. (Identity, derived from the Latin *idem*, means sameness.) These individuals seem comfortably at peace with themselves and at ease with their own bodies. They are not unduly disturbed by the pressures and demands of other individuals or events. They are in control of themselves; their actions reveal a sense of direction; they seem to be going somewhere.

We acquire a sense of identity first through a close, supportive relationship with others. In the words of Erik Erikson, whose writings on this subject have exerted considerable influence, we have "an inner assuredness of anticipated recognition from those who count."[2] Both identity and self-esteem are related to a feeling that "all is well." When children enjoy a warm, consistent, trusting relationship with their parents, they radiate a feeling of belonging. The development of a sense of self stems from a sense of oneness with another.

THE IDENTIFICATION PROCESS

The early closeness between parent and young infant described in the previous chapter is the beginning of a long process known as identification. Identification is a form of learning, mostly unconscious, that takes place continuously throughout life.[3] In this process, children whose parents have provided them from birth with physical and psychological security gradually absorb the personality traits, attitudes, values, and moral standards of their fathers and mothers. In becoming like their parents, they develop into mature, independent, coping individuals.

Early Forms of Identification

Identification begins in the loving, intimate relationship between the infant and his first caretakers, normally the mother and father. The first person who satisfies the infantile hungers becomes the object of the baby's first identification. Since each parent is a unique individual with distinctive traits, each will exert his or her influence on offspring.

As parents lovingly nurture and care for the young infant, the child begins, spontaneously and unconsciously, to absorb some of their personality characteristics. This baby has inherited from both parents a unique pattern of genetic physical traits—perhaps the father's brown eyes and the mother's skeletal build. Now there begins, through the identification process, an evolution into a new, unique, and eventually separate and independent personality.

Children are most profoundly influenced by their earliest caretakers, usually their parents, who during the first months of life repeatedly satisfy all their needs for food, protection, relief of discomfort, and loving attention. The parents literally become the child's world and his identification with them will be relatively permanent.[4]

Let us examine the identification process as it influences the development of a child we shall call Nancy.

At the beginning of life Nancy has no sense of herself as a separate human being. She perceives herself and her caretaker as one. Their identities are said to be totally "merged."[5] Erikson refers to this period as the stage of "basic trust."[6]

The first sense of separateness occurs some weeks later. The child gradually becomes aware of her body as distinct from its surroundings:

Little Nancy is beginning to take notice of the world around her. When she is being nursed, she looks up at her mother. One day she returns Mother's smile and both Mother and Daddy are elated. Within a few weeks she reaches out to touch their faces, later to coo and babble, and they respond in delight.

Here is little Nancy's first real (though wordless) communication, her first exchange of loving feelings with another human being. Here are her first steps toward feeling happy, being content with her little world, and above all, beginning to sense herself as a separate individual in that world.

At about the age of one year, Nancy enters the "age of autonomy." She not only learns to walk, but also acquires two other important tools:

Verbal communication. When Nancy learns to talk (at first in rudimentary, later more complex fashion), she develops her budding sense of identity, independence, and control over her environment. Now she can name objects and persons, voice her wants, express her feelings to others, carry on simple conversations. Words are also the foundation of her subsequent intellectual skills. She's beginning to think and deal in symbols; eventually she will handle abstractions. (Early development of speech is known to occur in children whose parents communicate warmly and affectionately with them at an early age.) In addition, language helps Nancy to develop her social skills; she can now begin to interact with others, exchanging information and feelings with them.

Throughout the toddler and preschool years Nancy's language and physical activities expand and grow in power. She is also beginning to develop another important personality trait: *judgment—the power to choose between alternatives.* When she starts school, leaves the protected surroundings of her immediate family and encounters new individuals and situations, she will have need of judgment. Her identification with her parents will help her make wise decisions and choices.

One area in which such choices will be made is in the selection of friends. Even in elementary school Nancy will meet contemporaries with a wide variety of family backgrounds and personalities.

In Nancy's grade there's a girl named Toni who lives on the same street, but Nancy doesn't like her. Toni borrowed Nancy's new ball and didn't return it for a long time. Nancy prefers to play with Jessie, who is careful of belongings. They become pals and soon enjoy playing in each other's homes.

In choosing Jessie instead of Toni as her friend, Nancy is merely gravitating to someone she feels she can trust, whose company she enjoys, and who contributes to her self-esteem. The reason? She has been close to her parents, and her growing identification with them is guiding her selection of honest, fair-minded playmates. For her part, Jessie reflects the influence and similar values of her own parents. The two children thus enjoy a comfortable relationship.

Judgment is also involved in choosing what actions to take. Because she is emotionally secure and confident that her needs will eventually be met, Nancy can take her time in making decisions. She looks ahead and anticipates the results of her behavior. She does not make impulsive choices. Sometimes this involves postponing an immediate pleasure for the sake of a more valuable future gain:

In the five and ten Nancy looks longingly at M & M's on the candy counter. At the end of the aisle there's a game of backgammon which costs more than the candy. After some thought, Nancy decides to save her allowance for a few weeks until she can buy the game.

The candy would be eaten up at once; the game can be played many times with her friends. Nancy is showing self-control, a trait absorbed from her parents. (In later years she will probably defer other instant pleasures, choosing to stay home to study for next day's important test instead of going to the movies with friends.)

Continued Forms of Identification

During the elementary school years identification centers chiefly around the child's most powerful models, father and mother. On entering adolescence the young person encounters other influences. Some of these are adults, others contemporaries:

Adult models. An adolescent may wish to emulate a favorite older relative, a teacher, or a Scout leader; sometimes the model is a minister, priest, or rabbi. Prominent sports heroes or entertainers may be idolized. Outstanding scientists, explorers, performing artists, even characters in fiction are other important models. Any one of these personalities may contribute to the building of the young person's character. No model, however, will be as profoundly and permanently influential as his or her father and mother.

During these years it is normal for young persons to draw gradually away from close parental influence and control. Gravitating to the company of *peers*, they will begin to rely on their own standards and personal value systems. They are away from home much of the time. The social pressures of contemporaries will often be overwhelming. There's always the need to be liked, the urge to be popular, to be viewed as a good sport and one of the crowd.

The dubious influence of peer pressure is only too well known. If young people's relationships with their first models, their parents, have been warm, trusting, and affectionate, however, the bonds of identification will already be close. The child will have internalized (absorbed) the values, attitudes, and standards of the parents.[7] Thus there is already available a firm foundation for judging the prevailing values and attitudes of contemporaries and selecting those with which the young person feels comfortable—in other words, those that enhance self-esteem. This foundation provides the child with the courage to be different, to stand apart from peers when necessary in defense of personal ethical principles and value system:

Charles tells his father he's staying home tonight, a Saturday. "Mike has his father's car and the gang is driving over the state line to buy a case of beer. I told them I had to baby-sit, so you and Mom can go out if you want."

MATURITY, INDEPENDENCE, AND VALUES

There [seems] to be some evidence that the formulation of a system of personal values is a concomitant of an integrated identity.[8]

As a group, productive young people maintain high standards of moral behavior. They are usually busy with constructive activities in and out of school. They tend to select friends whose values are similar to theirs, thus further contributing to their sense of identity.

After years of healthy identification with their parents and other important persons in their environment, young people have absorbed a code of sound ethical standards. They know the difference between right and wrong. They live by the ground rules of mature social behavior and interact with others accordingly. If they break any of these rules, they experience guilt, lowered self-esteem, and temporary loss of identity. They therefore assume responsibility for the results of their actions:

Charles, who has borrowed his father's car, has committed a parking violation. On returning home, he reports the matter to his dad, who will eventually receive notice of the infraction. Knowing the fine will be $10, Charles hands the money to his dad and apologizes for what happened.

True maturity carries with it the capacity to be independent, to make one's own decisions with good judgment, to cope with one's environment effectively—all within a strong code of values. Only then can the individual function productively.

The achievement of mature identity is not dependent on chronological age. We have only to recall our five successful young people described in the second and third chapters. Although of assorted ages and ranging from the fourth to the twelfth grades, they all sense their identity and the meaning of their lives. Beneath their strengths and competencies is a basic trust in their parents. Because they feel accepted as persons, others feel comfortable with them. Free of basic anxieties about themselves, they go about the business of solving problems, working with others, formulating and carrying out plans. The history paper, the biology project, the next Scout merit badge can engage all the creative energies of Steve, Mary, Jill, and others like them. Personally secure, they can perceive their next goal. They have a sense of what they want to do with their lives. In essence, they are engaged in successful living.

Outstanding young adults often remember from their childhood years certain moments of closeness to their parents. Several years ago we gave a sentence completion test to undergraduates of two prominent eastern colleges. Some of the incomplete sentences evoked memories of childhood experiences. Here are responses given by two of the high achievers:

To the stem "My mother," one sophomore boy wrote: "My mother and I are very close."

To the stem "Father," an outstanding junior commented: "My father is an inspiration to me."

From the feelings of affection revealed in these comments, one detects the presence of identification at its best. These young people love their parents, want to be like them, and are striving to develop themselves into fine human beings.

GENDER IDENTITY, AN ASPECT OF IDENTIFICATION

Five-year-old Donny is glad to be a little boy. Sarah, his contemporary, is equally satisfied to be a little girl.

During the years of healthy identification, children naturally develop feelings about themselves as males or females. Youngsters with high self-esteem are generally happy with their biological endowment. Some become aware of their sex group at a very young age, possibly as early as one and a half years.[9] Between the ages of four and six, secure children accept themselves as boys or girls.

Most of the personality and behavior traits children acquire during their formative years are quite unrelated to gender. Happy, productive children like Donny and Sarah are aware of but not unduly conscious of their own bodies. They move about effortlessly. Accepting themselves as they are, they are free to cope with the demands of the environment. Currently there is a positive trend that encourages such youngsters to share interests and playtime activities without regard for gender stereotypes. As they grow older, Donny and Sarah can also share similar educational goals and personality characteristics. They will be coping, socially responsible, empathic, independent young persons who feel comfortable with their bodies. We say that they have good gender identity.

Gender identity includes much more than the acceptance of one's biological endowment. It embraces social and vocational roles as well. Young girls are now aware that women are accepted in nearly all vocations and professions. Sarah may well become the mainstay of the softball team and later go to engineering school. In future years Donny and his wife will share home chores and child-rearing responsibilities. Good gender identity merely refers to good social adjustment and high self-esteem in persons of either sex.

Boys and girls must be accepted as equals by both father and mother if they are to be comfortable with their biological endowment. They will identify to some extent with the characteristics and values of each parent, provided they perceive each as a nurturing and competent adult model.

Parents whose own identity is secure are usually not unduly concerned about their children's gender identity.

As a rule mothers spend more time with the youngsters than fathers during the infant years, although there is no doubt that fathers are becoming increasingly involved in a nurturing role with their young babies. The mother's affection and nurturance nevertheless promote her daughter's gender-role identification. As her son grows older, he will become closer to his father while still retaining his mother's values. His mother, if she is a secure person, will subtly support the growing father–son relationship.

An empathic father is of special importance in enhancing his son's healthy gender identity.[10] He is also significant in his daughter's development:[11]

Eight-year-old Sue is a tomboy, climbing every tree within reach. At sixteen, when she's invited to the junior prom, Dad will admire her new gown and growing feminine atrractiveness.

Elementary school youngsters who have good basic gender identity usually maintain it through adolescence. Feeling comfortable with their own bodies, they acquire ease with the opposite sex. During the late teenage years and early twenties their educational plans proceed toward implementation, and their social contacts— acquaintances and close friends—often evolve into a more serious and permanent attachment to one special person in their lives:

Twenty-four-year-old Sue, with college behind her and a diploma from business school in hand, will shortly marry her college sweetheart. A job is awaiting her in the same area where her fiancé is already established. They are making long-range plans for their future together.

Sue's father and mother were important persons in her early years, and her father may have played the more significant role as she grew older.

Promoting Healthy Gender Awareness

It is good to keep the following suggestions in mind:

● Do help your young children in particular to be comfortable with their maleness and femaleness. When praising them, you can occasionally make some approving reference to their sex grouping. Even simple expressions such as "Good boy!" or "Good girl!" will be absorbed and remembered. When you talk to them thus, you are helping them develop genuine pride in themselves.

● Never on any account suggest to a child that he or she is the opposite sex from what you had planned. You can always say, "We got just what we ordered!" If your children are all of the same sex, you can say, "Nothing is better than a family of all boys (or all girls). When you get married, we'll get the opposite sex anyhow!"

• Be careful not to show more affection to one sex group than to the other. In the past, parents have unwittingly displayed such preference. The tendency (which seems fortunately to be diminishing) has been to protect and shelter little girls and allow them to stay close to mother or be "spoiled" by father while pushing little boys out into rough-and-tumble play in the hope of making men of them. In the current world, concepts of masculinity and femininity are becoming less stereotyped, to the benefit of both sexes. Daughters need (and many are now receiving) more stimulation to compete and achieve; sons will respond to tenderness and nurturance, which will enhance the gentler, more expressive side of their natures.

• Don't, in matters of discipline, favor one sex over the other. Be sure you are being fair in settling even the smallest disputes. Be certain that you are not casting blame on your little boy because he is noisier and more obstreperous than his sister. She may have contributed to the problem. Your son's growing sense of identity is prey to disillusionment as he perceives that his parents prefer a sibling of the opposite sex.

THE CHALLENGES OF ADOLESCENCE

Growing up to the age of twenty is a challenging undertaking. Society expects youngsters to acquire year by year basic physical skills and to develop socially and intellectually according to the norms of the group in which they live. Apart from two periods—the rapid growth in infancy and the dramatic spurts in height and sexual development at adolescence—these growth increments are fairly equal. If children's home life is stable and their parents consistently affectionate and supportive, their physical, social, and intellectual development may proceed rather smoothly during the first twelve years of life.

At about the seventh grade, however, and at the very time when the physical changes of adolescence begin to manifest themselves, the educational and social expectations increase. Hence the young person's struggle for social acceptance and maintenance of self-esteem intensifies. This is also the time when parents, thinking that their young teenagers should become more independent and self-reliant, tend to withdraw some of their support and nurturance. Their sons and daughters are left somewhat isolated, without the supports that surrounded their earliest years, and often troubled by the rapid physical changes beginning to occur in their bodies as well as the numerous demands and expectations of the surrounding worlds of school and society. Anxiety renders many of these young persons moody, withdrawn, and uncommunicative. They tend to turn to their peers for support.

For all these reasons, adolescence has been described as a time of turmoil for youngsters and parents alike.

One source of confusion for younger and less secure teenagers in particular is the great variability of physical development patterns among their peers. In every adolescent group there are the early, the average, and the late maturers, with the corresponding differences in height and sexual development that have enormous implications for everyone's self-esteem and self-image. The tall girl with a woman's curves, the little pipsqueak of a boy who secretly envies the brawny fellow on the junior high football team, the little girl preoccupied with her still-flat chest—all have their private confusions, misgivings, even agonies. It is hard to say which is more difficult for young persons—to be expected to play a social role for which they are still unprepared emotionally or to suffer feelings of social inadequacy because their bodies are less developed than those of their friends.

During these hectic years their growth, defined broadly as growth in all three dimensions (physical, intellectual, and psycho-social), is seldom totally even and steady. There are ups, downs, and plateaus for many young people as they encounter crises of one sort or another. Yet some adolescents survive these years without any setbacks or interruptions in their development. The following research is illustrative:

In 1975 a team of midwestern psychiatric workers reported the results of an eight-year longitudinal study of 73 young men, originally selected when they were high school freshmen, who had been followed between the ages of 14 and 22.[12] The investigators used an in-depth psychiatric approach involving clinical interviews and psychological testing for the students as well as interviews with their parents, teacher ratings, and other measures. Three different psychological growth patterns, representing different "develop-mental routes" through adolescence, were noted among the boys as their lives and activities were observed over this eight-year period. These patterns of growth were called Continuous, Surgent, and Tumultuous.

The researchers found that students in the Continuous

growth group had many qualities attributable to ideal mental health: happy, coping, well-ordered lives lived in accordance with conscience, good interpersonal relations, a minimum of physical ailments and chronic complaints, and controlled aggressive and sexual impulses. These young men could dream about being the "best" in their class in various areas, coped well with difficulties and problem situations, could postpone immediate gratification, and were able to work toward future goals. A distinguishing characteristic of the members of this group—which comprised about 23 percent of the total—was an "overall contentment with themselves and their place in life" as well as a "quality of order in their lives." These are characteristics that are found in productive adolescents with high self-esteem and a good sense of identity.

The family backgrounds of these boys were stable. There was mutual respect, trust, and affection between parents and children. Parents encouraged their boys' independence and were willing to grow and change with their sons. Value systems of parents and sons dovetailed and the sense of gratification was reciprocal.

Neither of the other groups studied exhibited the above characteristics. Boys in the Surgent group (about 35 percent of the total) seemed to develop in spurts, alternating with periods of turmoil. The Tumultuous group experienced even more of such problems. The family backgrounds of the boys in these two groups—particularly the third—were less stable, less harmonious, and more conflicted than those of the Continuous group. Many of the problems these young men faced were not unlike those that characterize the psychological state known as *confused identity*.

CONFUSED IDENTITY

If a sense of identity is a harmonious functioning of all parts of the individual, denoting oneness or wholeness, then confused identity suggests that the parts are not functioning as a unified whole. One or more aspects of the individual's physical, intellectual, and social life are in some way failing to promote the young person's growth. Children in a state of confused identity are getting mixed and inconsistent messages from their parents—some supportive, others critical and negative.

The Surgent group of adolescent boys, constituting the largest group in the midwestern study described above, provide an excellent illustration of confused identity in adolescents. Because their growth pattern alternated developmental spurts with periods of turmoil, the boys' lives seemed a constant cycle of progression and regression. At times they moved ahead, at other times they seemed stuck and unable to advance. The self-esteem of these young men wavered. They differed from the Continuous group in degree of confidence and coping ability, became discouraged more easily, exhibited more anger, were more dependent on peers, and were inclined to blame others for their mistakes.

The relations of this group with their parents were marked by conflict of opinions and values. The parents disagreed between themselves on the importance of discipline, academic achievement, religious beliefs. The families were also more traumatized—more affected by separation, death, and severe illness than those in the Continuous group; in some cases the parents came from different backgrounds. Some mothers experienced difficulty in permitting their sons a normal opportunity to separate themselves from a dependent relationship. In the area of schoolwork, the parents' expectations were for "average" achievement, and their sons accordingly achieved at that level.[13]

These Surgent students typify many youngsters who are confused about their identity. The wavering self-esteem and lack of general confidence suggest an inconsistent parental background featuring periods of tension and conflict—prolonged and frequent arguments and disagreements which inhibit or block normal parent–child communication. Parents often have limited goals for such children.

Unevenness in productivity is characteristic of many "average" students and is reflected in somewhat erratic school achievement (grades usually average out to a C level). Such students are typically more interested in getting to basketball practice than in checking their homework carefully. Similarly, their physical appearance can be characteristically sloppy and unprepossessing; yet before a date they may spend considerable time before the mirror.

The fundamental cause of children's confused identity is insufficient parental love and support. When thus deprived, a child becomes sensitive to even subtle undercurrents of parental indifference, rejection, or hostility. A toddler, for example, may react by uneasy clinging and excessive demands for attention, refusing food at mealtimes, or wetting the bed beyond the normal age.

Parents may deprive a youngster of complete acceptance for a variety of reasons. Perhaps at the child's birth they were disappointed by his or her sex. They find fault with some aspect of physical appearance. Perhaps they are irritated by the youngster's behavior. Whatever the cause, their dissatisfaction and ambivalence will be evident to the child.

Such parents are often cold and unexpressive toward a youngster; they smile rarely and often frown, discipline the child for minor transgressions, criticize frequently, even inflict excessive physical punishment. Above all, they tend to be inconsistent in their feelings and attitudes toward their child.

Parental inconsistency is particularly demoralizing; it can make children feel both bewildered and helpless. Praised, they feel close to their parents; scolded, they feel abandoned. They never know what to expect. Such children either search for approval which is not forthcoming or try to protect themselves from further rejection.

A youngster in such an unpredictable situation doesn't really know who he is. He is forced to react to the two most powerful and significant adults in his life in two different ways—at one time with love and at another with anxiety and fear. In this dilemma he cannot function effectively as a person.

The Body Image

An individual's body image, or attitude toward his own body, is formed early in life. It is directly related to how the persons in his small world feel about him.

Awareness of the body is the young child's first sense of identity or "self" (a feeling that "This is me"). The body also serves as a mirror: it reflects the child's perception of the parents' attitudes and feelings about him. If the youngster views his parents as empathic and accepting, his bodily appearance will be appealing—posture and movements relaxed and effortless. Such a child will be relatively unconscious of his body and, if constantly supported during the growing years, will comfortably traverse the stages of physical growth through adolescence.

When, on the other hand, children perceive their parents as indifferent and uncaring, their bodies tend to reflect anxiety and tension. Listlessness, awkwardness of movement, poor posture, overweight or underweight, and possibly muscular coordination problems may be evident in some children. In adolescents the symptoms may include excessive preoccupation with personal appearance (the determined body-building regimes with which some youths endeavor to achieve massive muscle power or the inordinate concern with clothes, hairstyles, or makeup of some girls) and sometimes a tendency toward frequent minor illnesses.

These individuals have a common problem. They are basically anxious and insecure. Their self-esteem is low. They are uncomfortable with themselves and their bodies have become the focus of their anxiety.

Let us examine a few of these symptoms in more detail.

● Some youngsters seem plagued with poor muscular coordination:

Seven-year-old Tony is awkward, walks with a slouch, and detests competitive sports. On the playing field he's clumsy and makes a lot of goofs when he's railroaded into a ball game.

Poor muscular coordination occurs more frequently in boys than in girls. Tony should of course be examined by a physician for the presence of a possible neurological condition. If this is ruled out, it is possible that his problems have a psychological cause. Emotional immaturity has been found to be significantly related to boys' muscular coordination problems in the lower elementary grades.[14] Encouraging parents of such youngsters to express more nurturance toward them has proven to be an effective remedy for the problem.

● Another common problem is hyperactivity:

Freddie is chronically restless, impulsive, and fidgety; his limbs and body are always in motion. He's given to breaking things, forgetting tasks and obligations, falling, and bumping into objects.

Hyperactivity has been viewed as having possible neurological or chemical components. One school of thought maintains that the cause of hyperactivity lies in the presence of red coloring and other additives in foods. Acceptable scientific research, however, finds no valid connection between such factors and hyperactivity.[15] A somewhat related condition is accident-proneness, which is seen in an impulsive child who seems constantly involved in minor (or not so minor) mishaps to himself and with others. Such problems are typically found in authoritarian, critical homes where communication is poor, youngsters' verbal expressions of resentment toward parents are prohibited, and the child becomes constantly active in order to relieve his anxiety and hostility. Recent research has found low self-esteem to be a common characteristic of hyperactive children.[16]

The hyperactive child should certainly be seen by a physician to determine any neurological cause of the problems, but the drugs that may be prescribed will not in themselves remove psychological insecurity. Psychological treatment should focus on helping parents to promote the child's self-esteem. Once the youngster feels more comfortable with his father and mother and thus with himself, he will have less need of continuous uncontrolled activity.

• Another problem associated with bodily complaints is known as "psychosomatic conditions" (see Chapter Eleven). These conditions tend to appear in families where communication is sparse, praise and affection are rarely expressed, and individuals are afraid to verbalize their fears or resentments. Contradictory parental comments of the double-bind variety described in Chapter Four can, in certain cases, almost paralyze children, trapping them in an emotional dilemma from which they can't escape, either physically or verbally.

The body, or some part of it, may become the focus of anxiety. The skin and respiratory tract may be involved; disorders in the digestive, circulatory, or cardiovascular systems may develop. Overweight in both boys and girls may occur.

School Problems

Children who are uncertain of their identity sometimes encounter school-related problems which are of two general types, lack of motivation and learning problems.

Simple lack of motivation is not uncommon. These youngsters seem uninterested in school. A "don't care" attitude pervades their activities in and out of the classroom. This really signifies their feeling that no one cares about them. Their chronic anxiety interferes with their ability to cope with the demands of the school program. Sensing no genuine affection and reassurance from their parents, they feel no need to do well in school.

Children in the primary grades with learning problems primarily caused by psychological factors due to poor parent–child relationships are often confused in identity. They have trouble mastering the elements of reading, spelling, and arithmetic and are often described by their teachers as having a poor self-image.[17] Their low self-esteem does not give them the confidence to cope easily with new situations, especially the academic tasks that involve the use of symbols rather than tangible objects. Research by ourselves and by others demonstrates that merely teaching learning-disabled children to read does not usually get at the basic psychological insecurity which is almost always present in such youngsters. When systematic tutoring and remedial instruction in the child's deficient skills are accompanied by work with the parents—who are shown how to provide their child with more affection and nurturance at home—the child is usually on the road to improvement.

The Problem of Late Maturity

Research on adolescent boys whose maturity is delayed has found such characteristics as irresponsibility, poor self-image, attention-getting mechanisms, and rebellion against conventions and authority figures. Follow-up studies on this group further indicate that these traits tend to persist after the individual reaches normal physical maturity and even into early adulthood.[18] Late-maturing girls find this period less stressful than boys.[19]

Parents and teachers are too often prone to attribute the academic and social problems of late-maturing adolescents to their delayed physical development. The family backgrounds of these students should be explored before such judgments are made. Physical maturity, early or late, does not in itself determine levels of achievement. Many students of both sexes who are below average in stature are academically and socially productive. Coopersmith found in his study of 10- to 12-year-old boys that self-esteem was not related to height.[20] In light of research on personality development we suggest that the problems of self-perception and inadequate school and social functioning of these late-maturing young people probably originate in an early child–parent relationship lacking in affection, nurturance, and concern.

Confused Gender Identity

Adolescents with low self-esteem often suffer from confused gender identity. These young people usually lack coping skills, independence, creativity, and the motivation to be productive; they therefore tend to focus on social behavior that involves interaction between the sexes to compensate for their lack of competence in other areas. They overplay their masculinity or femininity in various ways:

Sixteen-year-old Joe affects a swaggering "macho" image. He revs up his motorcycle and joins the noisy weekend parade of vehicles that roar up and down the popular downtown strip.

Mary Anne parades her sexual charms in provocative attire.

Being vulnerable to peer influences, such youngsters are easily led by others with similar problems into experimenting with alcohol, marijuana, and sex. An adolescent girl may become pregnant; a boy turns to alcohol and drugs. The social life of such young people is usually passive; they prefer to sit at a pot party than to play a vigorous game of softball.

There is much misunderstanding of issues surrounding gender identity. Part of the trouble arises from the widely held attitudes about what is "masculine" and what is "feminine." Social expectations in past years have been sharply different for men than for women and they have been evident in the lives of even our youngest children. The boy or man has been deemed the stronger—the more daring, assertive, competitive member of society. The girl or woman has been viewed as the gentle nurturer—caring, empathic, home-loving. Therefore boys were put outside to play and girls tended to occupy themselves indoors, staying close to their mothers, who probably talked more with them than with their brothers.[21] (As a result, girls have been typically more verbal than boys.) In the past fathers have tended to be more openly affectionate toward their daughters than toward their sons, although they have been less expressive or empathic toward children of either sex than their wives. As a group fathers are also more authoritarian toward sons than toward daughters. Expecting from their boys toughness, daring, and aggressiveness, they try to develop in them stereotypical male characteristics. Athletic competition is encouraged, presumably as preparation for the competitive business world.

The net result of these sharply different expectations toward boys and girls (as well as men and women) is that boys as a group receive less basic nurturance and "tender loving care" than do girls. Somehow, in the effort to build a strong man, the male's need for tenderness and empathy is sometimes overlooked. This is particularly true when fathers express very little affection to their sons, who may consequently experience some basic low self-esteem. Boys who have received insufficient nurturance, who have seldom been praised, and who have been encouraged to be competitive and tough may come to overplay their masculine role. This type of behavior (actually masking deep insecurities) results in more physical and social problems of adult men as well as in the antisocial exploits that are statistically associated with men and boys—a higher incidence of automobile accidents, alcoholism, sexual exploits, drug abuse, and violence. Conversely, research on the backgrounds of productive boys reveals that abundant affection and support from *both* parents have made possible the development of healthy, coping, socially responsible young men. Many of the problems encountered by today's parents and teachers could be reduced if fathers could be admonished to express more affection and support to their sons.

ENHANCING YOUR CHILD'S SENSE OF IDENTITY

If your children are to grow into happy, productive adults, they must develop a sense of identity early in life. They will need certain things from you. First of all, you must let them know that they are special to you: each child is like no other individual on the face of the earth. In addition, you must nourish their self-esteem with warm affection, encouragement, and praise. You must provide them with consistent guidance and standards. Finally, you must have faith in their capacity to make something of their lives.

There are numerous ways in which you can enhance your children's identity formation. Some are illustrated below.

You can keep a record of your youngsters' growth from year to year. Among other benefits, this will provide them with a sense of themselves as continuously evolving human beings:

There's a special wall in the laundry with two columns of little penciled figures on it. One column is marked "Eddie," the other "Marie." Daddy has measured their height, in feet and inches, on each of their birthdays since they were two and could stand still long enough to cooperate. Now that they are ten and eight years old, Eddie and Marie comment in wonderment, "Was I ever that little?" There's additional proof in all the birthday snapshots that Daddy has taken each year.

You can be generous with compliments concerning physical appearance:

Carol, seventeen, comes into the kitchen wearing a new outfit she has just purchased with part of her summer earnings. "Gee, you look great this morning!" comments Dad. Mom adds, "It's a becoming color for Carol, isn't it? It fits you well, too, dear."

Such comments help Carol to feel accepted as a girl. They also demonstrate her parents' respect for both her taste in clothes and her judgment in spending her money wisely. It's equally important to compliment Carol's 16-year-old brother when he appears in his new sport jacket and his Mom's favorite tie!

You can and should try to find frequent opportunities for a

child to spend brief periods of time *alone with one parent*. When a child shares companionship with a significant adult in his life, his sense of identity is enhanced. That adult's full attention is temporarily his, and his alone; he doesn't have to share it with anyone. At such moments a child can feel unique, special, and significant because he and his companion are sharing their lives in a special way. These precious moments can occur spontaneously amid the routines of daily living. Merely letting a small child help with a task presents an opportunity:

At five o'clock in the afternoon 6-year-old Alan comes into the kitchen and says, "Mummy, I want to make something for supper tonight." Mother says, "Thank you, Alan. How would you like to help me fix the salad?" "Goody!" says Alan, and gets to work. Mother doesn't mind the messy kitchen counter. Together they put the greens into a big bowl and Alan mixes the salad all by himself. At supper everyone enjoys the salad. "You're a good cook, Alan!" says Daddy. Alan agrees.

Daddy is raking the lawn. Three-year-old Molly is helping. Her hand is on the long rake handle under Daddy's. For a few minutes they work together. This slows Daddy down but he doesn't mind. To be sure, Molly presently tires of this activity and returns to the driveway to cruise around on her tricycle. But she has felt close to her daddy for a little while.

Equally precious are moments of shared leisure, especially when working fathers and mothers have relatively few opportunities to be alone with individual family members. It's important that they plan such occasions, as the five productive families described in Chapter Three have done:

Young Jill has enjoyed long Sunday afternoon walks with her father. Steve and his dad go to ball games and play tennis together. Mary remembers the glorious fall day she and her mother spent gathering maple leaves.

Individual adult attention is particularly significant for a small child at bedtime:

Edward and Anne Smith are parents of little Nancy, who is two. Edward is in his last year of law school. Anne is trying to finish her master's degree and this year she must attend classes two evenings a week. The Smiths are devoted to Nancy and seldom hire a baby-sitter; instead, they divide the home responsibilities. When Anne has a class, Edward sees that his young daughter has plenty of attention at bedtime. They always read a story together, and Nancy loves it when her father sits next to her bed and they talk about what she's going to do the next day.

A rich sense of identity, both for individual children and for the family as a whole, is provided when everyone can share in moments of intense emotion. Grief at the sudden death of a beloved grandparent is felt by children of all ages and should be shared with their parents. Children, of course, love moments of uproarious merriment. The following incident is a precious memory in our own family:

Peggy and Jack have a great time trying to see who can tell the funniest joke at supper. They especially love to see their father laugh at their comical stories. Funniest of all, however, is the sight of Daddy telling one of his own "special" jokes and then doubling up with laughter at his own performance. One night Daddy is especially hilarious. "Look at Daddy!" says four-year-old Martha as Daddy, speechless with glee, wipes his eyes after one of his favorite joke stories. Mother explains to Martha that sometimes when we laugh very hard it makes tears come. Everyone feels good at the end of the meal and, somehow, all the children sense that they are close to their parents.

CONCLUSION

Identity and self-esteem are the basic prerequisites of productivity. Without a sense of identity, children's lives lack continuity, meaning, and direction. Every dimension of their activities will be affected. The source of their sense of identity, like that of their self-esteem, is found in the love, constancy, faith, and expectations of their parents.

SPECIFIC SUGGESTIONS

Do:

Do build strong bonds of affection with your children, thus enhancing the process of identification in their lives.

Do compliment your child's personal appearance.

Do help your children to be comfortable with their gender identity.

Do try to provide opportunities for each parent to be alone with individual children.

Don't:

Don't show more affection to one sex group than to the other.

Don't, in matters of discipline, favor one sex group over the other.

THE INFLUENCE
OF BIRTH ORDER

Mary and Joe Smith have three children. Ellen, the oldest, is thirteen, a model of good behavior, an excellent student, and rather shy and serious. Janie, the youngest, is six. She's an adorable, outgoing youngster who makes friends wherever she goes and always seems to be in charge of her playmates' activities. Jimmy, nine, is in the middle. He is somewhat awkward, impulsive, a trifle irresponsible, and not doing too well in school.

A child's personality development and productivity are in part influenced by his or her position (as first child, second, third, etc.) in the family. This influence is well illustrated by the three Smith children.

THE BIRTH ORDER PROBLEM

The topic of birth order (or ordinal position) has been the subject of much research.[1] It has been found that high achievement tends to occur more frequently in first-born than in later-born children. As a group, first-born children tend to be conscientious and responsible workers, often socially reserved people, and more adult in their behavior (though not necessarily brighter) than their younger brothers and sisters. The youngest child in the family is frequently more social and peer-oriented than the first. It is the middle child (whether the second of three, or somewhere in the midst of a larger family) who seems most likely to develop various kinds of learning and social problems.

There are numerous exceptions to these trends. In many families the middle children are just as productive as their older or younger siblings. It is also true that not all first-born youngsters are high achievers.

In some large families, devoted and hard-working parents have carefully nurtured the development of each and every child, regardless of his or her position in the order of birth:

The Antonellis, though in modest circumstances, raised four outstanding children. All are now grown and on their own. The eldest son holds a doctorate in history and is on the faculty of a well-known university. One daughter, after earning a master's degree in Romance languages, was a successful teacher; she is now happily married and the mother of a small son. The third and fourth family members are physicians. Andrew, with his nurse wife, has established a small clinic in an isolated part of northern Vermont, and Maria, also an M.D., is rearing two thriving youngsters with the help of a cooperative husband.

Many parents remark that their children are all different from each other. They fail to realize that, in spite of their best intentions to the contrary, they have not given equal amounts of attention to each.

Each child in a family grows up in a different emotional and psychological climate from that of his or her brothers and sisters, even though all the children in that family are living under the same roof and receiving the same physical care. The reason? Without realizing it, many parents tend to lavish considerable attention and concern on their first child. They are then somewhat more casual with subsequent offspring.

If, as we have previously pointed out, a child's productivity is nurtured from infancy by warm and empathic parents, it follows that differences in children's productivity probably result from the differing amounts of attention and stimulation they have received, particularly in their early years. In general, conscientious parents will try their utmost to treat all their children alike regardless of the family's size and the position of each child in the birth order. Nevertheless, the family environment is never the same for any two children.

EACH CHILD'S POSITION IN THE FAMILY

The following situations resulting from the influence of birth order will serve to illustrate the problems faced by many youngsters.

First-Born Children

Children who are born first in a family acquire traits associated with productivity and achievement because in their earliest years they are, for a time, alone in an adult environment. For them, life has some of the following characteristics:

> They generally receive much undiluted parental love, adulation, and solicitude. They are praised for each and every accomplishment—their first smile, their first tooth, their first steps, and so on. Early on, they become conditioned to receive adult approval for everything they do.

> Their fathers and mothers probably play games, read to them, laugh and talk freely with them so that they develop verbal skills rather early in life.

> They also acquire adult social values, problem-solving techniques, and other assets from their parents.

> Temporarily an only child, the first child does not at first have to interact and compete for attention with other children.

> Because of their inexperience, the parents tend to be somewhat unsure of themselves in their new role and may communicate some of this concern to their youngster, who may therefore be a little less relaxed or casual in social relationships than his or her younger siblings.

Second-Born Children

The next child to come along is usually in quite a different situation:

> The parents, for whom the novelty of having children has partly worn off, tend to be less anxious and more relaxed than they were with their first-born.

> They are also somewhat less attentive. Their time and energies are now divided between two youngsters and accordingly they may not make quite the same investment in the second child's achievement skills that they did with the first-born. (There's less time for the story, the little individual chat, the enjoyable little game that were shared with child number one.)

> Children who are born second probably spend more time with the older sibling and less alone with the parents. Their social environment is therefore very different. Playing and

conversing with a contemporary much of the time, they hear more child language as opposed to adult talk.[2]

If there are no more than two youngsters, and the second-born is either close in age or of the same sex as the elder child, there is some possibility of rivalry and competitiveness between the two. (The two-child family is discussed below.)

At the birth of a younger brother or sister, the second-born becomes a middle child. He or she will never enjoy the privilege of being an only youngster (as the youngest child probably will in later years when the older siblings are often out or have left home).

In this position, the second child can neither compete with the achievement of an older sibling nor secure the favored position of a younger one, who will be enjoyed as the baby of the family.

It is therefore possible, *though not inevitable,* that this child (or any youngster who is born somewhere between the eldest and youngest) will grow up with a certain degree of insecurity. If the family is large and the children closely spaced in age, this threat is increased.[3]

Later-Born and/or Youngest Children

For children who are born third or later in a family, life tends to go something like this:

From an early age they are surrounded by and forced to maintain and assert themselves with slightly older rivals. From sheer necessity they develop competitive skills.

As a result they may enjoy a leadership advantage with their own playmates. (There appear to be a large number of youngest children in professional athletics.)

The parents now have even less time and energy for individual children, although their increased experience and confidence permit them to enjoy and accept this younger family member. The child may, however, receive less of the attention and informal teaching that were given to the first-born.

The younger child is often praised as "a nice person." He or she learns early to relate well to others.

If a fourth or fifth baby comes along, the third child becomes a middle child.

Youngsters who are third or later in the birth order may not openly demand attention, but their school achievement is sometimes less than it might be. They may be inclined to be somewhat impulsive and aggressive, to lose possessions easily, to be more casual than serious, and even to be somewhat accident-prone.

Because such children are often socially mature, their parents may not be much concerned about them. Nevertheless, they should view these symptoms as indicating that the youngster is being denied his or her full share of parental love and attention.

Birth order is subject to two other moderating influences, the sex of individual children and the distance between their ages. If the second of three children is a boy between two girls, he occupies a unique place in the family by virture of being the only boy. Similarly, a little girl sandwiched between an older and younger brother can play a special feminine role in the family. (In other words, these middle children may fare better simply because they are supplying the family with welcome diversity of sex.) If a large family consists almost exclusively either of girls or boys, a single child of the opposite gender will usually be warmly accepted. In certain cultures, when the eldest child is a boy, he is accorded special preference and adulation.[4]

Age spacing is also an important influence. In any situation where there is a gap of five or more years between siblings, the younger child is virtually guaranteed sufficient individual adult attention (assuming that his parents are prepared to give it!) to assure his optimum development.

THE LARGER FAMILY: PROBLEMS AND GUIDELINES

As a family grows larger, its challenges and problems (including those arising from birth order) usually intensify. They sometimes influence the development of individual youngsters.

To begin with, there are greater economic strains on the family because there are more individuals to feed, clothe, and educate. In these days, both parents are usually working and there are heavy demands on the time and energy of each. Some fathers are supplementing their income by moonlighting at a second job; others are struggling to attain a promotion with its corresponding pay increase. Because of these demands, both fathers and mothers have limited time and energy to devote to the parenting tasks. In particular, fathers are less available at home than when the family was smaller.

With the father thus occupied, the mother (often working herself) may have to assume many child-rearing tasks. She tends to become the chief disciplinarian and chief arbiter of minor disputes, particularly among the younger children. (The eldest child is likely to remember Daddy as the main disciplinarian, while younger brothers and sisters recall their mother in this role.) The family structure also tends to become more authoritarian; there is less flexibility, less opportunity to hear and respond to individual views and preferences.[5]

Another possible problem in a larger family is that the marriage relationship is somewhat more vulnerable to strains and tensions than in earlier, less stressful years. Finally, in the larger family there are increased opportunities for the creation of both alignments and scapegoats (see Chapter Eight).

Under these circumstances, one fact becomes obvious. It is the younger, and particularly the middle, children who may be most deprived of sufficient individual care, support, attention, and intellectual stimulation. Consequently their achievement skills may be less well developed, especially in the early, formative years. The larger the family and the more closely spaced the children, the greater the problem of meeting the needs of those in the middle.

This situation can occur in all socioeconomic groups.

Precautions in Certain Family Situations
If you have more than three youngsters, and it appears that the achievement of your younger children is suffering, don't feel guilty over past slights. Remember there are still plenty of ways in which you can encourage your youngsters' productive development. The first step is to be sensitive to the *continuing liabilities* of each child's position in your family. The children's behavior will undoubtedly help to remind you of the problems they face. When a middle child sulks and takes little interest in his schoolwork, you can plan appropriate measures: his mother can take him by himself to a baseball game, or his father can take him to lunch and the aquarium. If two sisters bicker constantly, they can be encouraged to become engrossed in separate projects.

In large families, certain factors can sometimes work to the disadvantage of individual youngsters' development. It's well to be alert to the potential for harm in the circumstances described below:

● It is not enough merely to "enjoy" your younger children. They deserve just as much attention and stimulation as the first-born received. Parents of big families understandably become more confident, relaxed, and somewhat casual with the third, fourth, or fifth addition to their brood:

The Phillips family is growing. Now that Sam, the third child, has arrived, Mrs. Phillips breathes a sigh of relief. Sam seems so much easier than the first two babies. She worried a lot about Johnny and Meg. But she's thoroughly enjoying little Sam.

Mrs. Phillips must invest the same effort to develop Sam that she gave to Johnny and Meg. Otherwise he may grow up socially mature and pleasant but lacking in drive, competence, and productivity.

● It is not fair to turn the eldest child of a big family into a regular baby-sitter:

Ann is the eldest of five. At twelve, she has to take a good deal of responsibility after school for a 2-year-old brother and a pair of lively twin boys who have just turned six. Her mother gets home late from work every day, and she's always tired.

Ann would like to go to after-school chorus and Scout meetings more regularly, but she has to baby-sit a lot. (Her mother's helper isn't very reliable and she's been sick for the last three weeks.)

Is this the best arrangement that Ann's working mother can make? There is certainly no harm in occasionally asking a 12-year-old to take temporary charge of younger brothers and sisters, but expecting this kind of commitment on a regular basis and for several hours at a time is really asking too much of a child of Ann's age. She may grow up feeling a little bitter about having been forced prematurely into a parental role and also a little drained of motivation to develop her own academic skills and assets.

Working mothers unquestionably have very tough schedules. Nevertheless, their youngest children need continuous *adult* supervision. Mothers have three choices. They can try to schedule their working hours so as to be at home themselves in after-school hours. They can arrange with a mature adult (relative or close neighbor) to look after the household in their absence. Or, lacking these options, they can commit a portion of their earnings to hiring a *reliable* person in good health to take charge at home.

● It is unwise to allow the eldest child in the family to be the customary spokesman for younger siblings. The eldest child, as we have noted, is characteristically mature, responsible, and possibly more articulate than younger brothers and sisters. This does not mean that she or he should always be the individual to speak up for the others in relating the details of a given incident or problem.

You can remedy this situation somewhat by trying to give equal time to first, middle, and youngest children alike. At dinnertime or in general family conversation you can rotate among children the privilege of speaking and being recognized first. In this way, no one needs to feel slighted or inferior.

It goes without saying that you cannot permit an older child to dominate, control, or tease a younger one.

● Do not boast to friends or neighbors about the achievements of the "star performer" in your family without reference to those of the child's brothers and sisters. This is a great temptation, particularly for ambitious parents:

Mrs. S. volunteers to her neighbor that "Peter is doing so well—you know he got admitted to college early decision. . . ." To her neighbor's polite inquiry about Peter's younger sister Sally, Mrs. S. replies somewhat apologetically, "Well, she'll probably settle for a junior college. She's just not the student her brother is, you know."

What does this do for Sally's reputation? Mrs. S.'s pride in Peter is understandable. What is *not* fair is the implication of the rest of the conversation. These remarks and predictions are not only cruel but may also be inaccurate. With proper support, it's entirely possible that Sally may begin in a junior college, do well there, and then transfer to a university where she achieves with distinction.

THE FAMILY WITH TWO CHILDREN

Today's families are becoming smaller. Many couples want no more than two children. Sometimes—for economic, professional, or other reasons—a number of years may elapse between the births of the two youngsters, in which case each child can enjoy abundant parental attention during the important early years and get off to a fast start in life. In this situation there are rich possibilities for the individual development of both children as well as numerous options for their parents. There are ample opportunities for children and parents to share common interests and pleasures that would be less affordable in larger families. Life can be pleasant and rewarding for all concerned.

It's quite possible for two children in a family to grow up happily together into equally productive and successful adults. Certain risks, however, are inherent in the two-child situation. Rivalry, competitiveness, and even hostility may develop between the siblings, particularly when the two are close (two years or less) in age and when they are both of the same sex.

If you have two youngsters, you should be aware of these risks. There are ways of minimizing them, as illustrated in the following situations. It is well to keep certain points in mind:

● Be sure that you make an equal investment in each child's development, particularly in the early years:

Shortly after her fourth birthday Nell goes proudly off to nursery school every morning. This gives Mother a chance to take 2-year-old Carol for a little walk. On bad days they play little games, do lots of things together around the house, and talk and laugh a great deal. Before lunch Mother always reads Carol's favorite stories.

Later, during Carol's nap, Nell and Mother have a good visit together.

This mother is trying to provide her second daughter with the same individual attention, affection, and informal education that she gave to her first.

● When child number two joins the household, try to empathize with the older child's feelings as he or she adjusts to the presence of a younger sibling:

Mother is feeding baby Edward. Two-year-old Paul, still harboring mixed feelings toward his little brother, is watching. At four months Edward is still far from being a good playmate, and he seems to take a lot of Mother's time, too.

Mother understands how Paul feels these days. She lets him help with the baby when he wants to. They both laugh as Edward's strained carrots dribble down onto his bib. Paul gets a clean one for him, and Mother gives him a big hug of appreciation.

Before bedtime Daddy and Paul play a rousing game of "Bear" together. Daddy hears all about Paul's day. After a quiet story, he tucks Paul into bed.

Sometimes the first child has difficulty becoming adjusted to the presence of a new baby. After being kingpin since birth, Paul is suddenly dethroned and must henceforth share the spotlight with a potential rival. His feelings must be understood and respected.

It helps greatly when, as in the above situation, the mother is supported by her husband in handling the two small rivals.

● Be happy with the safe arrival of your second baby, regardless of his or her sex. By all means, avoid the following mistake:

When Joe and Maria were in their late thirties and expecting their second child, they were advised to have no more children after this one was born. They already had a little girl and desperately wanted a boy.

When another girl arrived some months later, Joe and Maria were deeply disappointed. For years they have had difficulty coming to terms with their feelings.

Now there are problems. The second little girl is not doing as well in school as her big sister, and the two often quarrel bitterly with each other.

The seeds of rivalry and antagonism between the two girls were sown in the attitudes of Joe and Maria long before child number two was born. In setting their hearts on their second child's sex, they have shortchanged their second daughter.

● Try to be scrupulously fair in disciplinary matters. Failure of parents to be evenhanded in adjudicating disputes can cause problems in a family of any size but it seems to be particularly damaging to relationships between two siblings. An older child may feel that the younger is always favored simply because of his or her age.

This mother has coped sensibly with the problem:

Despite a three-year difference in their ages, Fred and Greg get along pretty well. Once in a while there's an argument. If it comes to Mom's attention she listens carefully to both sides of the story. Although Fred, the elder, sometimes thinks his little brother has an unfair advantage, he's usually willing to accept what he perceives as an equitable settlement.

THE ONLY CHILD

Today we are seeing an increased number of one-child families. Eleven percent of American women of child-bearing age (twice as many as in 1955) are now reported as planning to limit their families to one youngster.[6] The uncertain times, the enormous cost of rearing and educating children, the large number of later marriages, and the trend of young women to prepare themselves for professional positions prior to raising a family are the principal causes of this trend.

What are only children like? Like the first-born with younger siblings, they generally have well-developed achievement skills as measured by tests of abstract reasoning, mathematics, English, and reading comprehension. They tend to have higher educational goals than their peers, to be somewhat less sociable than other youngsters, and to spend more time in intellectual and artistic pursuits. In later years only children seem to develop into more cultivated, more mature, and more academically oriented adults.[7]

Recent research points to three other personality differences between only children and others; these are found in self-esteem, gender identity, and attitudes toward the size of their future families.

● The only child's self-esteem is not noticeably different from that of other children, with one important exception: it is not quite equal to that of first-born children who grow up perceiving themselves as somewhat more advanced and competent than younger brothers or sisters. Children without siblings can only compare themselves with adults in the home, who are understandably viewed as more powerful and competent individuals.

● Only children also seem less concerned than their peers about gender roles; they enjoy a variety of activities without reflecting on their "masculine" or "feminine" appropriateness. This is probably the result of the fact that their parents, satisfied to be rearing one youngster, are themselves without any particular concern in this area. Rigid sex stereotypes appear to be of less importance in such a household.[8]

● Only children apparently intend to beget only children; they seem to have little interest in rearing a large family, thus reflecting their own satisfaction in the kind of life they have been able to lead.[9]

The home environment of only children is similar to others in respect to economic and social characteristics. Their parents are typically somewhat older than other couples. They also have higher educational goals and expectations for their youngster and impose higher standards of behavior. Consequently these children tend to identify with adults, to absorb adult values, and to relate comfortably to adults in general.

There are numerous advantages for both child and parents in

the one-child situation. The child can receive abundant attention, affection, and often tremendous intellectual stimulation from each of two adults, especially if both are highly educated and successful persons. In all likelihood financial pressures on the family are minimized if both parents hold professional positions. Possibly they will require less hired baby-sitting help and can spell one another in this role, much to the child's benefit. The youngster is freed of the stress of competition and rivalry from siblings near his or her age and can attend nursery school in order to gain the companionship of peers.

When an only child of a divorced couple lives with one parent, the amount of nurturance is limited. Research has documented the fact that children from one-parent families have lower IQ scores and do less well on achievement and Scholastic Aptitude tests than youngsters from intact homes.[10] Yet it should be possible for any devoted single parent to overcome these deficiencies and rear a highly productive, successful son or daughter.

In the past it has been widely assumed that parents should at all costs avoid limiting themselves to one child, who would surely grow up selfish, self-centered, shy, and unable to compete and make his or her way in the world. Although this notion still persists, there is evidence that, given the requisite parental devotion, support, and expectations, the only child can become not only a high achiever but also a compassionate, concerned, and effective adult, and even a leader. At all events, we are likely to see increasing numbers of one-child families. It is our prediction that they can make a solid contribution to the solution of society's future problems.

CONCLUSION

Whether you have one, two, three, or several children, it's possible to overcome the risk factors that are inherent in the special circumstances of each. Like the Antonellis, you can rear every youngster to productive adulthood. What is needed is alertness to the occasional developmental deficiencies that may confront certain children who are in a relatively disadvantageous position in the birth order.

It is well to take the long view. All is not won or lost in the early years. Each child is a continuously evolving and growing human being; each will respond to the changes you make to try to improve conditions for him or her. The little things you do for your sons and daughters day in and day out—sitting down for a brief chat, taking a short walk together, playing a game of catch, showing special interest in a school paper or assignment—will in the long run make a difference in their futures.

SPECIFIC SUGGESTIONS

Do:

Do maintain a strictly open mind about the desired sex of an expected baby.

Do remember that each child's position in the family as determined by birth order carries permanent assets and liabilities.

Do give as much careful attention to your second and subsequent children during the early months and years as you did to your first-born.

Do, at the same time, continue to appreciate your oldest child.

Do teach skills to all your children, not just the first.

Don't:

Don't turn your eldest child into a regular baby-sitter or permit the child to be the customary spokesman for younger brothers and sisters.

Don't boast to others about one child's accomplishments without mentioning the progress of your other children.

Don't be satisfied merely to enjoy your younger children.

7

DISCIPLINE, TRAINING, AND SELF-ESTEEM

On a sweltering July day 9-year-old Jimmy and his two friends, Paul and Sam, were playing with the garden hose in Jimmy's driveway. Mr. Smith, a salesman, came in his station wagon to deliver a large tin of laundry detergent to Jimmy's mother. While Mr. Smith was in the house, the boys, in a prankish mood, turned the hose on the contents of the station wagon. Mr. Smith and Jimmy's mother emerged from the house in time to see the act.

What was done about this situation (in which our own son was involved!) by way of discipline?

Although Jimmy's mother was both horrified and embarrassed, she did keep her composure. After the boys had made preliminary apologies, she decided further action was needed. The three families involved held a long conference, after which the boys agreed that: (1) each would earn money to be sent to Mr. Smith as some recompense for the damage done to his merchandise, and (2) each would write a letter of apology. The earnings were subsequently put into a single check and mailed with the letters to the unfortunate gentleman.

There was a surprising sequel to these events. Mr. Smith sent the boys a kind letter. He thanked them for taking responsibility for what they had done. He also wrote that he did not intend to keep the check. Instead he would send it to a camp for underprivileged boys in which he was interested.

Everyone concerned learned from this experience and the boys made appropriate restitution to the individual whose business they had thoughtlessly disrupted.

ESSENTIAL CONDITIONS FOR GOOD DISCIPLINE

The purpose of discipline, and especially of punishment, is widely misunderstood.[1] According to most dictionaries, discipline has two meanings. The first concerns training or teaching. The second meaning has to do with punishment. Parenthood is more properly concerned with the first meaning.

The family is an institution that should be primarily devoted to training, teaching, and learning. Only in a secondary sense should it be concerned with punishment.

Discipline in its primary sense, then, involves learning and training rather than punishment. The first center of this training is the home. The first and most important teachers are the parents.

This training is most effective when the following ten conditions are present:

The parents are understanding and affectionate.

They set a good example.

They provide sound instruction in the principles of right and wrong.

Their own behavior is predictable and their relationship with their children stable and consistent.

Their disciplinary measures (penalties for breaking rules) are also consistent.

The child has a high degree of security and self-esteem.

He or she clearly understands basic rules beforehand.

When punishment does seem necessary, it is handled as calmly, judiciously, and above all, appropriately as possible.

The child, having clearly understood what he or she did wrong and why, participates if possible in the penalty.

The penalty involves some restitution and is carried through to its conclusion so that the child is not left with a residue of guilt.

COMMON MISCONCEPTIONS AND PITFALLS

"If I could only be a better disciplinarian!"

This rueful comment, often voiced by mothers, betrays a fundamental lack of understanding of the discipline issue. Somehow it has been assumed for years, without much logic or justification, that parents should be strict, cold, and at times punitive. Let us look at two typical attitudes, each of which is essentially negative and counterproductive.

One common notion maintains that parents and children are antagonists locked in a perpetual *power struggle*. This presupposes that one side always has to win at the other's expense ("Do as I say!").

Psychological research does not support the effectiveness of such an attitude. Children will obviously be dependent on their parents for many years for the fulfillment of all physical and psychological needs. Simply because the parents are physically larger (at least in the early years) and possess much greater financial and other resources does not mean they should use their position to outwit or dominate their youngsters.

Mere assertion of parental power is futile. It teaches the child nothing about constructive behavior.

Another mistaken idea about discipline is that parents should *make life tough* for their child, especially a son. They assume illogically that a boy obliged to overcome difficulties in his early life will later be able to make his way in a competitive, complex world. Parents who subscribe to this notion make free use of criticism, caustic comments, and other forms of rejection:

Vic is in trouble. He got into a minor accident while driving without permission a car belonging to his pal's father. There's a big bill to pay for straightening the damaged fender and no insurance to cover it.

Vic's father just shrugs his shoulders. "Let him take the consequences. He'll have to learn the hard way."

Vic must of course pay the consequences of inflicting damage on someone else's property, even if it means parting with nearly one-half of his summer earnings. But his father's cold, unsympathetic, and indifferent attitude contributes nothing to Vic's morale or to the resolution of the problem.

Making it tough for a boy in order to make a man of him is a sure way of producing a man who behaves like a boy. Such a person can be either submissive and afraid or brazen, blustery, and generally immature. In either case he is likely to become a selfish adult.

There are other obvious pitfalls to avoid in dealing with disciplinary situations. Verbal abuse (shouting at a child, resorting to name-calling or—worse still—using profanity) is uncivilized and degrading to both you and your youngster. Lecturing and preaching (as opposed to explaining a given issue briefly and clearly) are a waste of time; the child makes no promises and pays no penance. It's futile to enact unenforceable penalties (trying to "ground" a teenager for an entire month). You should never humiliate a child unnecessarily (by shouting "Shame on you!") or invoke irrelevant and guilt-producing comments such as "What you are doing makes me feel bad." Threats that are not carried out only serve to undermine trust, and pious moralizing ("I'm doing this for your own good") carries no weight with any child. It's safe to say that not one of these measures solves any behavior problem without exacting an unacceptable price in terms of your relationship with your child.

Sensible discipline usually steers a moderate course between two extremes, excessive authoritarianism and abject permissiveness.[2] Authoritarianism is represented by the rigid, dictatorial parent described above who always feels he or she must win every confrontation. The permissive parent, on the other hand, weakly allows a child free rein to do whatever he or she wants without restriction or protection—an approach that is equivalent to pure and simple neglect. Children reared permissively grow up socially irresponsible, feeling that their parents simply don't care what happens to them. Young people *want* the security of living in a family that abides firmly by a few rules and standards. On the other hand they do not need, or desire, dozens of trivial prohibitions.

FOUR COMMON TYPES OF DISCIPLINE

Punishment is the infliction of physical or psychological pain upon an individual after he has committed an unacceptable act. We usually punish youngsters to discourage them from repeating their behavior. We hope they will act differently in a similar future situation.

Unfortunately, some parents punish a child before clearly informing him or her that the behavior is wrong. In effect, they punish first and teach second. Such an approach puts the cart before the horse. It also violates everything we know about the psychology of learning.

If we parents do a good job as teachers, we should not have to make extensive use of discipline in the punitive sense. However, there may be times when it is needed. Authorities usually distinguish types of punishment according to their degree of severity:

Simple Verbal Reasoning

This is the mildest, the most constructive, and therefore the most desirable form of discipline. It may consist merely of an expression of gentle disapproval, preferably couched in positive terms. One of us personally witnessed the following scene, in which the mother merely issues a tactful reminder:

Mother, Grandma, and five-year-old Melissa are Christmas shopping. As her mother and grandmother pause for a somewhat lengthy discussion of a prospective purchase, Melissa becomes restless. She begins to handle merchandise, to become a little obstreperous, and to wander up and down the crowded aisle, getting in the way of other customers. Without raising her voice, Mother finally restrains her with the polite request, "Melissa, please help us just a little longer." Melissa quiets down.

This type of discipline can involve explaining to a child why we do or do not behave in a certain way or pointing out the possible consequences of a given act for ourselves or for others.

Some Form of Isolation

A child may be temporarily removed from physical or psychological contact with others (by being sent to his room, for example):

Six-year-old Randy, Joe, and George are playing in Randy's back yard and becoming a little wild. Seeing that a few stones are beginning to fly, Randy's mother goes quickly to the scene. Her voice is firm. "Randy, you've been told time and again that throwing stones is dangerous." As a precaution against further reckless behavior, Joe and George are sent home, and Randy goes to his room for half an hour.

In the above situation, firm action by Randy's mother is justified since the boys are clearly behaving in a dangerous manner. Sometimes it is better to confine a child to an area other than his room (a chair, for example, may be quite enough isolation for a younger child whose room might otherwise become a place of banishment).

Denial of Some Source of Pleasure

This may include revocation of certain privileges such as seeing friends, television viewing, use of the telephone or (for older children) the family car. There may be a temporary cut in allowance which takes the form of a fine:

Seventeen-year-old Bill understands the ground rules clearly. He is to bring Jean, his date, home by 11:30 Saturday evening and his parents' car is to be in the garage by midnight. Bill arrives home at 1:30 Sunday morning. Both sets of parents are awake and anxious. No one attempts to deal with the situation that night. Sunday morning Bill and his parents talk the matter over. It is mutually agreed that Bill will lose the use of the family car for social purposes for one month.

This form of penalty is not determined arbitrarily by the parent but results from a discussion of the situation culminating in an agreement between young Bill and his father and mother that the penalty is justified.

Actual Body Contact

It is our position that this form of punishment should be invoked only rarely and always in a mild form, but that it can occasionally be justified when, as in the following situation, a small child is clearly endangering herself or others:

Active little Tammie, aged two, runs repeatedly to the gas stove and turns on the jet. Mother has said, "No, no!" many times. Finally she slaps Tammie's rear. Tammie whimpers, but now she leaves the stove alone.

Although most of us can probably recall at least one childhood incident in which we were spanked for some misdemeanor, we would surely agree in condemning severe whippings or beatings of the type that were approved in more authoritarian and cruel societies in the past.

PUNISHMENT AND SELF-ESTEEM

All forms of discipline deprive a boy or girl of psychological safety—in other words, self-esteem. The mild reproof, the temporary isolation, the denial of privileges, and the slap on the buttocks are all forms of saying, "I don't like you at this time."

No form of discipline, punitive or otherwise, will succeed with a child unless he or she has some measure of self-esteem. When parents complain that no discipline seems to be effective with their child, the central problem is that they have not yet learned to empathize with their child—to put themselves in the child's place.

Physical punishment may make children feel that their parents actually despise them. In such a situation, youngsters have literally nothing to lose. Their attitude toward their parents says, in effect, "Since I never feel any love from you, I've nothing to gain from trying to improve, no matter what you do to me!"

No child learns merely through enduring physical pain. Continual physical punishment (spanking, slapping, whipping, and the like) accomplishes nothing. Worse still, it gives a child feelings of bewilderment, helplessness, pent-up resentment, and rage. Such children, assuming no responsibility for their actions, are likely to grow into adults who are not only hostile toward others but also generally dependent and incompetent.

In summary, most types of physical punishment are futile, brutalizing and destructive of self-esteem, identity, and the capacity to learn and to solve problems.

In rare situations such as little Tammie's, where safety of life is at stake, you may have to resort to a mild slap (which should certainly be followed by some form of loving reassurance). Otherwise, you should rule out the use of physical punishment in dealing with your youngsters. It is seldom really necessary.

THREE AREAS OF CHILD TRAINING

Let us consider the three principal areas in which child training is carried on. The first of these concerns children's personal care, the second relates to their physical safety, and the third pertains to their relationships with other people.

Personal Care

As parents, especially of small children, we are naturally concerned about training them in good habits of health and personal care. We want them to eat properly, brush their teeth, bathe, use the bathroom properly, go to bed at the proper time, wash their hands before meals, wear clean clothes, pick up their clothes and toys. These concerns can consume a considerable portion of their lives and ours.

As our children grow older, they begin to develop reasonably sensible habits of health and personal appearance. Somewhat regularly, however, some of us continue to remind, urge, cajole, warn, criticize, or scold as the situation dictates. Most of these comments can be identified by the term *nagging*. We have all done too much of it at one time or another.

It's helpful to keep one basic rule in mind: *Keep your priorities clear!* Some issues are definitely more important than a bed left unmade, a sweater that was not picked up and put away, or hair that could have been combed more neatly before dinner. After a time, children no longer hear the nagging anyway. Worse, they may tune out comments or suggestions that are related to more important issues such as adherence to basic safety rules or respect for others' rights.

Personal Safety
We are all rightly concerned with safety, especially that of young children from the moment they begin to crawl and move about independently. Whether they eat their spinach, wash their hands before supper, or go to bed on time is considerably less significant for their survival than their basic safety.

To protect young children when they are still too young to understand and reason, we watch them with an eagle eye near the kitchen stove, near the bathtub, near light sockets, stairs, or objects that can tip over on them. We put dangerous medicines, cleaning compounds, and matches out of their reach. Outdoors we are mindful of other dangers—automobiles, strange dogs, sharp tools, and open water areas. As soon as our young charges can communicate, we start to say "No! No!" about these perils to life and limb, removing them physically, if necessary. There is never any question in such circumstances that the child must at all costs be protected.

Once children have reached the age when they clearly understand the meaning of basic rules for physical safety—fire prevention, use of bikes and automobiles, water safety, precautions when hiking or camping—one cardinal principle should prevail: *Safety rules are never broken.*

Normally such rules can be discussed, clarified, and formulated in family council meetings (see Chapter Eight). By all means let the children participate in this process.

It's very important for parents to consult together and reach advance agreement on any borderline safety matters such as the following:

Chris received a new bike for his fifth birthday. Where and how far is he to be allowed to ride it?

Mom thinks he's doing very well and is sufficiently skilled to take it down the street to the corner and back. Dad, however, feels he should still stay in the driveway.

Naturally, Chris gets two messages and is sure to test the limits of the rule.

The Safety and Rights of Others

We also want our children to get along well with other people and especially to respect their safety and rights. In this regard there are many things to be taught. When a child is very young, raw aggression (pushing, hitting, throwing stones, and so on) must be curtailed. Then the child must learn fairness and respect for others' rights; generosity and honesty; sharing, taking turns, waiting in line; watching out for younger children; the niceties of common courtesy.

As children grow older they learn to apply these principles on an increasingly mature level—in other words, to internalize them.

TRAINING WHILE PRESERVING SELF-ESTEEM: FOUR TRYING SITUATIONS

How can you promote your child's training in these three areas while at the same time protecting his or her self-esteem? The answer is not excessively complex.

The only valid and permanent discipline is self-discipline. A self-disciplined person has learned to govern his life so as to avoid behavior that is disapproved by others and that interferes with his attainment of long-range goals.

Self-discipline is not developed overnight. Like competence and maturity, it comes about as part of the identification process described in Chapter Five. Time, and also much patience on your part, are needed for its development.

Children's attempts to act safely, cautiously, sensibly, generously, fairly, and honestly represent genuine effort on their part. Reward these efforts with approval and recognition. Overlook occasional slipups when possible. Don't nag about unimportant details. Keep rules to a minimum and be sure that these are needed for basic reasons of safety and consideration of others' rights, and that they are clearly understood and firmly enforced. Finally, reserve punishment solely for situations in which your children have clearly or knowingly been reckless of their own or others' safety or well-being.

When, as can sometimes happen, there has been a misunderstanding or an error of judgment on your part, be quick to offer your apology ("Sorry, I was wrong about that"); you are thus modeling responsible and mature behavior. Moreover, your child will be less on the defensive and more willing to discuss his or her responsibility in a given situation.

Chronic misbehavior is usually a sign of emotional insecurity. It is *insecure* youngsters who misbehave, who need to draw attention to themselves by inappropriate clowning, who tease younger siblings or bicker with older ones, who are chronically reckless or impulsive, who are inconsiderate of others' possessions or selfish with their own, who stubbornly refuse to cooperate with family rules or who say, "I don't care." Almost always these behaviors are but symptoms of their own low self-esteem and a feeling that, for the moment, no one cares for them.

In many cases such misbehavior is only minor or temporary. In the normal course of family life typically trying situations arise that may eventually lead to the eruption of small disciplinary problems. In the four examples that follow, it is evident that a little parental foresight and ingenuity can often keep problems from occurring.

An Unstructured Day

Sometimes the regular routine is suddenly interrupted. A school day becomes a snow day, or a long-awaited Saturday excursion is canceled because of rain. Weekends can be particularly difficult if the days are not well organized. Children left with unplanned time on their hands tend to become demoralized. Small scuffles, arguments, or worse can break out unless substitute activities are quickly arranged.

A little advance planning is a great help. You can provide some insurance against the problems of that rainy Saturday by always maintaining ready at hand a supply of projects (including suggestions, plans, and available materials) on which you can draw at a moment's notice. Cooking, sewing, minor carpentry, or simple crafts offer possibilities for appealing and constructive activities. You may need to improvise quickly and ingeniously in order to get youngsters of various ages started on appropriate undertakings. But you and your family can certainly make productive use of the day.

A Long, Tedious Delay

Any long wait, particularly in a confined area, can produce discomfort and frustration, especially for young children. The check-out counter of the local supermarket at rush hours can try the patience of any mother with a heavy load of groceries and several small youngsters in tow. Similarly, a hot, uncomfortable drive home from the beach in heavy midsummer traffic is taxing for all concerned.

Here the remedy lies in possible alternative action. If you

must bring the children with you, try to do the grocery shopping early in the day when the store is less crowded. As for that midsummer excursion to the beach, consider in advance whether it's going to be really worth the tedium of the long, hot ride. A back yard picnic may well be less nerve-wracking and more enjoyable for everyone.

Extreme Fatigue

Fatigue can always contribute to the eruption of minor forms of misbehavior. When both adults and children are tired (at five o'clock in the afternoon, for example) sheer exhaustion can turn a relatively unimportant incident into a major encounter.

At such times your best course of action may be to avoid direct disciplinary measures. Your own judgment, your sense of perspective, and especially your self-control are likely to be at low ebb. Without comment you can separate the antagonists. Merely letting things cool off may be all that is needed and is preferable to an uncontrolled outburst of temper from you.

Excessively Long Adult Telephone Conversations

A frequent and familiar cause of behavior problems in any home is a lengthy phone conversation, particularly between one parent and an unseen relative, committee member, or friend. In the children's eyes, Mother or Daddy is at this moment completely unavailable to them, devoting complete attention to an invisible "someone." It's normal for youngsters to react by feeling left out, forgotten, and rejected and to behave accordingly. Moreover, the parent at this point is in no position to deal with little Susie's wail ("Johnnie hit me!") and matters usually worsen until the phone chat is concluded. (Such conversations are annoying to spouses, too.)

Any long telephone call within a household is a potential cause of resentment. You can explain to your chatty friend at the other end of the line that you'll call back after the children are in bed or have gone to school.

(We might add that children are equally annoyed when their parents sit for hours before the TV set.)

THREE QUESTIONS TO ASK ABOUT ANY BEHAVIOR PROBLEM

Determining the Cause

What is the actual cause? Children often misbehave for a variety of reasons of which they may not be fully aware. Apart from sheer fatigue, the causes of the problem may lie either in the home itself or in outside influences:

Mr. and Mrs. W. have had an argument. For the moment neither is speaking to anyone. Without much warning, little Johnny and Susie start to quarrel bitterly.

Ellie has had a tough day at school. Her teacher bawled her out because she was whispering to her neighbor. At recess her two best friends ganged up on her on the playground. Ellie comes home in a bad mood and is disagreeable toward everyone.

In the first situation, the cause is clearly the tension that is generated in the household by the parents' conflict. In the second, Ellie's mother or father may have to talk with her at an opportune moment, listening carefully in order to find out what the trouble is.

Devising a Constructive Solution

How can we handle the problem so that the child *learns* something from the experience and makes adequate amends for her or his wrongdoing?

Several things will help, if you can remember them in the emotional heat of the moment. First of all, maintain your own composure. Second, try to arrange an early conference with the child in which, speaking quietly and gently, you hear the youngster's version of what actually happened. Gently insist on a completely truthful story. Under these circumstances you will usually obtain at least a partial explanation as to why the behavior occurred.

Then try to devise an appropriate penalty, letting the child be involved in the process.

Effective punishment involves some kind of restitution whenever possible:

The two little Watson boys have come to blows. Donny, the five-year-old, has almost finished the jigsaw puzzle he received for his birthday and is pondering where to put the last ten or twelve pieces. Lou, three years older, sees just where the pieces should go and unwisely tries to interfere. Donny resists. In the ensuing scuffle, the puzzle gets stepped on and some pieces are bent and damaged. Donny is heartbroken.

Adult intervention is clearly called for. Lou and his daddy talk the matter over. Why did he interfere? How would he feel if someone three years older had interfered with his puzzle? What can be done about the broken pieces?

Lou apologizes to Donny. The puzzle is spoiled but Lou decides to save his allowance and buy Donny another one.

Ending the Incident
How can the matter be brought to a definite conclusion? The story of the three boys and the hose at the beginning of this chapter (which is still vividly remembered by the authors!) throws interesting light on this question.

The boys could not, of course, compensate the salesman for having disrupted his delivery schedule. Their penalty was a largely symbolic one, but their written apologies and modest monetary contributions demonstrated that they were being held accountable for what they had done. Once they received Mr. Smith's letter, the incident was closed. For years it was never referred to again.

Twenty years later, however, there is a sequel to this story:

Recently, we asked our thirty-year-old son whether he remembered the hose incident. His reply astonished us: "I don't remember a thing about it."

Effective punishment is complete. The penalty is administered and brought to a definite conclusion. The offender can feel that he has "paid his dues." Incomplete restitution leaves an uncomfortable residue of guilt, a feeling that one still "owes" something (see Chapter Ten). The boys with the hose were able to forget the incident because they had made amends for their thoughtlessness at the time.

If you can deal with wrongdoing in this manner, you will also be helped as a parent. You need not (and should not) have any lingering feelings of anger against your child. There is no need to hold grudges; bygones can be bygones.

We must not conclude this discussion without citing the remark that our son made immediately following his previously quoted comment:

"But I *do* remember the time you made me eat peas for supper!"

HANDLING DISCIPLINE WITH SMALL CHILDREN

It's usually fairly easy to deal with minor misbehavior in children under the age of four. Small children have an abundance of energy but they can easily become overstimulated and tired. Their coping skills are still somewhat limited. Their sense of time and place is only partially developed; they live in the here and now. Their attention span is short and they are easily distracted.

You can generally take advantage of some of these characteristics and limitations in handling small behavior problems. Don't expect too much of small children, especially if you know they are tired. When possible, ignore their acting up, which is usually a symptom, anyway. Rely on strategy to divert their attention from counterproductive activities. If necessary, simply remove them physically from the scene. Act quickly, keep your sense of humor, and avoid lengthy explanations and lecturing. If discipline is necessary, rely on the milder forms such as physical isolation. *Above all, be loving and kind even when you are obliged to act firmly.*

CONCLUSION

The manner in which you discipline your children profoundly affects not only their self-esteem but also the manner in which they relate to others. Thoughtful techniques such as reasoning help them to develop empathy and social concern. On the other hand, when you inflict physical punishment or harsh deprivations, you plant the seeds of future hostility, rebellion, and selfishness.

By stressing a positive rather than a negative approach, you are on safe ground. The tone of your voice can convey the importance of the message. Judicious planning ahead can forestall many tension-provoking situations, especially where small children are involved. If a difficult situation arises suddenly and you must take quick disciplinary action, talk the matter over afterwards with the child. Try to institute discipline that is appropriate to the situation and allow the offender to be involved in determining the penalty. See that restitution is part of the penalty when appropriate.

Discipline involves the long process of learning to become a responsible, mature adult. To be effective, however, it must preserve self-esteem. It will then keep the child's anxiety level low. Only thus is the young individual free to develop all his or her capacities and skills for productive later years.

SPECIFIC SUGGESTIONS

Do:

Do try to teach your children when you discipline them and before punishing them. They must know exactly what they have done wrong and why.

Do try to recognize the actual cause of a child's misbehavior. Experiences at home or school or on the playground can lower youngsters' self-esteem, causing them to act out their frustrations and hurt feelings within the family group.

Do, when possible, permit the offender(s) to choose an appropriate penalty and be sure it involves restitution when applicable.

Do bring a disciplinary incident to a definite conclusion. Don't dwell on the situation. Let bygones be bygones.

Do plan ahead. You can forestall many potential disciplinary problems with a little imagination, understanding of human limitations, and especially, advance planning.

Do explain all safety rules explicitly and enforce them firmly. Normally these rules can be formulated in a family council.

Don't:

Don't preach. Preaching does not change behavior.

Don't nag on unimportant issues; keep your priorities clear. Matters of safety and concern for others' rights are more important than minor lapses in neatness or appearance.

Don't rely on physical punishment to solve any discipline problem effectively.

Don't expect too much of small children. Instead use strategy to divert their attention from counterproductive behavior.

Don't fail to be kind, even when you are obliged to act firmly. Preserve your child's self-esteem at all costs.

EFFECTIVE MANAGEMENT OF FAMILY LIFE

Lucy, Diane, and Nick regularly argue about who's going to do the dinner dishes.

Pete doesn't see why his older sister has a bigger allowance than he does.

The TV is a chronic source of friction in the Smith household.

The Johnson boys always seem to be picking on their sisters.

Familiar problems? Of course.

The family as a small social and economic unit must serve many needs of its members. It must provide and pay for physical shelter, food, clothing, and perhaps some luxuries. It must keep its affairs in order. It must give its members psychological reassurance and support. Finally, it must provide its younger members with an environment in which to prepare for the physical, social, academic, and vocational demands of life.

To meet all these requirements effectively, family life needs some structure. The larger the family, the more organization is required. Even in small households life can become very complex and hectic. The parents *cannot* do all the planning, deciding, and work themselves. Ground rules and schedules are needed. Members must keep each other informed of their special plans and whereabouts. Good communication is essential. Appropriate responsibilities should be assigned to everyone; even a small child can carry plates each evening from the supper table to the kitchen sink.

Studies of problem families find them notoriously disorganized. Poor communication, inadequate or nonexistent planning, casual attitudes toward money and finances, television addiction, and a general tendency of individual family members to "do their own thing" regardless of others' welfare all result in pervasive uneasiness, tension, bickering, and frequently outright conflict.

How, then, on a day-to-day basis, do we keep a family functioning smoothly, pleasantly, and productively for all concerned? This chapter will try to provide a few answers to this question.

The chapter is divided into four parts. The first discusses the value of a regular meeting (sometimes called the "family council") as a democratic means of giving the family unit some basic structure and organization. The second section deals with the important issue of sensible money management. The third is concerned with television, an overwhelming presence in virtually every American home. Finally, there is the problem of managing relationships among family members so as to prevent the formation of undesirable alignments and the creation of scapegoats.

THE FAMILY COUNCIL

This week

Nancy	*Set dinner table*
Bobby	*Help Mom clear dishes*
John	*Take out garbage*
Beth	*Do yard while Dad's away*
Bill	*Cook dinner Friday*
Mom & Dad	*PTA meeting 7:30 Wed.*

These instructions (and others) have been posted on the family bulletin board by 14-year-old Bill. As this month's secretary, he wrote them out after the regular Sunday evening meeting. They were voted on by Nancy (six), 4-year-old Bobby (whose mother had explained the proceedings to him as necessary), John (eight), and the two teenagers of the family, Bill and Beth.

Do You Need a Family Council?

Effective management of a family (particularly a large family) is like managing any business or professional organization. You need short- and long-term goals and guidelines to achieve these goals.

Progress is ensured when members, whether in a family or on a board of directors, meet regularly to review and discuss pending activities and concerns. The family council was suggested some years ago by Rudolph Dreikurs and has since been advocated by other parent education programs.[1]

Successful executives accustomed to the routine of regular staff meetings may be reluctant to implement weekly family council sessions in their own households, but once they are undertaken, their value becomes evident.

Modern living proceeds at a fast pace, leaving no time for inefficient handling of daily, recurrent household chores and responsibilities. The family council is especially needed in the millions of homes where both parents hold full-time jobs. Even though these working fathers and mothers are trying to share the additional burdens of home management, it is still the mother who carries the heavier load. (If she is the sole head of the household, her situation is even more difficult.) In any case everyone, regardless of age, can and must share the task of helping the family to run smoothly.

Regular family council meetings provide numerous benefits:

● They are a democratic means of allocating household chores.

● They help family members keep abreast of each other's activities.

● They can be an effective forum for discussing and resolving major problems of mutual concern to all family members.

● Because these problems are solved as a group and each child feels his or her input is important, everyone's self-esteem and identity were enhanced.

● When everyone in the family, regardless of age, contributes suggestions for rules and regulations, everyone shares responsibility for seeing to their enforcement. The parents no longer need to "rule the roost" in an authoritarian manner.

● Decisions on controversial issues need not be arrived at impulsively or hastily. (One can always say, "Let's put this on the agenda for next week.")

● Since opportunities for tension are reduced, everyone's energy is saved for more productive functioning.

Families differ in the way they run council meetings. In general, three requirements are observed.

Someone presides, at least informally. In the beginning this can be a parent, who can remain somewhat more objective than a teenager, for instance, in discussions of such sensitive issues as use of the telephone. Later other family members may take turns as chairpersons, depending on the circumstances.

A secretary—and a teenager can fulfill this responsibility admirably—is appointed to take notes of all decisions reached at the meeting and post them afterwards.

There is some kind of an agenda. At first parents may have to provide topics for this, but children should be encouraged to add their suggestions. Sometimes one child can be made responsible for polling the others for ideas; it's even a good idea to keep suggestions for future meetings in a special "agenda jar" in the kitchen.

"We're a small family. We don't need so much structure!"

Your family may prefer a more informal approach than that described above. Nevertheless, communication and planning are needed in all households. How you adapt the council concept to your own needs depends on your particular situation. Parents of an only child can perhaps sit down with the child at regular intervals for a relaxed, three-way discussion of pending schedules, problems, and concerns. (Such sessions should not be allowed to evolve into a parent–child confrontation.) Two-child families also report considerable success with council meetings, particularly when youngsters are near in age and in elementary school. There are a variety of ways of modifying the organization of the council while retaining its numerous advantages.

The First Meeting

Getting started is the hardest part. You'll naturally be apprehensive as to how your children will respond. Don't force the family council on them. You can begin as this family did:

Dad, a self-employed salesman, and Mom, a teacher, are parents of Jean, fifteen, eleven-year-old Jimmy, and Judy, four, who attends nursery school until midafternoon.

After Sunday supper Dad restrains family members who are about to disperse in various directions:

"Say, Mom and I just realized that the first of this week looks pretty complicated! I need my car all day Monday and Tuesday. Mom has to leave hers at the garage tomorrow morning and can't get back until late afternoon. She has to be back at school for a PTA meeting early in the evening. Jean has Monday afternoon Scouts. Judy can stay with Mrs. Brown [next door] until someone can bring her home. Any ideas about how we can work this out?"

Or you can start an informal discussion about household duties and each individual's responsibilities for carrying them out.

Little children can be introduced to the family council concept in an occasional bedtime chat. ("What's Molly going to do tomorrow? Let's plan it together!") Thus they will learn to think ahead, sensing some control over their lives.

Some Words of Caution
Before we discuss some specific topics suitable for council meetings, here are a few words of advice:

● Don't have long meetings. From fifteen minutes for small children up to an hour for adolescents is appropriate.

● Be sensitive to special needs of individual children, especially teenagers. Don't force a child to attend a meeting at a time that conflicts with a previously planned and important activity.

● Never use the family council to preach, lecture, or criticize.

● Keep the proceedings issue-oriented rather than personality-oriented; do not permit children to tattle on others in the meeting.

● Be sure that the topics brought up for discussion affect in some way the daily lives of all members.

● Treat all family members as equals in the council setting. Encourage everyone to express views and opinions. Be sure everyone is listening attentively.

● Be careful not to dominate the discussion yourself. At the same time provide tactful leadership.

● The council setting is not the appropriate place or time to discuss private matters. (These include discipline in an isolated situation, inappropriate dating behavior, or sex education.)

Some Topics for Family Discussion
The following topics lend themselves to discussion in a family council:

● Begin by taking an inventory of household chores. Let everyone contribute to the list. Setting and clearing the table, dishes, trash, laundry, and the lawn are only the beginning. Someone has to shop, cook, take the car to the garage, vacuum, dust, clean the bathrooms, pay bills, and balance the checkbook. Some of these are obviously adult concerns. In addition, children have their private responsibilities and commitments: care of personal possessions and/or pets, homework, music practice, choir rehearsal, Scouts or team practice—in general, keeping life in order.

● Talk over problems involving schedules. If your family includes teenagers, you probably experience some difficulty in scheduling dinner hours, family activities, and use of the family car. The council meeting can be used to keep everyone informed of individual schedules. Afterwards these can be posted prominently in a central location. This practice also helps put into perspective the demands that are made on every family member's time.

● Basic home rules are an ideal topic for discussion; you have an excellent forum for formulating rules concerning behavior that is expected of members in various situations, in or out of the home. It is wise periodically to review, clarify, and revise these rules (and penalties for their infringement) in a general discussion:

Where may bicycles be safely ridden? What are the curfew hours? Does the family have a plan for emergencies (fire, accidents, sudden illness, and so on)? Are the older children familiar with such a program? Is a list of emergency phone numbers posted in a prominent place? What are the rules for use of the family car? For entertaining friends in the home? For dealing with strangers who come to the door?

You want family council procedures to be viewed as democratic. The trick is to let such subjects come up for discussion, to encourage everyone who wishes to contribute an opinion, and then, if necessary, quietly to interject your own observations.

If your children participate in making rules, they will be more likely to observe them. In matters pertaining to safety and health, you may be surprised at their good judgment. If necessary, make your own views clear in a nonauthoritarian manner. And be sure to follow through with the decisions reached. The children may test you to see if you are doing so!

● Television viewing (see below) can be a tremendous problem if it is not well monitored. Sometimes the issue can be resolved through democratic family council discussions. These enable family members to assess the influence TV has on their lives and productivity. Perhaps each person can list his or her favorite programs in relation to other routine responsibilities. Each family will have to develop its own regulations with due regard for the occasional outstanding program that everyone wants to see.

● The family telephone is an even more chronic source of conflict than the TV set, especially if there are adolescents in the household. They use the phone for a variety of seemingly unimportant reasons. In the interest of family harmony and productivity, telephone usage must be controlled. No one of any age should monopolize the phone at others' expense.

Here's how one family solved the problem:

With three teenagers and one phone in the Wilson household, there has been growing friction. Finally Jane, Don, and Art resolve the issue themselves in a Sunday evening council meeting. Then they post the following notice over the phone:

Ten-minute limit on all calls.
No calls at dinner.
No calls after 9:30 on school days.
Penalty: You can't use the phone for three days!

● The council is an excellent setting for discussing family vacations. It's especially good fun to plan an August camping trip on a dreary January afternoon. Each person can voice suggestions or preferences. How much time will we have? How much money? Where do we want to go? What do we want to do or see? The children can help write the budget, develop the itinerary (they love to pore over maps and charts), and even begin to make some advance preparations.

Two Final Suggestions

The rules and regulations you and your children formulate in council meetings are important. In addition, we would leave you with two pieces of advice, neither of which is always easy to implement.

The old adage "Time and tide wait for no man" is particularly applicable to productive family life. All conscientious parents would agree that their household functions most smoothly when they themselves are "ahead of the game." This, of course, means being up in the morning before their youngsters, getting a "handle" on the day's activities, setting the machinery in motion. It also means some preparatory rituals the night before, particularly when school is in session (laying out next day's clothes, assembling books and materials, and so on). Instilling habits of advance preparation even for nursery school youngsters provides a sense of control over life and also reduces the tension and anxiety that invariably accompany the morning rush.

Keep in mind, too, that all functions of a family have to be kept in balance. Occasionally some must be assigned priority. Your overemphasis on neatness and cleanliness—keeping rooms tidy and beds made, picking up clothes or taking baths—may detract from your children's success in carrying out school tasks or other responsibilities. An unexpected but important test, a major athletic event, a long play rehearsal may occur in any family. Any program of assigned home duties should be flexible. Try to be understanding! It may, for example, be more important for Beth to spend a few minutes after breakfast reviewing for her chemistry exam than making her bed.

MANAGEMENT OF MONEY

The MacDonald kids have begged all winter for a motorboat. Finally Dad and Mom confront them with some questions to ponder:

"What will the new motorboat cost? How is it going to be paid for? Where will it be stored? If we buy it, will we still have money for our groceries, our heating oil, our phone, our electricity, our clothes? What about our insurance? The orthodontist? The mortgage? The taxes?"

How we handle money involves emotions and values. In making decisions about how to use money, we reveal our basic attitudes toward money, our tastes and priorities. Inevitably, our children observe our spending habits and are influenced by them.[2]

You can tell much about an individual's tastes and underlying needs by the way he or she handles cash:

Carl heads for the Yankee box office while Albert buys a ticket to a chamber music recital.

Louisa splurges on a high-style evening gown while Diana invests in a rugged topcoat.

Tim, the free spender, empties his wallet to purchase treats for all his buddies.

Elaine, the impulse buyer, comes home laden with the merchandise she saw temptingly advertised.

Miserly John, refusing to part with any of his cash, hoards it for years.

In most homes the subject of money comes up continually, requiring constant clarification and frank discussion. Some of this can take place in the family council; some is more properly dealt with on an individual basis.

Try to confine general family discussions about money to basic principles. At appropriate times you can talk about good programs of money management. When your children are young, do not go into detail about your family's financial circumstances. You *can* instill the principle of regular allocations for savings and gifts to church or charity, leaving the rest for personal needs. An occasional discussion such as that about the MacDonalds' motorboat can also help your children become more realistic about what it costs to live and how to establish sensible priorities in handling finances. In today's world there is an acute need for each individual to manage his or her personal funds prudently.

As children mature, they gradually learn how to use money sensibly. They do this by watching the way it is handled by you, by other family members, by their friends and others—and also by managing it personally. They acquire direct control of cash either by receiving an allowance from their parents or by earning it themselves.

Allowances

It's best for children to have a small amount of spending money; they should not be obliged to rely on casual parental handouts in response to chronic pleas for cash. Even if your own resources are limited, you should consider some structured plan for giving allowances as part of your responsibility. The amount can be small in the beginning and gradually increased, but it should be given regularly and for specific purposes thoroughly understood by the child. In the adult world money, unless inherited or otherwise provided by others, must be earned. Children must gradually learn this lesson. First, however, they must acquire some early experience in handling personal funds on a small scale, learning something about prices, values, shopping, and bargain hunting, and even profiting from an occasional mistake. The allowance is not paid as compensation for the chores youngsters agree to perform for the benefit of the family as a whole. As they grow older, you can provide opportunities for them to earn extra cash from performing nonroutine household tasks (cleaning the garage and the like), and additional opportunities for doing odd jobs in the neighborhood usually arise.

If you give allowances, be sure your younger children understand that their older brothers and sisters receive more money because of increased expenses and obligations. This practice keeps misunderstandings and jealousy from developing among siblings.

Paid Employment

In these days even elementary school youngsters are looking increasingly to earn spending money from a paper route, baby-sitting, or mowing lawns before they are old enough to be on the payroll of a local supermarket or gas station. If your young people assume the responsibilities of paid employment, you play a delicate role. You should try to respect their growing ability to decide how much of their time and energy they can devote to such employment. At the same time they should understand that schoolwork—building solid achievement skills and acquiring a good academic record—should be their first priority.[3]

A youngster's commitment to a paid job such as a paper route should never be made lightly. The neighbors have a right to demand and expect regular deliveries in all kinds of weather. Sometimes you may have to provide back-up:

At six o'clock on a frigid January morning young Nick awakens with a bad sore throat and a temperature of 101 degrees. His dad, already facing a stressful day, gets the car out and delivers half the route; Mom takes over and finishes the job.

Whether your teenagers do regular part-time work outside of the home depends on a number of factors. As their incidental expenses increase, they will be tempted to accept job offers for the sake of additional spending money. They should *not* accept a job with heavy demands during the school week. Bear in mind, too, that managers of supermarkets, gas stations, and fast-food establishments sometimes put pressure on their young employees when someone else has called in sick or has quit. Unless your family is in real financial straits, it's generally wise to discourage paid employment when school is in session. All work is draining on young people, particularly if they are carrying a heavy academic load. It may be more important for your child to expend energy compiling a good school record. Weekend baby-sitting or lawn jobs or summer work are preferable to after-school employment.

Whether your children receive allowances from you or work for an outside employer, you should have some idea of how they are spending their money at any age. Frank discussion is especially important with your adolescents. Make it a point to sit down with them every few months and work out a detailed budget together:

Martha and her Dad are reviewing her financial situation. Her father asks her just what her budget is to cover. Is it for all her needs including major articles of clothing? What about the new winter coat she may have to buy later in the fall? The junior prom? What happens to her baby-sitting money? Does she really need it to supplement her allowance or can she put some of it into her savings account?

In talking about money with your adolescents, you will need to show empathy and respect for their special sensitivities in this area. If your basic relationship with them is affectionate, you should find no difficulty in resolving financial issues.

Other Financial Issues
The following notes regarding money management may be useful:

Care of surplus amounts of cash. Do not allow children to accumulate sizeable amounts of cash in the house. Open a savings account in a local bank for each child at an early age with one of you as trustee (meaning that all withdrawals require an adult's signature). Into this account can go special gifts from grandparents or relatives or summer job earnings.

Children and the law. Although children's money is their own, they are considered minors in the eyes of the law until the age of 18. Prior to that time their parents are legally responsible for their unmet financial obligations and also liable for any damage they may inflict on others' property.

Supervision or consultation about large purchases. It is advisable to have a standing rule that all purchases above a certain amount should be discussed with you in advance.

Training in the use of a checking account. A checking account and its proper use should be seriously considered at least for older adolescent children. Be certain that they master the simple procedure of balancing their checkbooks regularly!

Charge cards, credit, and borrowing. You have a particular obligation to teach your children responsible use of credit. Discourage the borrowing habit among school-aged children, even if the amount is small. Do not permit your children the use of your credit cards.

Older teenagers can learn the procedures of installment buying, although it's vital that they understand the actual cost of borrowing and the safeguards and limitations required whenever loans are negotiated. Instill the principle that everything we buy must ultimately be paid for.

It's impossible to overestimate the importance of your own example. Children learn habits of thrift and honesty from their parents. You must be able to say pleasantly but frankly to your children, when it becomes necessary, "Sorry, but we can't afford [a certain purchase] at this time."

Or you can handle a child's request for a financial outlay in a more positive manner:

This year Myra has invested her spending money in order to join the local swimming association.

At the end of January, when the Ski Club advertises its midwinter weekends, Myra asks if she may participate in these also. Her parents kindly reply, "You chose the swimming this year, Myra. Next year you can save your money for the ski weekends."

Keeping up with the Joneses. Currently there is evidence that some school-aged children, particularly in certain suburban areas, are bringing appalling pressure to bear on their parents by constantly begging for clothes, gadgets, or lifestyles that will conform to prevailing fads. Much of this is the result of peer pressure, but much is also related to the emotional insecurity of these children and their families.

If parents give in to extravagant and unreasonable demands, it is clear that they do not dare to strain a fragile parent–child relationship. They are afraid to say no.

Discussion of family finances with other children. This is to be discouraged. School-aged children are intensely curious about their respective families' financial affairs and often make them a topic of casual conversation among themselves. Blatant curiosity as revealed in the query "How much does your father make?" or "What did you pay for your house?" is rude.

To a child who is being annoyed in this way by a chum, you can suggest that he or she reply, "You'll have to ask my father." It is neither wise nor in good taste to discuss private family financial matters with school friends or, for that matter, any outsiders.

MANAGEMENT OF TELEVISION

The following candid remarks are part of a letter sent to *The New York Times* a few years ago by thirteen-year-old Monique. Monique describes how she has lived happily and productively for five years without any television at all:

I think one of the dumbest questions from TV watchers has been, "What do you do in your spare time?" The answer is easy. I am in 4-H, I take care of a flock of chickens, I'm on the basketball team, I'm on the track team, I am taking tennis lessons, I swim, I have three pet gerbils and I go to the track field by my house and practice long jumping and high jumping. I also sometimes ride horseback with my friend. I read a lot, I do homework, I have had a poem published, I collect stamps, I've had recorder and flute lessons, I cook a lot, and I have to keep count of the food my chickens eat and the eggs they lay and write it down. See what I mean by a dumb question?[4]

Television is important in contemporary life for many reasons. It keeps us informed of the ever-changing world scene. It acquaints us with developments in politics, science, the arts, literature, religion, and other areas. It serves as a forum for discussion of all kinds of human problems. It entertains us through its coverage of sports events and theatrical and musical presentations.

But television, particularly commercial television, has many drawbacks. It has been justifiably criticized for crassly promoting materialism, false values, sex, and violence. Its powerful, fast-paced presentations exert a peculiar grip on the average undiscriminating viewer; it has mesmerized all of us at one time or another. In the 95 percent of all American homes with at least one set (many have two or more) people are obviously deriving some benefit from television. Yet misused, as it all too often is, television viewing is undeniably counterproductive.

For people living alone or for shut-ins who are elderly, ill, or physically immobilized, television serves many legitimate needs. Providing its viewers with companionship, support, and some contact with the outside world, it fulfills a genuine need in their lives. Our chief concern here is with the huge number of school-aged children who have become television addicts. Beginning as young as age three, thousands of them sit before the set three or four hours a day (six or more on weekends), thus totaling more viewing hours per week than are spent in the classroom. It is no secret that over a twelve-year period these youngsters probably spend more hours before the TV than they spend in school.

Parents of such children complain bitterly about this problem but are puzzled how to deal with it. Their remedies are usually short-range and futile: threats to remove the set, repetitious criticisms of the child's excessive viewing without suggesting appealing alternatives, unenforceable directives ("No television while we are out this evening!"). Some parents may suggest another activity, such as reading a book or going outside to play, without offering to share their own time and companionship.

In the average American home television sometimes becomes an instrument of severe conflict. Often parents are unaware of its influence on personal relationships within the household. You should therefore examine the actual dynamics underlying a child's excessive viewing before suggesting a solution for the problem within your particular family.

The Psychological Appeal of Television

Television differs from most other forms of communication in a number of ways:

It is a one-way conversation. The viewer is talked to rather than talked with. This one-way aspect provides a certain amount of emotional safety for the insecure person. He can remain passive. He is not expected to respond to what is said to him. No one is going to argue with him or challenge him.

In particular, constant TV watching can become a kind of sanctuary from critical and authoritarian parents. Television announcers and speakers do not nag their viewers with admonitions of something they must do "this very minute," or reminders of things they haven't done. The conversation does not begin with "Now you listen to me!"

Much TV communication—especially the commercials—is offered pleasantly, enthusiastically, and usually with a smile. The speaker looks directly at the viewer, often addressing him as "you." The message often implies, if it does not state directly, that the speaker believes in the viewer, trusts him, and has confidence in him. Programs full of laughter and jokes also meet the needs of children or adults who feel depressed or rejected.

TV commercials and most popular programs are filled with promises of quick and easy fulfillment. "If you do such-and-such your life, in one way or another, will be better." "You'll be more accepted, more alluring, more successful." These typical messages subtly bolster the morale of the insecure person.

Children sitting in front of the TV set are not required to listen to their parents' problems and complaints.

They are not, at least for the moment, being teased, ridiculed, or physically attacked by siblings.

TV provides the restless or lonely child with an opportunity to identify with persons or objects that are pictured on the screen as moving rapidly through space. In a home where there is constant criticism, a child's resulting insecurity can take the form of wanting to be perpetually on the move. Being active serves to relieve this anxiety. Some parents remark that their child is never still except when he or she is in front of the set.

Television offers such a child an opportunity to identify vicariously with the swiftly moving motorcycle, automobile, or airplane as well as with people in action. Police and cowboy shows are the favorites of some children and, indeed, of some adults. One of the great attractions of sports events is the speed accompanying auto racing, swimming events, basketball, and hockey. Moving in fantasy is a release from the emotional and accompanying motor tensions that can occur within the individual.

It has been observed that children who are addicted to television viewing lack self-esteem, even to the point of being depressed. In their homes there is usually little empathy and much criticism. The parents talk *at*, rather than *with* the child. They seldom offer praise and encouragement, and they rarely smile. In many homes conversations between parent and child are a one-sided affair— similar to TV but characterized by frowns and corrections instead of the cheerful acceptance provided by most TV programs. In such a home the child quickly gravitates to any person, animal, or object offering some acceptance and recognition. Pets sometimes serve this need; TV, however, offers a special kind of immediate acceptance. A child whose basic self-esteem has thus been undermined naturally develops a craving for television. We have said that empathy can be transmitted by a smile, an affectionate word, and a hug; television readily furnishes the first two.

Television's Influence on Children
Social behavior. Parents are justifiably concerned over the potential harm to children from TV programs portraying violence and aggression. Research reveals convincingly that youngsters do indeed acquire aggressive behavior from watching scenes of violence. The influence of such scenes has been shown to be both immediate and long-term. It can also reduce children's cooperation and sharing with their peers.[5]

On the other hand, studies demonstrate that children will also imitate the behavior of characters who are portrayed as helping, sharing, and offering nurturance to others. After viewing such programs (public television's series on Mister Rogers, for example), subjects were found to be more persistent at tasks, more obedient to school rules, and more able to tolerate delays. They gained in levels of cooperation, nurturance, and sympathy as well as in the ability to express feelings. What is more, these effects could still be seen two weeks later.[6]

Nonetheless, commercial television's impact on children's social development is fundamentally undesirable, especially in the case of the young addicts who watch the more sensational late-evening shows. These programs deal with every aspect of human depravity. They throw the child immediately into the sordid regions of the adult world, erasing all boundaries between childhood and adulthood.[7]

Intellectual development. There is increasing evidence that excessive television viewing is seriously hurting youngsters' school achievement and general intellectual development. Recently the California Department of Education gave an achievement test to the 500,000-odd pupils in the sixth and twelfth grades of the state's public schools. Besides measuring reading, math, and language skills, the survey asked the question (to which 99 percent of the students replied): "How much time do you spend watching television each day?" Not surprisingly, the highest scores on the test were earned by students who reported one hour or less of daily viewing. For each additional hour of watching, the test scores declined. The most marked drop in scores occurred for youngsters watching three, four, and more hours a day.[8]

The students' reports also showed that television was replacing their recreational reading. As one educator pointed out, ". . . it's obvious that if you don't spend any time reading, you aren't going to read very well." It's easy to understand that not only reading, but also mathematical and other important cognitive skills develop poorly in these heavy viewers. There was universal agreement among professional observers of this study that responsibility for controlling children's TV watching rests squarely on the shoulders of the parents.

But the problem exists on a deeper level, as is pointed out by Neil Postman, professor of communication arts and sciences at New York University.[9] Television viewing does not require a child to deal with the process of symbolization (recognizing what words and mathematical figures stand for or represent), which is an essential function in thinking and imagination. Symbols are involved in all communication. The response to TV pictures is sensory rather than intellectual. The formation of ideas that accompanies the reading process does not usually occur.

Another essential intellectual skill hindered by TV viewing is the ability to concentrate. The fast-moving pictures make little demand on the child's power of attention.

Intelligent Regulation of Television
Parents, it is absolutely essential for you to monitor and control your family's viewing habits! Only in this way can you curb the instrument's potential for abuse.

Be sure everyone in your family understands that during the school week homework receives priority over viewing. It's very risky to tell children that they can watch TV "after homework is done." The temptation is simply too strong for a child to rush through the assignments, completing them just before a favorite program goes on the air.

In most highly productive homes children are so busily involved in top-notch academic performance and other concerns that they have neither the time nor the inclination to sit for hours in front of the TV set.

Our young friend Monique, whom we met at the beginning of this discussion, has no need of television at all. Her athletic activities, her chickens and pet gerbils, her musical projects, the long horseback rides with her best friend, and her numerous literary and academic pursuits all fill her days to the brim. Monique is too busy for TV. It's safe to wager that she would be bored with the programs and have very little time for them even if a set were available. She is so secure emotionally that her energies are released for all manner of creative and productive activities of her own devising.

Monique's letter thus gives us the clue to one part of the solution of the TV problem. We do not know her parents, but our correspondence with their daughter assures us that they have given Monique some precious assets. First and foremost, they have fully met her self-esteem needs.

If you feel that your children are making excessive use of television, examine your relationships with them. Ask yourselves whether they are growing up as truly secure individuals. Perhaps in your family, as in many households, there isn't enough time for companionship—*away* from the television set. Often there isn't enough of this kind of sharing, whether it be informal athletics, creative projects, or merely enjoying a snack and some chatty talk at the kitchen table. Today's parents are extremely busy people, but surely they can find brief moments such as these.

Television at its best has much to offer. Selected programs of high quality can be watched by everyone even though such occasions do not lend themselves to good family conversation. Many a family has remained glued to the set during the closing Wimbledon matches, the final innings of the World Series, presidential inaugurations and royal weddings, not to mention numerous events of world-shaking proportions. Witnessing such scenes of common interest to parents and children can only enhance a sense of family solidarity.

This said, however, we must insist on one warning. It is vital not to allow television to grow into a monster that destroys communication, steals time from more important pursuits, and obstructs the resolution of family tensions.

AVOIDING FAMILY ALIGNMENTS AND "SCAPEGOATING"

Whenever an argument erupts in the Smith household, the family seems to take sides. Regardless of the issue at hand, people divide into two predictable factions. Teenage Marie and Denise are usually their Mom's allies while the boys come to Pop's defense. In one way or another, there's chronic friction between the two groups.

Lucy Brown is pudgy, awkward, and always clashing with someone in the family. According to reports from the other kids and her parents, Lucy just can't seem to do anything right. Whenever anything goes wrong, it's usually Lucy's fault.

What is going on here?

When any family member—parent or child—feels neglected in the family group, he naturally reacts negatively. In a small social group such as the family, one insecure person can easily disturb the general equilibrium. A child suddenly pokes a sister in the ribs or scuffles with a brother; an adult loses his temper, swears or stalks out of the room.

The challenge of parenthood is to meet everyone's basic emotional needs, admittedly not an easy task. There are bound to be moments in every household when someone feels temporarily overlooked. If the individual could at that moment verbalize his feelings of loneliness, he would in many cases be criticized. Such remarks as "What's wrong with you?" "My, you're sensitive!" or "You just can't take criticism—that's your trouble!" do nothing for the individual's already depressed self-image.

Sometimes one child in a family feels more or less continuously deprived of attention over a long period of time. He then tries to make himself the center of attention. He teases or makes fun of siblings, leaves chores undone, carelessly spills milk at the table, or acts like a clown. These behaviors give him temporary attention, but not the basic assurance and affection that he needs. The parents, on the other hand, become progressively more annoyed at these attention-getting devices. The child, in turn, feels increasingly rejected.

This type of acting-up can eventually evolve into an unconscious form of revenge directed at parents. More serious problems (deliberate neglect of schoolwork, skipping classes, running away overnight, or drug involvement) may then emerge.

Alignments

In some families an insecure child may seek to enlist one or more other family members as allies, special friends, or confidants. An alignment of this sort that marshals two or more family members against the rest of the family group indicates that someone is not receiving enough recognition.

The larger family, with its complexity of human relationships and opportunities for tensions and grievances, is especially vulnerable to the formation of harmful alliances:

Danny, the youngest of the seven Jackson children, has a perpetual chip on his shoulder. He regularly seeks help from his 15-year-old sister, Sarah. He can count on her to take his side when he gets into trouble.

The three older O'Brien youngsters are bitterly antagonistic toward their younger sister and brother, who always seem to get away with things for which they used to be punished.

In the Smith family referred to earlier, one parent sides with some of the children against the other parent and the remaining children. In certain extreme cases all the children may organize against the parents, and the family's entire organization and direction can become paralyzed.

Alignments may occur in any group of three or more persons. In the average happy family the implications are usually not serious. Normally they shift, depending somewhat on the issue involved:

Jane, George, and Dad think the family should go camping in the state park next summer; Josie and Mother would prefer to stay at home and make day trips to the beach.

Such matters merely reflect individual differences of interest and taste.

However, when alignments become rigid and long-lasting and two or more persons always side together regardless of individual preferences, the situation becomes more serious. In such circumstances the family is no longer united but consists of two or more competing factions, and this situation indicates that some individuals' emotional needs are not being met. An identity problem is involved here that requires everyone's concern.

The Scapegoat

When alignments take the form of a coalition of several family members against one, a scapegoat situation is created. The scapegoat becomes the individual upon whom other family members can blame their difficulties. Scapegoating is a form of *displacement:* blame for unsolved family or individual problems gets displaced onto one person in the family who is in some way vulnerable.

A family with a scapegoat is a family that has failed to face and solve some of its own problems. In most such homes there is little or no free, easy, spontaneous communication. Members need a scapegoat to keep the family in balance.

Scapegoats may appear in any group of people who live, work, or socialize together. Moreover, as the group becomes larger, its tensions and its vulnerability to scapegoating increase. An authoritarian leader, particularly an authoritarian father, can create conditions conducive to scapegoating because members of the group under his control have no opportunity to talk out their problems; they need to displace their hostility upon a weaker person. Sometimes a family living in a neighborhood where the prevailing lifestyle of other homes is different from theirs can become a scapegoat, a butt of gossip or subtle discrimination.

The scapegoat, then, fulfills the family's need to relieve tension. Tension is partially reduced (though not resolved) when the family can habitually divert attention to one problem-person. "If Johnny weren't so hyperactive, things would be all right" is a typical attitude. In focusing on Johnny's problems, other family members can relieve their own anxieties to some extent.

Usually an individual so censured will progressively withdraw from family activities and turn to other sources of support such as a peer group.

Sometimes a family with unsolved problems will deliberately create a scapegoat out of one child. They may neglect him systematically, or they may impose such harsh and arbitrary discipline on him that he has no choice but to misbehave. Unfortunately, a child who has been made a family scapegoat continues to play this role, since it is only this behavior that secures any attention. When he continues his irresponsible actions in school, he faces other problems.

What kind of a person becomes the scapegoat? Usually it is a child. In other cases the target may be a vulnerable adult such as an alcoholic or chronically unemployed father. The child is an especially easy victim because he is helpless to combat his parents.

A family's choice of a scapegoat may reflect its particular values or interests. Thus, appearance-conscious parents will focus on an unattractive child. Those oriented to intellectual pursuits will fixate on the poor student. The family of athletes will single out the clumsy, uncoordinated youngster.

Sometimes excessively insecure parents convert a child's chronic health problem into a scapegoat situation; in such cases they are displacing their own tensions and anxieties onto extra care and attention for the afflicted child, thus failing to deal with their own problems.

How can you discourage the creation of family alignments and scapegoats in your household? It may be helpful to ask yourselves periodically some of these questions:

Are the family's goals and purposes designed for the maximum welfare and development of each and every person?

Are you adequately providing for each child's physical and, especially, psychological needs?

Are you maintaining free and easy communication between yourselves and your youngsters? Are you giving equal recognition, expressing equal affection to everyone?

Are you permitting your individual children the occasional freedom to ventilate their feelings and express grievances? At such times do you give them the support and understanding that will bolster their own security and ensure against further problems in family relationships?

Be especially alert to symptoms of feelings of neglect in an individual youngster who seems to withdraw frequently into imagined illness or excessive television viewing, or who bickers continually with brothers and sisters. At such times the two of you should sit down quietly together. Encourage your child to talk. Listen without criticism, and try to learn why this child feels that he or she is being treated unfairly. Your support and understanding at such times can be insurance against further problems in family relationships.

CONCLUSION

All four issues examined in this chapter are an inescapable part of daily family living. Schedules, chores, budgets, TV and telephone usage, occasional airing of individual grievances—all these and much else need some kind of rational control. How we manage them can make a big difference in our success as parents.

A democratically oriented family council, a wise and systematic approach to money matters, firm control over abuse of the tube and other potential distractions, and constant awareness of every individual's emotional needs will all help us attain our central objective, *structure* in family life. The structure should be flexible but very much there, for in providing children with a predictable social environment, we reduce unnecessary tension and anxiety and enhance both their self-esteem and their capacity for caring and for functioning productively.

SPECIFIC SUGGESTIONS

Do:

Do plan your first family council meetings carefully, introduce them tactfully, and conduct them along democratic lines.

Do see that decisions made during meetings are prominently displayed afterwards.

Do discuss money matters freely and often with all your children.

Do recognize that your own style of money management is a powerful influence on your children.

Do, if possible, give each child a regular allowance.

Do recognize the educational, social, and cultural value of television at its best. Help your family to cultivate sensible and discriminating viewing habits.

Do firmly enforce time limits on viewing, especially on school days. These rules are best evolved during family council meetings.

Do understand the reasons for TV's psychological appeal, especially to insecure viewers.

Do discourage any tendency toward alignments or creation of scapegoats in your family by being scrupulously fair and equally supportive toward all your children.

Don't:

Don't let family council meetings become too long.

Don't dominate meetings yourself or use them to preach or lecture.

Don't deal with private matters during meetings.

Don't hesitate to say, "We can't afford [a certain purchase]," when necessary.

Don't let television substitute for family companionship and communication.

Don't promise children that they can see a favorite program after finishing their homework.

Don't deny any child's right occasionally to express individual grievances to you in private.

THE PRODUCTIVE CHILD COPES WITH THE LEARNING PROCESS

My child—

doesn't enjoy school.
is immature.
wasn't in kindergarten, so he's behind.
was in kindergarten, so she's bored.
is hyperactive.
has a learning disability.
has changed schools.
isn't as bright as his older brother (or sister).
has a teacher who doesn't like her.
changed teachers in the middle of the year.
doesn't have a high IQ.
doesn't know how to study.
is lazy.

Who hasn't heard these typical parental excuses for a child's poor schoolwork?

Fortunately, such comments are not always necessary. In many families the children do extremely well in school.

In Chapter Two we met five such young people—Steve, Mary,

Dan, Jill, and Adam—all good students. They complete school assignments and other tasks easily and well. They meet their responsibilities on time. They deal effectively with daily problems. In out-of-school hours they find time for other productive activities. More than likely, they will continue to function in this manner throughout their adult lives.

COPING, PROBLEM SOLVING, AND SCHOOL ACHIEVEMENT

This chapter will consider children's competence in the realm of school performance. An understanding of the learning process is basic to encouragement of your child's academic progress.

Coping means having competence in solving problems. Broadly speaking, it involves much more than merely doing well in school. It refers to the thinking, reflecting, evaluating, choosing, deciding, and acting that we all engage in countless times daily, throughout our lives.

THE MEANING OF MOTIVATION

The term *motivation* is frequently misused in reference to a child's school achievement. In the strictest sense, being motivated means being impelled to engage in some form of behavior in response to a governing force or influence that is causing an individual to move or act. In the psychological sense, being motivated means that there is something meaningful to work for—some reward. Children are motivated to learn in order to satisfy a desire to gain or retain the rewards of parents' affection and recognition—in other words, to maintain self-esteem.

The first motivation to learn is seen in infancy. All normal babies are inherently curious; from about the age of six months they explore ceaselessly, want to learn about nearby objects, to grasp, feel, taste anything in sight or within reach.[1] This normal urge to explore the immediate surroundings is a baby's first motivation and chief means of learning. Unless the baby is scolded or slapped by an adult, the explorations will continue.

As toddlers, children acquire powers of locomotion and rudimentary verbal communication with surrounding adults, the ability to identify objects and people, to understand adults' verbal responses to their behavior, and even to sense adult expectations. At this age youngsters are quick to perceive approval (reward) as well as disapproval. In a sense they are beginning to perceive their actions in terms of outcomes. If praised for an act, they will want to repeat it. In a very rudimentary sense, they are becoming "future-oriented" although their concept of the future is still limited—probably to what happens within the succeeding few minutes. In any event, the capacity to view their actions in terms of even immediate future rewards is a form of motivation.

Motivation underlies all meaningful efforts at coping and problem solving. It is an inescapable factor in the development of an achieving, productive child—a child who does not hesitate to project himself into the future. In its best sense, motivation always entails the young individual's belief and assurance that his efforts will be rewarded and approved by his parents and the "significant others" in his life—as well as their expectations for his later attainments. If a father and mother have high aspirations for a youngster's future, the basis of that future is already established.[2]

THE IMPORTANT EARLY YEARS

Problem solving begins early in life, years before the start of formal schooling. We know that physical growth (especially that of the brain and nervous system) is extraordinarily rapid from the time of conception through the first six years of life. Researchers have now demonstrated the special importance of the first three years in the child's intellectual development.

When babies reach for toys on the other side of their cribs, they are attempting to solve problems. Later they take their first steps, try to feed themselves. They learn to use the bathroom, to dress themselves, to pick up their toys. Each task is an effort at first and should be rewarded (that is, praised and approved).

Informal education and training occur at home throughout the preschool years. If parents are patient, loving, and appreciative, children will learn easily. They will grow in confidence and self-esteem, learn to trust those around them. After each small success they will want to repeat their performance. Gradually they will gain confidence and skill to undertake more difficult tasks. Thus, during the first four or five years they learn to deal successfully with all kinds of small challenges.

Children who arrive in first grade after preschool years marked by loving support and affection at home have a clear advantage. They already acquired considerable informal education when their parents played with them, chatted with them, explored the outdoors with them, told stories, read aloud to them regularly, perhaps made music and shared other experiences with them. In such homes they have probably also been free to explore their small world for themselves. They have experimented, struggled with small tasks, made minor decisions, achieved small successes. Thus, as happy and already quite competent young individuals, they feel free to deal with new tasks and problems.

The earliest years of a child's development are undoubtedly important. However, even if your youngster is already in elementary school or beyond, there's still much that you can do. Don't waste time and energy in recalling earlier unused opportunities. It's never too late to make up for the past. You have undoubtedly done much already to give your child a good start in life. Now you must continue your efforts to develop his or her competencies and skills in every way possible.

In contemporary Western society, school is the first formal arena of competition and struggle. It involves homework, tests, report cards, and honor rolls; tryouts for varsity athletics and school plays; public speaking contests, art exhibitions, student concerts, and science fairs; campaigns for school office; applications to college and graduate school. For the rest of their lives, in school and on the job, your children will be evaluated, graded, and measured against their contemporaries.

Your youngsters must have tremendous reserves of self-esteem and emotional security to cope with ever-increasing competition. If they have been well supported with your affection and approval—*and if this support continues, day in and day out*—they will meet each new challenge with confidence and competence for years to come.

Achievement occurs in and out of school, in all places and at all ages. It can involve tying one's shoes, writing a good letter, building a stamp collection, or becoming an officer of one's high school class. But the best barometer of young people's ability to cope is the quality of their schoolwork.

TEN COPING CHARACTERISTICS

Let's look now at some personality traits and intellectual skills that are involved in problem solving especially during the school years. In reviewing the following list we will see one powerful influence continuously at work. This is the impact of emotional security (self-esteem) and of its opposite, a state of anxiety.

Sixteen-year-old Melissa's day has begun badly. Mom and Dad had another big argument and conversation at breakfast was minimal. Everyone in the family was uneasy, rushed, and tense getting off to school and work.

Melissa goes off to school feeling very "down." Her day seems to have no end of frustrations and, in fact, a number of small disasters.

Excessive anxiety is in some degree distracting, inhibiting, and even crippling to the problem-solving process.

Here are ten factors that are vital to the functioning of every child and that also are affected by anxiety:

Perceptual skills. Productive children perceive a situation clearly and realistically. They tend to gauge the dimensions of a problem much more accurately than do anxious children. They are clear-eyed, alert, quick to observe pertinent details. They are also intellectually curious and therefore tend to be much better informed than less secure children are.[3]

Nothing distorts one's accuracy of perception as much as anxiety. The anxious child is the confused child, the child who doesn't get the point of the teacher's explanation. Such students make hard work of math problems. They read sentences in their textbook over and over again without grasping the meaning; they fail to grasp easily the central thought of a paragraph.

Powers of concentration. Productive children concentrate well. They not only see a problem clearly but can focus their entire attention on it. Concentration takes mental energy. Children beset by anxiety find it very difficult to focus their attention. All successful people are able to concentrate effectively.[4]

By contrast, anxious youngsters are distractible. They typically have a short attention span; they daydream or fidget in class. Such children may have lived with constant criticism at home. They are so concerned about their own identity that they cannot devote full attention to schoolwork or other productive undertakings.

Independence in work habits. Another trait of successful, coping children is their independence. Given a task to perform, they go about it on their own. They don't require constant supervision. They enjoy working alone at original projects and are sometimes quite inventive and even unconventional.[5]

Insecure children are dependent. Their shaky self-esteem needs constant bolstering. They go to their teacher on needless pretexts or badger neighboring children for help with an assignment. Worse still, they may borrow frequently from others' work.

Judgment. Good judgment involves the power to choose between alternatives, to discriminate between two courses of action, to set priorities. Busy, successful, secure people—children or adults—have good judgment. They know that some matters are more important than others and should be attended to first; others can wait.[6]

Nothing interferes with good judgment as much as anxiety. Chronically insecure children find it difficult to choose between what is better or best—more or less suitable, right, fair, appropriate, justified.

Self-control. Productive children are levelheaded. They don't make hasty, impulsive snap judgments which can lead to mistakes. They check their arithmetic for minor errors, their written work for careless spelling or punctuation. They work efficiently but also accurately.[7]

Insecure children are often impulsive. Usually they have experienced constant criticism at home. Accordingly, they feel chronically empty, helpless, and uneasy. They are likely to be careless in the details that the high achiever carefully notes. Impulsive children also have a need to be perpetually on the move. A good example is the hyperactive youngster, whose constant movement serves to relieve anxiety.[8]

Memory. In order to build skills—academic or otherwise—children must have good memories. Memory is the storehouse of past experiences. It contains all the previously learned building blocks of learning from which more advanced academic skills are fashioned. All educational processes require memory. Children can't master long division if they've forgotten elementary subtraction and multiplication. Nor can they improve their reading if they don't remember the primary vocabulary they should have mastered in earlier years.[9]

Youngsters must be emotionally secure if their memories are to function well. If someone has criticized them severely in connection with a past incident or tasks they once tried to perform, their memory of those occasions will be painful and their future performance of similar tasks may be hampered.[10] (The little girl whose mother has severely criticized her piano practice is apt to panic in a performance or, worse still, to develop a distaste for further piano study.)

The most important factor in a good memory is high self-esteem and freedom from anxiety. The greatest handicap is low self-esteem resulting in emotional conflict. Poor memory is always characteristic of low achievement.

Organizing ability. Good students, and successful people of all ages, are effective organizers. They know how to manage their time, to make minutes count. They use outlines, lists, memoranda; they are systematic and methodical. They relish putting complex ideas into orderly patterns, and they seem almost to have a need for order. This need is based on their self-confidence, their conviction that they can control their environment. Thus they save time and energy for the most important matters, and they also have extra time for other projects and interests.[11]

It is the opposite with low achievers. They are more likely to bog down in detail, to fail to see the forest for the trees, to plan their time poorly, to flounder in a hopeless maze of complexity. They seem constantly confused about their work because they are confused about themselves.

Verbal and mathematical skills. Productive children are articulate. They have well-developed vocabularies, acquired partly through schooling, partly because of the educational level of their parents, and partly from the amount of reading they have done. A good store of words is a precious asset. Many parents of high achievers try conscientiously to develop their children's vocabularies through games and the encouragement of wide reading. But by far the most important factor in the development of a child's verbal ability is spontaneous, easy, warmly affectionate communication.

Mathematical skills are also important in a child's academic achievement. Society expects us to deal easily with basic numerical concepts. Mathematical symbols are abstract; they have no relationship to tangible objects. Thus they are especially vulnerable to anxiety. If a child has received considerable criticism at home and is chronically uneasy and preoccupied, he or she may well become panicky on a math test (misunderstand the wording of a problem, misplace a decimal point, or substitute a minus for a plus sign).[12] The consequences of such academic performances lead to further loss of self-esteem.

Persistence. Productive persons of any age are willing to work at a problem until it is finished.[13] They keep at it for hours, days, even weeks if necessary. Persistence in the solution of problems is particularly characteristic of scholars and scientists, who often labor patiently at research projects for endless years.

Productive children are persistent because they are hopeful. They expect eventual success. Having always received encouragement and approval in their previous undertakings, they are convinced that their present efforts will also be recognized as worthwhile. It is this conviction, this hope, that keeps them going.

Low achievers, on the other hand, are all too prone to become discouraged and to give up. They feel that no one (their parents included) really cares, and that it makes no difference whether they succeed, whether they try hard or merely go through the motions.

The ability to reach a decision. The productive, successful young person does not avoid the responsibility of reaching a decision when that is necessary. However, he or she is not impulsive in making such decisions. In a sense, coming to a decision is a creative act. It brings something to a close. Afterwards the individual can go on to pursue new goals. The productive child is not afraid of this process.[14]

Decision making sometimes requires considerable effort and skill. All leaders must possess to some degree the characteristics that we have discussed above. They must be perceptive and independent. They must have well-developed cognitive skills, good judgment, concentration, and self-control. They must know how to organize time, options, materials, and data. They must be persistent. Yet more than anything else, they must be decisive, possessing the emotional stability that will give them, if necessary, the courage to stand alone in the face of possible criticism of the action they have chosen.

HOW TO DEVELOP YOUR CHILDREN'S COPING STRENGTHS

During your children's years in school, particularly during the important early grades, you can nurture these ten traits and skills to maximize the development of your youngsters' learning and problem-solving capacities.

The first and fundamental step is to be sure that your child is secure in your love. You should also take ten additional steps to give him or her the best possible start in a successful school career. Your child will need the following kinds of support from you:

Hope

Be sure your child approaches tasks with hope. This is your youngster's inner assurance that someone believes in him.[15] All productive children have this precious asset. They are confident that their accomplishments—great or small—will be rewarded with approval by their parents (or parental surrogates), who are the really significant persons in their lives. No one of any age engages successfully in an undertaking of any kind without hope, without the conviction that someone really *cares* about his or her success. This attitude of hope forms the basis of productive children's approach toward life's tasks and challenges, their achievement in all areas of activity. It remains with them throughout their lives. A hopeful child becomes an optimistic adult.

Expectation and Goals

Provide expectation, goals, and a sense of direction. Children's goals and levels of achievement will be no higher than those you envision for them. If they are close to you, they will probably sense your aspirations. Nevertheless, you should discuss their future with them informally from time to time, especially as they grow older.

In defining expectations and setting goals, you keep school grades in perspective. You do not make them an end in themselves. You don't drive your child with continual pressure (by insisting, for example, that an 88 on a test should have been a 92). Rather, you regard grades as one means by which an individual attains future objectives. Be sure to make this clear to your youngster.

Interest and Enthusiasm

Show interest in and enthusiasm for daily school activities. Your child's teacher has expended effort and ingenuity to present material to the class. Be enthusiastically receptive to each day's account of what happened at school. *Talk* about it with your son or daughter. Listen patiently to a detailed description of the current goings-on. This daily exchange accomplishes at least two things. First, you help the teacher put ideas across by responding and reacting to them at home. Second, you communicate your own excitement about each day's experiences to your child. Enthusiasm is contagious and is part of any fruitful effort toward real learning.

In such talks you will also hear about negative happenings: the little setbacks, frustrations, moments of feeling low. The time to heal these small wounds is now, before they grow into a real injury.

Daily Recognition

Provide prompt recognition of each school day's accomplishments. When children bring home spelling papers, arithmetic tests, or short themes which their teacher has praised, they need immediate and *visible* recognition. One of the most effective ways of providing this kind of approval in the early grades is by maintaining a family bulletin board in a central location of the house (the refrigerator door is excellent):

> *Each time he walks through the kitchen, Neil sees the arithmetic test on which he got 100. He's resolved to be just as careful on every other test he takes this year. And fourth-grade Josie glances proudly at her theme on "What I Like About Autumn" on which Mrs. Goodwin has written, "I like your colorful description, Josie!"*

The bulletin board can of course be used for other things—finger paintings or drawings from the nursery school contingent, as well as announcements of coming events that are important to older children in the family.

In the elementary grades the learning of basic skills involves considerable drill, repetition, and hard work for your child. Each successful effort, a tiny step forward on the long journey of formal education, needs whatever small recognition you can provide at home.

Young children live chiefly in the present. The future rewards of these academic chores mean little or nothing to them. They need approval of today's work in order to go on to tomorrow's.

A Quiet Household

The household atmosphere should be conducive to learning. What do you provide at home on school days, following the brief afternoon hours of relaxation and (preferably) outdoor play?

A reasonably quiet household is essential. Television viewing must be carefully controlled. Evening television (yes, even the professional athletics!) is best eliminated altogether. The telephone should be used only for brief conversations. Stereos and radios can be quieted or silenced. Finally, your presence in the household is crucial to monitor these and other potential intrusions.

Admittedly, these conditions—particularly the last—are not easily provided, especially when working mothers come home late, tired, and preoccupied. But these provisions help create an atmosphere in which your youngsters can make productive use of their out-of-school hours.

A Setting for Homework

A child needs a congenial setting in which to do homework. Where do children do their homework? The answer is usually in their rooms, but this need not always be the case. If they want to work near one of you, by all means let them. They may need your quiet support. Perhaps ninth-grade Dorothy prefers to spread her history assignment out on the dining room table where she can occasionally exchange a friendly glance with the adult who's paying bills nearby. Sent to her room to "do" her homework, she may study halfheartedly and ineffectively.

Help, When Needed
Your willingness to help with problems can make a difference:

The ninth-grade Spanish class is moving at a pretty fast pace. There's another vocabulary quiz tomorrow and Larry's been making a lot of errors on them recently. Both his marks and his self-confidence are shaky at present.

If Larry agrees to your tactful offer to listen to his Spanish vocabulary for ten minutes each evening, it can make a difference in that next quiz and others to come. Foreign languages all involve systematic memorizing and drill as well as continual review.

You can of course offer such help in the lower grades, too. A brief run-through of spelling and number facts, a calm, matter-of-fact explanation of a hard word in a reading assignment, a pleasant hint or suggestion about where to find a given piece of information quickly—these take only minutes of adult time and can make a big difference in a child's morale at any age. At all costs, avoid a curt "Go look it up yourself!" Looking up a piece of information with your child will not destroy his or her "independence."

Priority for Homework
Give homework priority. Schoolwork is equivalent to the adult's responsibilities. During the grade school years you should help your children form disciplined study habits. In seeking to establish routines at home that will support the objectives of school and teacher, you should assign priority to homework over other activities.

In the early school years homework is a cooperative venture. You do not do the child's work yourself. Instead you stand by, quietly and continuously alert to the possibility that he or she may need an occasional lift over some small hurdle.

In the upper elementary grades your role concerning homework is still vigilant and supportive, but less conspicuous.

During these years extra projects are often assigned to introduce children to simple research problems, and these usually put youngsters relatively on their own. In this less familiar, less structured situation they may need some support.

You want your children to become increasingly independent in their work habits. Simply by showing your interest in a new project, you can often help them to get started on it. They may want to talk about it with you and thus clarify their own thinking. It's *not* appropriate for you to become heavily involved in helping with the details. Instead you should be receptive and attentive to any questions they may raise and be ready with hints or suggestions about how they might proceed. Be alert to special problems. Perhaps they need to obtain supplementary material. In today's sprawling urban and suburban areas they may require transportation to and from the public library.

Finally, be tolerant about the inevitable clutter of papers that normally accompanies an ongoing school project and can sometimes last for days.

When your children move from elementary to secondary school (whether via the route of the traditional junior high grades or the transition of middle school), they are faced with unfamiliar surroundings, vast corridors, myriads of regulations, strangers on the administrative staff and faculty. Their teachers are now more impersonal. It's clearly up to your youngsters to make their own way. Typically, there is much less support for individual students in secondary school than was available in the more intimate environment of the early grades.

At this stage young people who have had a solid academic start and consistent support at home normally take complete charge of their homework. They will adjust to the expectations and demands of secondary school if they have had your steadfast empathy and encouragement until this point. Now you need only be a sympathetic bystander, always remaining alert to signs of temporary floundering or uncertainty.

Reassurance and Encouragement

Offer gentle reassurance and encouragement whenever necessary. Things do not always go well in school, even for the successful student. Some days are a succession of unexpected quizzes, unwelcome and tedious chores, temporary frustrations with new and difficult material. After such days you may need to provide special empathy, understanding, and even consolation: Tomorrow things will go better; the teacher will explain the new math procedure again because everyone else is equally confused about it.

Freedom to Grow

Permit the freedom to explore, experiment, and grow independently. This means not pressuring a growing child with continual planned activity. Some after-school hours need to be free; an unbroken sequence of extra language classes, ballet dancing, figure skating, music instruction, swimming, and the like can lead to fatigue and disenchantment. Sometimes a child is best left alone—to think, to sort things out, possibly to work on a project, to dream a little. Research on the backgrounds of outstanding scientists and others has shown that they recall having been allowed as children much freedom to explore on their own. Such childhood freedom can enhance the later development of a person with a well-defined sense of purpose and drive.

ENCOURAGING A LOVE OF READING

Your child can possess no greater academic asset than well-developed reading skill.

Reading is at its best a total, exceedingly demanding intellectual activity. Individuals who are wholly engrossed in a book or other printed material are unconsciously mobilizing a complex array of mental processes. Their immediate perception of the meaning of the words and sentences before them is only the beginning. They are imaginatively projecting themselves into the situation described on the printed page. They are reacting either favorably or unfavorably to characters and events being presented. They are marshaling their background of previous information about the subject. They are questioning, comparing, judging, shaping an opinion. Often they are oblivious to the immediate physical surroundings. We call such individuals bookworms, and we comment on their powers of concentration and intellectual skill.

A true reader is developed, not born. The child who at age six is already absorbed in third- or fourth-grade material is the child whose parents have lovingly nurtured his or her verbal abilities from the earliest years. The friendly little chats, the continual exchange of observation and comment between parent and young child, the stories told over and over again, the favorite picture books, the bedtime reading aloud—all these come first. It is only a step to the colorful picture dictionary, the excitement of identifying the big GULF sign at the downtown gas station, the games with pencil and paper, the growing acquaintance with words and letters, and finally, the easy preprimer.

Once children are hooked on reading, their skill develops rapidly. The more they read, the better they read and the more they bring to each new reading experience. Often the only problem is finding them an adequate supply of materials.

Such children obviously have a tremendous head start over their contemporaries when they arrive in the first grade. But what about their less advanced classmates?

Helping the First-Grade Reader

There are usually wide differences in reading readiness and skill among first-grade youngsters. The teacher normally has little choice other than to divide the class according to levels of advancement:

Ray, an average 6-year-old, is coping word by word with the standard first-grade reading workbook. It's hard work and he's not sure that he enjoys it very much. Not everyone in the room is reading as slowly as he is. The "Bluebirds" seem to be much further along in the manual than his group, the "Robins." The "Robins" aren't as slow as the "Sparrows." . . .

Such a discovery is, of course, hard on Ray's self-esteem; he's sure those Bluebirds are smarter than he is. Yet Ray is by no means stupid and it's more than likely that he will eventually become a competent reader. But he needs a lot of support—from his teacher and especially at home. Most important, *reading must become enjoyable for him.*

Here are some things that Ray's parents can do, in addition to following the suggestions already presented:

They can obtain from his teacher additional reading materials at Ray's *current* level of skill. Armed with these, they can sit down with him at home for short daily individual reading periods. These sessions should be regular, without interruptions, free of adverse comments. Gentle help over the more difficult words may be necessary. Relaxed, friendly talk about the reading, and frequent praise and encouragement, should mark these one-to-one sessions.

They can take Ray for a weekly visit to the public library. If Mom and Dad both work, they can go on Saturday. (When Ray is older, he can go on his own.) Ray can browse among the books in the children's area. If he prefers, he can simply look at their illustrations. He can select whatever looks inviting and bring it home. Maybe he will choose certain old favorites again and again. This is fine at Ray's stage. In the process he is making friends with books. Also by rereading familiar material he will solidify his skills and acquire some sense of fluency, mastery, and above all, confidence. Often the children's librarian can make helpful suggestions regarding other appealing material.

They can purchase books for Ray's own library and encourage his grandparents and other relatives to give him books for Christmas and birthdays. Paperbacks from a school list are cheap and popular, and Ray can select his own titles.

They can give Ray his own subscription to one or more of the high-quality children's magazines.

If they have not already done so for an older child, they can invest in a good junior encyclopedia.

Continued Support

As Ray begins to read independently in the third or fourth grade, his parents should refrain from criticizing his literary tastes. He may become enamored of one of the popular mystery-adventure series. As his older sister once plowed through Nancy Drew, he may become intrigued with the exploits of the Hardy Boys. Maybe the pasteboard characters in these volumes or in the daily comic strips seem contrived, artificial, and unconvincing to sophisticated adult readers, but temporary exposure to them will do Ray no harm, and in time other literary personages will take their place. Tastes—in food, clothing, literature, the arts, or other areas—evolve slowly over the years through experiment, trial and error, and gradual refinement. Parental criticism of Ray's current reading preferences will stifle his enjoyment of recreational reading.

The public library is a particularly valuable resource. The trained and knowledgeable professionals who staff the children's departments can give helpful guidance. A child browsing in this inviting atmosphere is unconsciously soaking up learning. The rewards to a family of regular library usage are rich indeed. What does it matter that books are sometimes lugged home, ten at a time, left in various places around the house, temporarily misplaced? An occasional fine for an overdue book is a small price to pay for the enormous educational benefits involved.

From his independent reading Ray will gain much. Books will bring him heroes and models. He will observe them solving problems, travel with them to far-off places, and admire their exploits. With them, he will confront ethical and moral issues. He will begin to gain a sense of history. Best of all, *he will be engaging in an active, demanding intellectual process.*

BUILDING CONFIDENCE IN MATH

Grace gets uptight every time there's a test. She's always putting the decimal point in the wrong place, mixing up her plus and minus signs, and ending up with a poor mark.

Grace has a lot of company, especially among other girls in her sixth-grade class. She has what has been called "math anxiety." Grace is not stupid; she loves to read, is interested in her social studies, English, and (were it not for the nasty problems) her general science as well. As soon as she has met all graduation requirements, she plans to take no more math.

Grace will deeply regret her plan to discontinue math during her high school years. In today's world, skill in this area is increasingly indispensable to a satisfying career. There is no reason why proper encouragement cannot motivate Grace to improve her competence with numbers. Right now she needs some friendly, relaxed, informal help from her family to supplement her school program. (She does *not* need critical comments about the careless mistakes on her most recent test.) With a little imagination and ingenuity, her parents can devise effective strategies, games, and simple problem-solving situations which will challenge her pleasantly and reinforce her skill and confidence without threatening her with a low grade.

In certain situations Grace can find math both useful and fun. At the supermarket she can be encouraged to do some comparison shopping. (Finding out whether a family-sized can of tuna is really less expensive than a smaller one of a different brand means calculating prices and weights, handling fractions and decimals.) She can become an unofficial assistant family bookkeeper, recording and totaling monthly food expenditures. She can plan and cook occasional family meals and learn how to adjust recipes for large and small numbers of servings. She can help plan the family Christmas party, making preliminary estimates of quantities and prices of ingredients needed for the refreshments. She can keep weekly track of the local baseball team's performance by computing and comparing the players' batting averages.

Playing games of numbers may help. If an older brother who is very good at math is intimidating Grace with his high scores and self-confidence, Mom or Dad can intervene tactfully. It may be better for one of them to play separately (and less competitively) with Grace until she acquires more confidence.

It would be especially helpful if her Dad took some special interest in Grace's mathematical development. Fathers are known to enhance skills of analytic thinking in their sons. They have probably favored their sons in this respect because it has been generally assumed that men and boys are better at math than their wives, mothers, and sisters. The assumption seems unfair; it may also be incorrect. Representatives of college and university mathematics faculties report few differences between their men and women students. Some believe that the women outshine the men.[16] (Whether this holds true for girls' achievement at higher levels of abstract mathematical reasoning is perhaps difficult to say.[17] But young women—and young men too—certainly deserve to progress as far as they wish in mastering any branch of mathematics.)

As Grace enters the junior and senior high grades, it's vitally important for her Dad to continue his friendly interest and support. By all means she should have a small checking account and become proficient in balancing it regularly. She can be given a small pocket calculator. Though she will probably not be allowed to use it in algebra, she can have fun experimenting with it, and as she gains practice in its use, her confidence will be enhanced. The important thing is to preserve her confidence as she encounters the increasing challenges of the high school mathematics curriculum. She should be encouraged to give special attention to math in her homework schedule, preparing these assignments first, while her mind is fresh and alert. If she's comfortable having Mom or Dad check her work, she'll be spared the embarrassment of having errors pointed out to her in next day's class. (Her parents can also remind her that the male math shark in the class may be doing less well in history or Spanish than she is.)

The field of mathematics is a giant intellectual edifice comprised of many components. To attain any degree of mastery, one must deal successfully with its two principal aspects.

First, one must gain skill and facility in the basic processes of calculation (addition, subtraction, multiplication, and division), which are all utilized at higher levels of study. It takes extensive practice to sharpen these skills to the point at which they are readily available for a variety of mathematical tasks. Usually one builds this foundation in the elementary grades.

The second and more elusive aspect of math study involves learning to solve problems. One must analyze a given situation from a quantitative point of view, determine what is needed for its solution, and then apply the appropriate calculating procedures. While competence in calculation is gained from drill and memorization, problem solving demands more complex and diverse intellectual functions. One needs insight, analytical powers, concentration, flexibility of thought, curiosity, organizing power, and often persistence—in other words, the same coping strengths that have been discussed above.

Recently, several hundred teachers of remedial college mathematics attending a conference agreed that there are serious flaws in today's teaching of math. Specifically, one participant criticized "the excessive stress on memory instead of thinking, with the result that pupils forget how to transfer what they have memorized to problems they meet in a different context."[18] It is not enough to be able to calculate rapidly; one must also be able to "read mathematics." Only thus can one comprehend the vast quantities of scientific data that are published for specialist and general public alike as well as understand the complex political, economic, and social issues before us today.[19]

Throughout Grace's high school years her parents must give her sympathetic support that will help her build both calculating and problem-solving skills. In the words of Dr. Stephen Willoughby, she must learn to "use mathematical thought to solve problems that are real [to her] and important to society."[20] Always her mom and dad must remember this word of warning: nothing handicaps the young math student's efforts as much as anxiety (fear of criticism).

Finally, Grace must keep a steadfast eye on the future. Occupational analysts now say that "some basic math—above all the willingness to learn more math—is required for upward mobility in two of every three well-paying occupations."[21] If she persists, Grace may yet prepare herself to deal with these new realities. Other young women are making a successful leap into the computer world of the 1980's, as this recent (and true) report testifies:

Susan [not her real name] has just been named director of a newly established administrative data processing department of a well-known women's college. Susan has had more than fifteen years of financial and administrative experience, including her work as information systems analyst for a national firm that handles data systems. She oversaw the first in-house computer system in two business firms. Although her college major was English, she later earned the MBA degree in a nationally ranked graduate school of business.

Part of the trouble for girls like Grace seems to lie in the "math anxiety" referred to above. Recently one investigator has pointed out that as a group, girls tend to be anxious when confronted with problems involving numbers (particularly very large or very small numbers) and quantitative reasoning. The notion that they are stupid in math has no basis in either biology or neurology. According to this authority there is no reason why girls cannot learn to handle numbers or problem-solving tasks with ease and confidence.

It is at least partly a question of attitude. Often a girl's mother (who says she never could do math) communicates the impression to her daughter that she, too, is doomed to the same incompetence. In recent "math anxiety workshops" women have recalled childhood experiences of "humiliation, frustration, and failure that had persuaded them . . . that they did not have 'mathematical minds.' "[22]

The time to build confidence in numerical skills in such children as Grace (and boys with similar anxieties) is when they are in the elementary grades. In these years parents, with a little imagination and ingenuity, can encourage their young people to improve their "math mental health" (i.e., their confidence). In later years their daughters and sons will thank them.

THE REPORT CARD AND GRADES

Your children's report cards are important to them, to you, to the school, and to the community. The following true story is illustrative:

Jim, a junior high school boy and son of a poorly educated truck driver, had been doing very mediocre work at school. After an interested teacher had talked at some length with his parents, Jim's work began to improve. When his report card arrived, showing that Jim had actually received one B grade, his father broke down and cried right in the kitchen. He had felt that because of his own deficient education, he would never see his child receive a B. The joy of seeing Jim achieve in this manner was a tremendous contribution to his father's self-esteem.

All of us, regardless of our educational level, have an emotional investment in our child's report card. How do we react when it comes home? Certainly our attitude should, if possible, be positive and approving.

If the record is consistently good, there is usually no problem. Sometimes, however, things are not going as well as they might. At these times we must first try to be understanding. We can say something like, "That's too bad. Let's see what we can do about it. I'm sure you can do better next time."

It's best to take specific action, as this family does:

At the end of the first marking period seventh-grade Janice comes home with a D in history and a C in science. Fortunately, her parents are understanding and also sufficiently concerned to do something about the situation. After a general talk, a plan is worked out whereby Janice's mother helps her work on her history assignment while her father lends a hand with the science. A definite time is set aside each day for this work. Results on tests and homework are evident within a few weeks.

This type of short-range rescue operation serves to restore Janice's confidence and morale. She is more fortunate than many pupils who are struggling to make the transition between elementary and junior high school grades:

Young Stan has goofed off during the same marking period. Although his parents are annoyed, they are doing little to improve the situation. Stan's report card shows a C, two C minuses, and near-failure in math. His prospects for achievement in secondary school are poor at this time.

It's difficult to offer Stan's parents a specific program that is guaranteed to produce improvement in his school performance. Almost certainly they have failed to provide him enough general support and encouragement at home.

Tempting though the following measures may be, none will help raise a child's marks:

Criticism. As previously noted, criticism is almost always damaging. Criticizing a child's performance of any task inhibits the expression of his personality in that activity. It also kills his motivation, dampens any enthusiam, and, at worst, can throw him into a panic.

Punitive removal or curtailment of privileges. It will not improve Stan's math work merely to dock his allowance or keep him at home on Friday and Saturday evenings. (It would probably be helpful if his Dad arranged to spend time pleasantly with him on weekends and possibly work with him informally on his math problems.)

Threats. Threats of any kind are usually ineffective; moreover, they are difficult to carry out.

Taunts. Telling Stan that he "can do it if he wants to" explains absolutely nothing and makes no positive suggestions to him. Nor is it fair for his parents to call him lazy. Psychologically speaking, there's no such thing as a lazy child. Stan may be floundering, confused, and bewildered as he tries to adjust to the increased academic and social demands of the junior high school, but he is not lazy. He needs sympathy, support, and active parental concern at home, not critical and deflating comments.

Comparison with other children's academic performance. Nothing is more stinging than the comment, "Why can't you get the marks that Tim gets?" Stan will only be made miserable by the suggestion that someone else's son is better than he is.

Unrealistic optimism. It's unwise to rationalize Stan's poor school performance by saying, "Well, he'll grow out of it." If he is achieving at this level one-quarter of the way through the seventh grade, he will only be further behind in each successive marking period—and probably in higher grades—unless he is given sympathetic help with his present problems.

Grades need to be kept in perspective. It's important not to become discouraged by occasional setbacks. Sometimes a child, after having improved in a specific school subject (math, for example), reverts to a lower grade level in a subsequent marking period. Progress in any skill has its ups, downs, and plateaus. As parents, you should talk with your child in a positive manner about such problems.

YOU AND THE TEACHER

Good teacher–parent–child relationships are especially important during the early grades. The elementary school teacher is usually a warm and understanding person. You should try to establish a good relationship each year with your child's teachers.

As a professional educator, a teacher can be assumed to have certain qualifications. Among other things, she or he usually knows what can be expected academically of the class during a given school year. Viewing children both as individuals and as members of the group, the teacher will assess their special traits, their strengths and weaknesses, in reference to those of their classmates. A teacher is likely to be somewhat more objective about your youngster than you are. However, a teacher is a human being as well as a professional and will also have subjective reactions to your child—and to you.

Most schools arrange for routine parent–teacher conferences once or twice a year, but additional ones may be helpful. It is an excellent plan to arrange a meeting with the teacher as early in the fall as possible, even when everything seems to be going well. Take the initiative by calling in advance for a short appointment after school. Even a brief meeting will allow you to become personally acquainted. You can show your interest and support of the current program, ask for suggestions as to how you can help, possibly obtain extra materials for supplementary home drill.

Do not wait until there are signs of trouble. And do not rely on Parent–Teacher Night to provide you an opportunity for a personal interview.

In the course of the conversation, do not proceed to tell the teacher what you perceive to be your child's poor qualities and do not compare the child's schoolwork with that of an older or younger brother or sister. Don't encourage the teacher to make such comparisons. If they are made, simply make some positive comment about the child. You do not want to undermine his or her reputation. At the same time you can be supportive and positive in your attitude toward both the teacher and the educational program.

THE IQ MYTH

What is an IQ test? Simply defined, it usually consists of a series of questions designed to measure an individual's intellectual capacities and functioning. Of the many types currently in use, the individually administered test yields more reliable results than those given to a group.

A professional examiner trained in diagnosis and evaluation can, by individually administering one or more IQ tests to a child, determine with some accuracy the strength of his verbal skills (vocabulary, reasoning powers, and comprehension) and his memory as well as his social judgment and skills with numbers and arithmetical reasoning. This individual can also measure the child's nonverbal skills such as those involved in handling and arranging small objects.

Despite the care with which they have been constructed and standardized, IQ tests, particularly group tests, have numerous limitations. The scores are subject to error and should not be viewed as precise. A subject's performance can be adversely affected by surrounding conditions or by the way the person is feeling at the time of testing. Moreover, scores usually do not remain stationary during a child's life; they may increase during the growing years, particularly if the child's home life is intellectually enriching, affectionate, and secure. Finally, the tests are widely criticized, with some justification, because of their cultural bias. For example, children from homes where parents speak little or no English will be severely handicapped in coping with verbal material, although they may have sound mathematical and other aptitudes.

IQ test results are not entirely accurate in predicting future scholastic achievement. They do not measure a child's motivation, ambition, or capacity to persist at long-range undertakings. Consequently there are often puzzling discrepancies between youngsters' IQ test scores and their school achievement. Some children with high scores do poorly in school while others whose test performance is more average may do surprisingly well.[23]

Below-average school grades do *not* mean below-average intellectual ability. They are more likely an indication of a child's emotional insecurity and lack of motivation associated with inadequate parental nurturance and support.

Yet the IQ concept (or myth) exercises a powerful influence on many parents, as the following anecdotes show:

Mr. and Mrs. S. are high school graduates. Their ninth-grade son's grades are not of college admission caliber. Mr. and Mrs. S. tell the school counselor that they don't care whether Arthur goes to college, implying that he probably doesn't have the ability.

However, when an individually administered IQ test places Arthur in the very superior mental ability range, Mr. and Mrs. S. completely change their attitude toward him. Never again do they mention his not going to college. They are now making a determined effort to change Arthur's environment, praising and encouraging him, and hoping he will be able to qualify for college.

Here is a different situation:

Eleventh-grade Lewis has been called a brain. His parents boast that he has a high IQ and earned 700's on his Scholastic Aptitude Test. Lewis's grades, however, hover in the D to C-minus range.

Lewis's parents, both very busy persons, don't appear to be worried. "Lewis does well in the things he's interested in," they say, adding with some embarrassment that there are few things in which he is interested.

These insecure parents have a greater emotional investment in their son's IQ than in his academic productivity. If they do not soon realize the cause of Lewis's poor performance in school, he may drift aimlessly and eventually be bypassed by college admission offices. His latent talents and potentialities will not be realized, and society will be the loser.

Sometimes, although a professional should be aware of this pitfall, it is the teacher who worships the IQ concept:

Mark brought home a C report card. The teacher told his parents that since Mark's IQ on a group intelligence test was about 110, he was "working up to his ability." The father doubted the validity of the teacher's statement. On the advice of a sympathetic relative, he began to take a more active interest in Mark's schoolwork, in his activities, and in him as a person. Both parents made a point of expressing more approval and appreciation of Mark's efforts to improve his schoolwork, even offering to help him on occasion.

Mark's grades began to improve. He became more alert, more communicative, more intellectually curious, and in general more productive. Subsequently, on an individually administered IQ test his score was 135 rather than the 110 previously reported by the teacher.

We can only conclude that once his family took a real interest in Mark, his schoolwork (and his academic skills in general) improved. Accordingly, he was able to perform at a higher level on the second intelligence test.

Misconceptions About "Heredity"
"Uncle Joe never was a student, and Carl is just like him!"
How often we hear a child's indifferent school performance excused in this manner! The remark suggests some misunderstanding of the heredity–environment issue.

For decades people have discussed and argued the relative influence of inheritance as opposed to what we acquire or learn from our early environment. *Heredity* refers to the particular content of chromosomes and genes at the moment of conception which determines sex and other physical attributes of the fetus. From that time on the individual's rapidly developing nervous system, including the brain, is subject to all kinds of stimuli from the *environment*, including any disease, infection, or accident before, during, or after birth which can influence physical and psychological growth. Research on the influence of prenatal and early parental environment on the child's permanent acquisition of intellectual competence, musical and motor skills, and personality characteristics has greatly diminished the alleged role of heredity in determining the direction of our lives. Inheritance of physical characteristics (skeletal build, the unusual height favoring a basketball player, the structure and size of hands and fingers in a future instrumental performer) may make later athletic or musical performance easier. But the individual's motivation for high achievement in these areas comes chiefly from the support of early environmental influences.

Many parents refer to heredity to explain or justify their child's behavior in numerous situations. Like Carl's parents, they may ascribe poor school performance to a relative in a previous generation. If, on the other hand, a youngster shows unusual talent or intellectual ability, they credit her or his forebears and deny their own role in its development.

Carl was born with an unknown potential. Barring accident or injury there are really no limits to what he can accomplish in his life. He has not inherited his study habits from Uncle Joe but has probably been influenced by certain family attitudes about education and study in general. In any case, it is inappropriate for his parents to indulge in either of the following comments:

"We'll be satisfied as long as you're working up to your ability." At this point no one really knows Carl's limits. If he has recently taken an IQ test such as was described above, the test score may not be an accurate measure of his ability, particularly if it is a group test. Nor is it likely to indicate what Carl, properly motivated, might accomplish in later years.

"Just do your best." One's "best" cannot be defined by performance on an IQ test. Nor can it provide any sense of goal or direction. Parental urging that encourages a child like Carl merely to do his best relieves him, his parents, and his teachers of responsibility for his achievement.

There may be times in life—during an athletic contest or an important test, for example—when individuals may rightly feel they did their utmost under great pressure. However, the "do your best" expression is too often invoked by both parents and teachers merely to justify a child's mediocre academic performance.

THE INTELLECTUALLY ADVANCED CHILD

Ron, eight, was reading when he was five. He's always been articulate and talkative. His curiosity seems insatiable; he asks questions continually, wants to know how things "work," enjoys trying to solve difficult puzzles and complicated math problems. School bores him much of the time. Keeping him busy in class creates something of a problem. His energy seems limitless; he's "into everything."

Ron's classmate Trudy has much the same characteristics.

Children like Ron and Trudy are often called "gifted." The National Association for Gifted Children and other such organizations describe such youngsters as possessing a number of intellectual assets. Conspicuous are their unusual verbal and mathematical skills, their large vocabulary and general verbal fluency, their exceptionally quick and accurate memory, their ability to concentrate easily for long periods of time, their well-developed reading skill and omnivorous reading habits, their ongoing intellectual curiosity.

Such children are further described as typically energetic, highly motivated, and task-oriented in areas that challenge and interest them. They relish the process of grappling with a complex problem and reducing its intricacies to simple basics. Their judgment is sound; though willing to take risks, they are equally ready to assume responsibility for their decisions and actions. Often quite creative, they are also characteristically independent, tending to stand apart from others in their convictions and occasionally quite stubborn in defending their views.[24]

The degree of empathy and social awareness of these advanced and precocious children is also noted. They seem to grasp the meaning of kindness toward others at an early age, to become concerned about ethical issues and values, to surprise their families with their idealistic and empathic involvement with adult problems in the sphere of international politics, religion, and other areas.

Children who at an early age display unusual intellectual, musical, athletic, or other abilities are often described as "talented," "gifted," or "brilliant." Such performance always has a reference point. They are more skilled or capable when compared with their peers and thereby should be called "advanced" rather than gifted. They have reached a certain level because their parents and/or other concerned persons have exposed and stimulated them in some special area quite early in life—even during the first months of infancy. The rapidly developing nervous system, including the brain, readily absorbs these stimuli which become a permanent part of their personalities.

It is unfortunate that research on the family backgrounds of gifted children is somewhat sparse. What information we have, however, supports the claim that such qualities and talents arise in essentially stable, supportive, and educationally oriented family environments. Three studies are illustrative:

● *The famous study by Terman of his "gifted" group of some 1,500 11-year-olds originally selected in 1922.* Follow-up studies of these youngsters over several subsequent decades showed that subjects whose talents were equal in the beginning traveled different routes of success in later years. Contrasts in family backgrounds were dramatically evident in two subgroups: the "A" group comprised of the 100 most successful and the "B" consisting of the 100 least successful. The four traits in which the two groups differed most markedly were "persistence in the accomplishment of ends," "integration toward goals, as contrasted with drifting," "self-confidence," and "freedom from inferiority feelings."[25]

● *A study by Barbe during the 1950's of 456 children in the city of Cleveland.* Barbe examined the families of these children and found that an overwhelming proportion (about 88 percent) had been reared by their own parents in intact marital situations and had lived in essentially middle-class circumstances. The parents' educational level was higher than average, with the mothers' education slightly superior to that of the fathers.[26]

● *Results of a survey on the "roots of success" originally published by* Family Circle *magazine.* This survey of the mothers of 60 adults who have been unusually successful in widely differing walks of life indicates a significant quality in the maternal attitudes. From the time of their children's infancy (sometimes even earlier) these women had determined that their babies would have a promising future and they realized that this future lay in their care as parents.[27]

We are aware that individual cases of unusual talent can be found in disadvantaged and isolated families living in rural or ghetto areas. It is beyond the scope of this text to attempt to explain such situations. Usually little or nothing is known of the emotional quality of the backgrounds of such young individuals. From reading current research on unusually gifted youngsters, we can only conclude that self-esteem, enhanced from some source, is an essential prerequisite for the development of any kind of talent.

Let us return to Trudy and Ron. Their parents deserve great credit for the job they have already done in stimulating their children's rapidly developing intellects—a job that is, however, far from complete. Since both children will probably be more advanced than their peers at all grade levels, their parents will be continually challenged to provide them with opportunities for learning at home and in the community in addition to their work at school.

During the elementary school years parents of unusually advanced youngsters can be helpful in various ways. Building a good relationship with the teachers at each grade level is important; these individuals will be more likely to appreciate youngsters like Ron and Trudy and provide them with sufficient stimulation to keep them interested in school. Boredom with classroom routine is a common problem with such children.

The current practice in most areas is to keep children like Ron and Trudy within their own age group and have them participate in the regular curriculum for that grade while offering them opportunities to do extra work in areas of special interest. In a few states the schools provide special "enrichment" classes in which bright students spend a portion of their time. In the absence of such a class Trudy and Ron can certainly use the resources of the reading center and/or the school or public library for special reports that they can occasionally prepare for careful presentation to their classmates. If there is a small computer center in the school, they may be allowed to embark on some project of their own making. Or they can become part-time tutors for one or more classmates who need a lift over academic hurdles that they have previously surmounted.

Beyond the school walls parents can explore the resources of the community. Urban areas are, of course, especially rich in cultural and educational opportunities for persons of all ages including talented youth. Museums and other institutions offer well-taught Saturday classes in a wide variety of arts and sciences that are geared to the interests of such children as Trudy and Ron. Moreover, in these groups they will meet new friends of comparable intellectual advancement.

In high school there are normally opportunities for qualified students to enroll in courses at the advanced placement level. It may not be necessary or even wise for a child to load his or her program with too many accelerated courses. Such youngsters are not always equally advanced in all areas (the young math wizard may be less interested and less proficient in languages). If the high school is in a small community and unable to offer diversified courses such as the advanced placement subjects, families of advanced youngsters may have to search further afield, perhaps looking into courses offered by a nearby college or a branch of a state university.

Two Words of Counsel
 • As the Terman studies amply demonstrate, being unusually advanced in one's early school years does not automatically ensure later accomplishment. Parents should not take their child's "brightness" for granted. A gifted youngster may not have a future unless his or her parents steadfastly continue their affectionate concern and support over many years. Other things being equal, the gifted child will probably rank highly among his or her school-mates. In the teenage years, however, such youngsters are sometimes surpassed by hard-working, dedicated contemporaries.
 • For children of such promise there is always the possibility that their own enthusiastic involvement in numerous activities together with their parents' continous zeal for encouraging and rewarding them may leave them insufficient time for recreation. Trudy and Ron should have time for an occasional movie or softball game; they might prefer a free Saturday instead of that special class. These students often work long hours, but as long as their fathers and mothers support and encourage them and they take appropriate time for some carefree relaxation, there is little danger of their becoming "burned out" or discouraged.

LEARNING DISABILITY: THE STORY OF HENRY

Early in the fourth grade ten-year-old Henry began to experience difficulty with reading, spelling, and arithmetic. His teacher observed him to be somewhat restless, inattentive, lacking in confidence, and poorly motivated; he also seemed to be having difficulty with his peers on the playground. She recommended a staff meeting on Henry's problems and the members agreed that he probably had a learning disability.

The staff told Henry's parents that he should take extra work at the reading center twice a week; the tutor at the center was described as a good teacher and a warm and empathic person.

Henry's parents were puzzled as to why he should suddenly be having a learning disability this year; after all, he had been getting along as an average student. (His older sister had breezed through elementary school with straight A's.) After some discussion, they consented to the school's recommendation that Henry attend the reading center. At the same time they contacted a psychologist for a series of interviews.[28]

Let us look in on these conversations, which closely resemble many that have taken place in our office.

During the first interview the psychologist asks Henry's parents to reflect carefully about their relations with him during the past several years. Under discreet probing, they acknowledge some of their previous feelings about Henry. His sister was a good student so they had assumed Henry would do well, too. But because he was a boy, it was important for him to become a strong, assertive fellow, able to make his way in the world. It hadn't occurred to them that he also needed warmth, praise, and affection. They wanted him to hold his own in rough-and-tumble encounters with peers, to be tough and unemotional and never cry. It didn't matter that Henry, now occupied with strenuous and competitive outdoor activities, had little time, energy, or inclination to settle down indoors with a book in his spare time or to expend much effort on his spelling or arithmetic homework.

His parents also confess that they have been quite critical about the mistakes beginning to appear on Henry's papers; the work in the fourth grade is quite hard but they saw no need to offer much help.

The psychologist's recommendations are tactful but explicit. If Henry's schoolwork is to improve, he will need help from home as well as school. From his parents he must have more affection; more approval, even for completing small, insignificant tasks; and less criticism. There must be no adverse comparisons between his sister's good marks and his own mediocre performance. In particular, Henry needs some genuine interest, support, and friendly concern from his dad. And finally, he must have systematic, supportive help with daily schoolwork assignments from both parents under specific guidelines that will be provided by the teacher and the learning center.

Let us see what has been done with these suggestions:

Haltingly at first, but with gradually increasing confidence as they noted their son's responsiveness, Henry's parents tried a new approach. Henry was thrilled when his Daddy took him out for a big Saturday outing replete with a sitdown restaurant lunch where they talked for a long time about many things–sports, school, friends, even Henry's future. Other excursions and other conversations followed. Letters from Daddy and little notes tucked into his lunchbox by Mom began to brighten Henry's day at school. He was pleased when Daddy gently suggested they look over his arithmetic homework together or when Mom said it was time to review the next day's spelling words. They even became engrossed in Tom Sawyer *and found his adventures actually more appealing than the tube.*

Henry's big sister was not left out of the picture. Following another of the psychologist's suggestions, the family began to hold regular pow-wows once a week. The children were free to talk and get things off their chests; everyone came up with good ideas about how life at home could become better organized; plans were formulated for the summer, and in general people felt good about themselves and each other.

Mom and Dad kept faithfully in touch with the school while Henry was attending the learning center. Within two weeks some changes began to be evident. Henry seemed less tense, more communicative at home, more affectionate toward his sister. His teacher reported a better attitude toward school; he seemed less distractible in class and there were fewer problems on the playground. By the end of the month Henry's reading showed signs of improvement; there were fewer errors on his arithmetic and spelling papers because he was learning how to check more carefully for mistakes; he was doing his homework without urging and speaking up in class discussions. At the end of eight weeks his teacher in the learning center felt he no longer needed her assistance.

Educators have been puzzled for many years about the causes and treatment of learning disabilities—or "LD," as they are sometimes called. The case of Henry illustrates some recent developments in the diagnosis and treatment of this problem. (In the discussion that follows we are not dealing with "dyslexia" which, according to medical specialists, probably occurs in no more than 3 to 5 percent of the population and is often confused with learning disability.)[29]

Some form of LD is alleged to afflict between 10 and 15 percent of all schoolchildren; vast sums of public money have been spent in an effort to cope with the problem. The term was coined about thirty years ago to describe a hypothetical injured condition in the brain that would supposedly interfere with a child's learning. Without the support of thorough research the term "minimal brain damage" was used to describe this condition. Later, as its validity was questioned, the term "minimal brain dysfunction" was substituted, although it too cannot be definitively identified through tests. Researchers are currently recommending the elimination of these terms.[30] Nonetheless both labels have influenced teaching and remedial methods, which have consequently been directed from a neurological point of view toward developing sensory-motor and perceptual-motor skills. There is no evidence that such methods have improved children's reading or general academic achievement.[31]

During the past 30 years learning disability has become a nebulous umbrella term. As many as 60 different definitions have emerged, each depending on the parameters, terminology, and design of a given piece of research.

The possible role of psychological factors in learning disability cases has been almost totally ignored. The LD problem is found three to five times more often in boys than in girls.[32] This fact may be linked to the finding in recent research that parents give less support and affection to sons than to daughters. LD is common in disadvantaged, disturbed, noisy home environments where parents are beset with numerous economic and social problems. Among delinquents the percentage of learning disability is quite high.[33] Yet LD is also found in many middle-class families when emotional tension, marital problems, and general lack of concern for the children's academic development are present.

Although LD students' typical problems of poor self-image, hyperactive tendencies, and social immaturity have been attributed to their inability to read, it is likely that most of these problems are at least partially caused by anxiety.[34] Traits that interfere with the learning process such as inattentiveness, short memory span, and impulsiveness are associated with emotional insecurity as well as with the inability to read. Understandably, a poor reader's anxiety will be increased as he perceives himself coping inadequately with the multitudinous intellectual tasks for which good reading skill is essential. But anxiety has probably preceded the current problems—it is not merely a result of poor reading.

Basically, a single factor underlies the vast majority of learning disability problems: lack of security caused by insufficient parental concern and involvement in the educational development of their children. Parents of youngsters like Henry would do well to reflect on the implications of his story. They ought to ask some questions, both of the school and of themselves. By all means they should seek educational and psychological advice, the earlier the better. Private intellectual (and, if indicated, neurological) testing may be helpful. There is still time in the elementary grades to institute a systematic tutoring program to meet a youngster's specific academic deficiencies. But the problem is an emotional as well as an educational one. No program can achieve success without parental involvement, commitment, and support.

NONACADEMIC SKILLS

Hobbies and Creative Activities

"Their house fairly bulges with unfinished projects!" Thus a proud grandmother describes the household of her busy daughter and son-in-law, parents of three youngsters aged four through eight. They live in a beehive of activity that verges at times on the chaotic.

Hobbies are an important outlet for the energies of many grade-school children. Some youngsters become omnivorous collectors: they gather stamps, trading cards, dolls, coins, rocks, insects, models of rockets or space vehicles. Their interests may shift from one year to the next. No matter. Each young collector is building up his or her own particular store of general information about a given area: about other lands, peoples, or historical periods; about favorite sports and sports heroes; about biology or engineering. In maintaining a collection over an extended period of time the child is also developing persistence, patience, and intellectual curiosity.

An ongoing and expanding collection can present storage problems. If it represents a considerable investment of its owner's time and thought, it should be respected as well as protected from the hands of a younger sibling. Providing adequate space can be difficult in today's homes, and tolerating clutter isn't easy either. Take the long view if you can. When your 9-year-old has gone off to college ten years hence you will find the house neater, but quite empty!

How a child pursues a hobby or any creative project reveals much about his personality, particularly his independence and his capacity for perseverance in a long task:

Jerry, ten, puzzles over the minute directions for the model F-15 fighter plane, refusing help from anyone. Bit by bit the plane takes shape, and Jerry doesn't neglect a single detail. The job is complete in about three weeks and Mom and Dad are invited to inspect it proudly.

Fourteen-year-old Marion embarks one summer on her most ambitious sewing project to date, a tailored jacket and skirt. She painstakingly copes with the intricacies of the pattern–cutting material, lining, and interfacing with utmost care, and following the step-by-step directions for preparing and assembling the numerous pieces for final stitching, pressing, and even buttonholes! With patience and occasional help from her mom, Marion turns out an attractive outfit.

The typical household offers literally dozens of opportunities for creative activities, especially for observance of holidays, birthdays, and other celebrations. The materials for pot holders, aprons, placemats, artwork, greeting cards, and special desserts are almost always ready at hand; the results can be immensely meaningful to the grandmothers, favorite relatives, or old friends to whom they convey a child's love.

Some children will express themselves in unusual ways:

Nineteen-year-old Jane, with a genealogical bent, has painstakingly constructed a family tree for her brother and sister. She has scoured the house for every available baby snapshot as well as old photos, scraps of yellowed correspondence, and miscellaneous memos from her parents' files, and has succeeded in tracing several family lines back nearly one hundred years. The project, which has taken her several weeks, has involved the expense of photographic reproductions and considerable care in mounting the materials for display.

During the week before Christmas Grandmother, ill in a nursing home, is visited by 10-year-old May and her 4-year-old brother Matthew. May performs a little dance that she has composed especially for Nana. Not to be outdone, Matthew then executes his own choreographic interpretation of "Rudolph, the Red-Nosed Reindeer."

Jane's gift of her own time, research, and careful synthesis of family records not only has enriched her personally but has given her brother and sister a new awareness of themselves as part of a continuous family heritage. The memory of the visit from May and Matthew will sustain Nana through many long days and nights of illness and discomfort.

Original work, no matter how modest, is a precious commodity in these days when material goods are to be had for the mere outlay of cash. It should *always* be encouraged and appreciated.

An Appropriate Investment in Athletics

There are only twenty-three varsity hockey jerseys at the senior high. From the age of nine or ten there are two hundred boys out there vying for them.

The coach at one of Boston's suburban high schools adds ruefully that an average parent can go insane at an ice hockey game, particularly if his or her child is involved. A similar situation prevails in basketball and football. The vast majority of aspiring youngsters never make the team. The resulting stresses on some are often a source of concern to school coaches, counselors, and administrators; they are also troubling to many thoughtful parents.

Ann and Jim Brown, both sixty-five and retired to Florida, still play year-round tennis. Whenever their grown children visit them, family doubles in various combinations are in order. Each and every member, in-laws included, joins in low-key family competition spiced with friendly humor and private rivalries among certain more vigorous members of the clan.

The Browns' tennis-playing skills are not of expert or professional rank, but they all play well enough to enjoy the game as a lifelong recreational pursuit.

Viewed in proper perspective, athletics are unquestionably valuable in youngsters' all-round development. Only a very few, however, will reach genuine star status, while thousands of others and their families pay a heavy price.

It's important to keep priorities in balance. Your children most probably will *not* earn their living as star athletes. If they choose to become athletic teachers or coaches, they will still need a good school record to qualify for admission to a college of physical education. Any athletic program that regularly drains a child's energies from satisfactory completion of her or his basic academic program should be questioned.

Special Performance Skills
Nat has studied piano for seven years. He plays well enough at sixteen to be assistant accompanist for the school glee club. Because of homework, Nat now has little time to practice but he enjoys helping at choral rehearsals.

Molly, the first accompanist, began piano study at five with her mother, a professional pianist. She is considerably more advanced technically than Nat, practices several hours a day, is preparing to play a concerto with the local symphony orchestra, and hopes to attend a conservatory for further training.

The situations of Nat and Molly illustrate two approaches to the training of young people in special performance skills, whether they involve a musical instrument, figure skating, ballet, dramatics, gymnastics, or some other area. They represent two possible routes—one leading to amateur, the other to professional status.

A child who remains a musical amateur, for example, typically grows up in a household where music is viewed as one part of a full, balanced, and essentially normal life. The family members enjoy informal singing, they listen to records, possibly someone plays an instrument. A few years after entry into school, if a child indicates sufficient interest, he or she is allowed to start formal lessons on either an orchestral or keyboard instrument under the aegis of the school, in a special class, or in private instruction. Many such youngsters practice with a reasonable degree of regularity at least into the junior high school years. If they can participate in a group such as a small orchestra, their interest and willingness to continue music study are enhanced and sustained. As the academic program in the secondary school becomes more demanding and other interests claim their attention, their commitment to music is often modified. They may still go on to play in a college orchestra or explore simple chamber music with friends of similar competence. Lacking these options, they may become faithful members of their local church choir or community chorus.

The progress to professional status, on the other hand, typically requires an early start and also extreme dedication on the part of the entire family. It is no accident that professional musicians are often developed by professional parents; both before birth and during the earliest months of life such children receive continual aural exposure to music which indubitably sensitizes the ear. With any performing skill, it is usually the family who first notes budding aptitude and decides on the child's behalf to embark on its development. They willingly shoulder the commitments and the expense of providing continual private instruction and personally supervising the youngster's practice. The road to a professional career is rigorous, and preparation for it must be dedicated and meticulous. Only after the child has reached the late teenage years will he or she probably make a commitment to pursue further training. Such young people must endure constant evaluation and criticism if they are to survive the stresses of possible entry into a specialized school, mastery of an extensive repertoire, theoretical training, special coaching, auditioning, and possibly further hurdles toward achieving success and critical recognition. Amid all these efforts, however, those who throughout their development have received the encouragement of parents, relatives, and friends will not relinquish their efforts toward the goal of becoming respected artists.

Parents who undertake to groom a child for a professional career of any kind must weigh carefully the realities of their entire family situation. In preparing one champion, they may risk seriously neglecting the development of other siblings.

There is another risk. It is not always wise for fathers and mothers who are themselves professionals to undertake to teach their own youngsters. If you are teaching them or supervising their practice in a skill in which you yourself have reached considerable competence, you may find it difficult to keep your instruction free of tension. As a parent, you love your child; as a professional, you know the crucial importance of maintaining the strictest standards in training. Many professional musicians freely acknowledge that as children they hated the long and arduous practice hours and their parents' barrage of criticism and correction. It may help to engage a colleague who is not emotionally involved to instruct your child.

In developing one special performance skill, children may travel the road to either amateur or professional status. Possibly they will combine the two approaches; countless adults (the organist-choirmaster-private teacher, the actor-director, the dancer-choreographer, the figure skater who turns coach) are productively wearing several hats. Some amateur skills later become professionalized though this is probably not likely in the case of a world-class solo performing artist.

Two things are worth remembering. You and your child must be realistic in accepting the roles, demands, commitments, and constraints of the choice you have made as well as your expectations for its future outcomes. Second, you as parents must provide never-failing support for the young person's efforts; in either case it is a long, often lonely road to attainment of the objective.

Additional Suggestions

A little imagination will suggest countless ways in which to enhance your youngsters' problem-solving and achievement skills. Here are three possibilities for stimulating young children in particular.

Let a small child "win" at a game when you can do so unobtrusively:

The game of checkers is approaching the final moves. Jack, seven, is rapidly learning how to exploit every opportunity. Somehow his daddy has just missed a chance to block the beautiful double play he's plan-

ning for his next turn. Triumphantly, he jumps his red checker over Daddy's two remaining black ones and pronounces himself the winner. Daddy winks slyly at Mom and writes down the score.

Games are not only fun; they also stimulate logical thinking and concentration. For example, Scrabble, a great favorite in many households, is a helpful vocabulary builder.

Let a small child make frequent choices:

"Janet, where shall we take our walk today?" The three-year-old ponders the alternatives: a trip to feed the ducks in the park or a good workout on the jungle gym at the nearby playground. After a moment of reflection she decides that the ducks could use a meal of stale bread crumbs.

We learn to make important decisions only after long years of practice at making a multitude of minor ones.

As far as possible, let children finish tasks they have started, and do not interfere:

Tommy wants to frost and decorate Daddy's birthday cake. He's seen the beautiful creations in the local bakery window and wants to try his hand with the tools in the kitchen cupboard. The job becomes rather involved and somewhat messy. Mom tactfully retires from the kitchen so that Tommy can finish by himself. The final product is much admired.

General Enrichment of Family Life

Productive child rearing is a many-sided undertaking. Important though they are, school and schoolwork are only part of the picture. In the genuinely productive home, a quality of indefinable enrichment permeates the lives of all family members:

The gentle strains of a Mozart string quartet emanate from the record player while dinner is in progress. . . . The newly arrived Geographic lies on the living room table ready for perusal along with yesterday's Sunday Times, which Mom hopes to catch up with later in the evening. . . . Someone has been paging through the beautiful catalogue of paintings in the National Gallery. During dinner, teenagers and parents participate in a lengthy discussion of the Middle East problem. . . . Plans are afoot for the family canoeing trip next August. . . . Everyone hopes to catch the newest BBC Shakespeare production on public television. The last big basketball game at the high school comes off this week.

The days are full indeed for such a family.

CONCLUSION

If you are successful parents, you will develop boys and girls who have alert, intellectually curious and acquisitive minds; who attack problems with enthusiasm and intensity, but also with good judgment; who act independently of others; who possess good verbal and mathematical skills and retentive memories. These young people will efficiently manage both their time and their talents, and they will remain with projects until they are completed. If necessary, they will not hesitate to take a stand or to arrive at a difficult decision.

You look forward to the future years when your children will make their special contribution to society. You are not concerned that they amass great wealth but you hope they will gain respect, status, and sufficient economic rewards to afford them and their families some security. The key to this accomplishment is not only your abiding love for them but your confidence, your hope, and your ultimate expectation that it will come to pass.

Good school performance is one sign that your children are well on their way. But marks are less important as an end in themselves than as a means to future attainment.

Marks do, however, symbolize the continuing approval of the educational system. As a parent you can say, "What a great job you did on that paper!" but the evaluation that finds its way into the permanent cumulative record is the final testimony of your child's strengths, competency, and promise.

In this chapter we have discussed the various kinds of skills—particularly those related to school achievement—which will help prepare our young people for a useful adult life. Skills and problem-solving capabilities are intimately related to self-esteem. Youngsters build these abilities through our encouragement and continuous affectionate support; furthermore, as they acquire and improve their competencies in numerous areas, their self-esteem is continually enhanced.

But skills, the ability to cope with and solve problems, and general competence are only one dimension of the young individual's personality development. The other dimension is the caring, the compassion, and the active concern for others' welfare that are the subject of the next chapter. In Freud's words, we want our children to be able to "love" as well as to "work."

SPECIFIC SUGGESTIONS

Do:

Do show affectionate interest, enthusiasm, and pride in all your child's accomplishments, in or out of school.

Do keep your long-range expectations for your child high.

Do allow children as much freedom as possible to explore on their own, solve problems, make decisions, and bring tasks to completion.

Do encourage your child's enjoyment of reading from the earliest years.

Do encourage your child's interest and competence in mathematical subjects.

Do be sure your child completes the daily homework assignments, beginning in the elementary grades.

Do provide prompt and visible recognition of daily school accomplishments through a bulletin board or other display.

Do find a few moments each day to listen empathically to your child's account of school experiences.

Do keep in touch with your child's teacher.

Do show interest in and encourage creative hobbies.

Do enrich your home with good music, good conversation, contact with the fine arts, good literature, and the best of television.

Don't:

Don't assume that your child's "ability" has limits.

Don't deal with poor schoolwork in futile ways (curtailment of privileges, threats, taunts, and other negative comments).

Don't bias your children's teachers against them or compare their work with that of a brother or sister.

Don't become discouraged by occasional setbacks; realize that progress in any skill has its ups and downs.

10

THE PRODUCTIVE CHILD IS CONCERNED FOR OTHERS

Eleanor has learned about the starving refugees of southeast Asia. For several days she has collected pictures of their plight and pasted them into an improvised scrapbook. Armed with this, she now goes from door to door in her neighborhood pleading for donations to CARE.

Social relationships and attitudes can be approached from three different perspectives:

In general philosophical terms, most people agree that our basic concern should be for the general welfare of humanity. This is the altruistic ideal.

In more specific terms, we all live with certain principles we've accepted concerning how we *ought* to behave toward others in our everyday dealings. We try to be honest and dependable. In return, we expect to be treated in like manner.

Finally, each of us continually faces the question of the morality or immorality of our actions and their inevitable impact, for good or ill, upon the lives of others.

All these issues affect our children as well as ourselves.

ALTRUISM, THE GIVING ATTITUDE

The word altruism (derived from the Latin *alter* meaning other) denotes unselfish concern for others' welfare. Like Eleanor, altruistic persons give but ask nothing in return. They anticipate no personal reward. Often their giving involves some sacrifice of time, money, or energy. It may even entail some risk. They devote themselves selflessly to programs for helping the needy, raising the level of education, promoting the cause of justice in the local community or the world at large. They are, in effect, world citizens.

Basic to altruism is a capacity for empathy. To be genuinely concerned about another's welfare, we must be able to put ourselves imaginatively in that person's position.[1]

Even young children can possess the traits of altruism and empathy. We personally know of one precocious 5-year-old who was seen leading a discussion of an international crisis among his kindergarten peers. Observers of children as young as two have watched them go to the aid of nursery school classmates in need or distress.

Research has also found that children's capacity for empathy is related to their own self-esteem and security. In one study of kindergarten youngsters, the generous subjects were described as bright, considerate, dependable, creative, responsible, and relaxed. Their less generous peers were deemed aggressive, restless, impulsive, immature, and rattled after stress.[2] Boys low in empathy tend to be aggressive.[3]

Altruistic children of all ages have been found to be more self-confident, more satisfied with peer relationships, and more self-assured than less secure peers. They are better adjusted, more socially responsible, more expressive, and more active and outgoing than other children. Females of all ages are more empathic than males.[4]

Altruism is related to achievement in older students. A survey of National Merit Scholars in 1961 found that they showed greater social presence, greater social skills, and greater interest in people in general than nonscholarship winners.[5] The same trend is evident in these typical responses to a sentence completion test given to high school and college students:

The best thing that I . . . (high school seniors)[6]

High achiever: "have ever wanted is to help others."
Low achiever: [like is] "having a good time."

The best thing that I . . . (freshmen at Massachusetts Institute of Technology)[7]

High achiever: "ever did was for my fellow-man."
Low achiever: "ever saw was Boston."

There is some association between altruism and creativity. Creative adolescents have been found to be "humanistically oriented and empathic" toward others.[8] An altruistic attitude is characteristic of highly creative architects. They not only possess high ethical and artistic standards but are also unselfish toward colleagues.[9]

Young individuals in leadership positions have similar traits. A study of persons who had been leaders in college found them deeply concerned with issues of civil rights, international peace, and honesty in all forms.[10] Abraham Maslow conducted extensive studies of persons of all ages whom he called "self-actualizing" (they appeared to be utilizing to the full all their talents, capacities, and potentialities). He noted that one of their most conspicuous traits was "a genuine desire to help the human race."[11]

SOCIAL INTERACTION, GIVING AND RECEIVING

Responsible social interaction involves both giving and accepting. We live, work, and socialize with family members, friends, fellow students, teachers, business associates, and casual acquaintances. These interactions are governed by the simple principle of reciprocity. We try to get along with others in a friendly, decent, fair-minded, dependable, honest, punctual, and considerate manner. And we expect similar treatment from them:

Mrs. Smith uses charge accounts but pays her bills promptly. . . . In the Brown household each child leaves the kitchen picked up for the next person. . . . When Mary Ellen goes out, she always tells her mother where she's going and what time she'll be back, and her mother does the same. . . . Jimmy and Ronnie take turns shooting for the basket. . . . The wealthy couple donate to the local hospital and in turn reduce their income tax. . . .

Such behavior is expected of all of us. Normally children are aware of its importance by the age of eight or nine. They know the rules and expect others to observe them. We need only to watch them on the playground, where they are quick to spot and censure the cheater who isn't playing "fair."

Responsible social interaction, like altruism, is characteristic of productive children. Both qualities are usually consistent and permanent parts of their personalities.

MORAL RESPONSIBILITY

Webster defines morality as implying conformity with generally accepted standards of goodness or rightness in conduct and character. A sense of moral responsibility has been more specifically defined as an attitude that views actions in terms of their possible consequences for others.[12] Frank Barron defines this attitude well:

Psychologically healthy people do what they think is right, and what they think is right is that people should not lie to one another or to themselves, that they should not steal, slander, persecute, intrude, do damage willfully, go back on their word, fail a friend, or do any of the things that put them on the side of death as against life.[13]

Any act that purposively injures someone else directly or indirectly can be considered immoral.

For morally responsible persons, all social actions—moral or immoral—involve both a capacity for empathy and a sense of self-esteem. If, for example, they give generously to a worthy cause, they feel good about themselves because they are aware of another's benefit. If they injure other persons physically or psychologically, they suffer lowered self-esteem and guilt because they can empathize with the suffering their actions have inflicted on other individuals.

By contrast, morally irresponsible persons have a limited capacity for empathy. Because their self-esteem is low, they have an inordinate need for support and attention. In the process of seeking such attention, perhaps through an illicit sexual adventure, they may injure someone else.

Productive children or adults who possess both high self-esteem and a capacity for empathy are concerned about helping other people. They have a highly developed conscience. Their altruism is closely related to their sense of moral responsibility.

THE SOURCE OF CONCERN FOR OTHERS

Ten-year-old John decides to give up his favorite Saturday morning Little League practice so he can stay home and cheer his newly widowed grandfather with a game of catch. Later his parents praise John's generous action and Daddy adds, "You were pitching well, too!"

The roots of caring are planted at home in the early identification process that has already been described in Chapter Five. If parents are themselves loving, unselfish, and socially and morally responsible, their children will absorb these traits even at nursery school age. The parents' values in relating to others become the child's. The basis for John's relationship with his grandfather is the empathy he has acquired from his parents. Feeling secure with them, he is learning to reach out emotionally to others, to understand how they feel and even to extend them help.

In early childhood the parents' nurturance and generosity become a model for the child to observe and imitate. For every unselfish act, a youngster needs and should receive praise. Thus he learns to feel for others' needs. Once learned, such behavior tends to persist.

Parents can teach concern for others not only by their own acts but by explaining to their youngsters the importance of kindness and generosity. In cases of discipline they can reason gently with a child. In numerous ways they help him or her develop caring and generous attitudes.

Children thus raised with kindness will by nature be generous and outgoing. They will empathize easily and instinctively with others. They will *want* to be helpful, to share, to play fairly and honestly. Youngsters who have been raised in cold, rigid, authoritarian families find it more difficult to relate to others in this manner. They may have been told time and again how they should act socially; they know the rules, but lack the flexibility, spontaneity, imagination, and emotional security to act on them.

How Children Learn to Live with Others
The process of learning how to live with others is called *socialization*. It begins in the home when children are very small. Gradually they progress from the total self-centeredness of infancy to awareness of the existence, the needs, and the rights of other people. At first this awareness includes only the members of their own family. Later it extends to associates outside the home. Finally, in its most mature form, it includes an attitude toward the whole of humankind.

Your children acquire attitudes of social responsibility in three ways. They learn, first, from the example of adults around them. Second, they learn that all behavior is labeled or judged by society (as good or bad, right or wrong, fair or unfair, and so on).

Finally, they learn from experiencing the consequences of their own behavior.

Youngsters learn first from the example of people within their own family whom they love and trust.

In a loving, nurturing home young Alison has learned how important it is to be truthful about everything. One day, however, she comes in tears and agitation to her mother. "I just spilled ink on Daddy's desk! Don't tell him I did it!" Mother, quick to understand and reassure, says gently, "Of course we'll tell Daddy, and I know he'll understand." So Alison does tell Daddy what happened, and Daddy understands.

No such lesson, however, is taught in this home:

Mr. Smith, a plumber, works for a small firm. As required by law, his employer reports his earnings to the Internal Revenue Service, withholding the proper taxes. But Mr. Smith also does some extra jobs, for cash, which he doesn't bother to report. Over the year these extra earnings have amounted to a fairly sizeable figure.

Shortly before the annual April tax deadline, Mr. Smith's fourteen-year-old son Mike hears his father telling his mother that he plans not to list the extra cash he's earned during the year. "Everybody's doin' it these days–it's the only way a guy can come out a bit ahead. I'll take a chance on gettin' away with it."

We can easily imagine young Mike cheating in small or possibly larger ways as he conducts his own affairs in subsequent years.

Your child learns that all actions are labeled, or judged, by society. Some actions are "right"; some (like stealing or throwing stones) are "wrong" because they may injure others. Some are merely inappropriate (being noisy in church, for example). A 4-year-old knows that it is "good" to share his toys but "bad" to hit his little brother. A third-grader finds out the difference between fair play and cheating on the playground. A 10-year-old knows he or she must never break a promise. Junior high school students are aware that it is dishonest to copy a neighbor's paper on a test or to plagiarize material on a school paper.

The law of cause-and-effect is always with us. A child must learn that our actions inevitably produce consequences for ourselves and (sometimes indirectly) for others:[14]

*Amy, ten, carelessly leaves her new sweater on the bench at the play-
ground and finds it next day rain-soaked or torn by a dog. . . . She
oversleeps in the morning and misses the school bus. . . . She gorges
herself on rich pastry and is sick to her stomach. . . .*

The consequences of Amy's acts will primarily affect her
personally. Her new sweater is damaged. She may have to walk to
school on a frigid morning and arrive late. She endures several
hours of disagreeable nausea. Yet someone else besides Amy is
usually affected, too. Her parents' money has probably bought the
sweater. Mom may have to drive her to school before leaving for
work. She probably looks after Amy until Amy recovers from her
stomach upset. At the least, the child's behavior produces some
inconvenience for busy adults.

Some actions affect others more directly:

*Nick fails to show up Saturday morning at his grandfather's house
after promising to help him rake the leaves. . . . He brings his juice
and cookies into the living room and leaves a trail of sticky crumbs on
the new carpet. . . . He borrows his daddy's expensive tools and
leaves them out in the rain instead of returning them to the basement
workroom. . . .*

Amy and Nick are normal youngsters. They're not delinquents, deliberately stealing or vandalizing property. However,
they are showing some degree of social irresponsibility.

The Development of Conscience
Through identification with loving parents a child growing up in a
productive family with a structured value system will naturally and
easily absorb many social values. Through wise and rational discipline, ground rules are taught and understood. The child knows that
right actions bring approval and therefore increase self-esteem and
that wrong ones are to be avoided because they will be censured.

In such a family, a child gradually develops a conscience, a
"still, small voice" within himself that tells him he should do certain things because they are right and should not do others because
they are hurtful and therefore wrong.

Conscience is therefore an internal mechanism by which one
can either enhance self-esteem by doing right or threaten it by doing
wrong. If children are secure, they will be able to look ahead to the
consequences of their actions. They will choose behavior that will
enhance, not damage others' welfare.

GUILT AND SELF-ESTEEM

Guilt is an uncomfortable feeling that arises in us when our behavior has violated the guidelines of our conscience. It is our "anticipation of rejection"—specifically, our fear that someone we love and depend upon (or have depended upon in the past) will disapprove of our act. We can experience this feeling even if that person (who is most often our father or mother) is no longer alive.

When we suffer guilt, we also have lower self-esteem. In order to feel guilty an individual must have some degree of self-esteem—something to lose. Generally, persons with high self-esteem are relatively free from crippling guilt. Having learned from previous experience that guilt is painful, they avoid guilt-producing situations or cope with their guilt either by apologizing or making some form of restitution. On the other hand, persons with little or no self-esteem have literally nothing to lose if they commit an antisocial act:

Sylvia, a happy youngster living in a secure, affectionate, nurturing home, loses a library book. . . . Teresa, a lonely, alienated delinquent, is caught shoplifting. . . .

Sylvia will suffer more guilt from her unfortunate oversight than Teresa will over committing a major act of theft. The reason? Sylvia has self-esteem. Teresa has little or none. Undoubtedly Sylvia will pay for replacing the lost book while Teresa will probably be sullen and unrepentant as she is taken into custody.

Children who have lived in an inconsistent and constantly critical parental environment can be conditioned to anticipate criticism and rejection from relatively harmless behavior, wrongdoings in which they were not directly involved, or even acts that they have fantasized but have never carried out. These memories may be carried into adulthood. The self-esteem of these individuals remains low: they bear the burden of guilt over some past action that remained unresolved because no opportunity was provided for discussing the incident or making apology or restitution. In a structured, civilized society few people of any sensitivity are completely free of some degree of guilt. Nearly everyone has done something he wishes he hadn't done. Thousands of others, however, carry an unnecessary burden of unresolved guilt that can be damaging to their mental health. Guilty persons are often chronically anxious and ineffective people. They usually do not cope well with daily problems; in particular, they do not work well with others.

Parents therefore have a responsibility to prevent severe guilt

feelings from developing in their children. Guilty youngsters probably feel even more threatened than guilty adults, for their main
source of self-esteem (namely, their parents) is directly at stake.
They cannot stand to lose this approval and support—which should
be there in the first place.

A child like Sylvia, whose self-esteem is normally high, feels
guilt even after a minor sin. If, however, her parents are wise,
affectionate, and understanding, they can keep guilt-producing
situations at a minimum in her life.

Children who are involved in secret wrongdoings are under
special tension. First, they must always be on guard lest they be
discovered. Second, by hypocritically acting as if nothing is happen-
ing, they also carry the burden of knowing they are being dishonest
with themselves and others. Finally, by keeping their activities
secret, they are depriving themselves of possible sympathetic understanding from the very persons who might help them.

The Role of Confession
*Marijuana lies on the dressing table. . . . Cigarette stubs are found in
a coat pocket. . . . A note from a secret boyfriend is left in plain
view. . . .*

Before guilt feelings can be resolved, there must be some sort of
confession to others who, in the case of a child, are you, his or her
father and mother. Children whose self-esteem is shaky will usually
lack the courage to reveal their problems directly. They are afraid
they may hurt you and also that they may open themselves up to
further rejection. They may therefore use indirect methods of asking
for help such as those above.

It is usually unwise to try to draw out a child who seems
unduly preoccupied. Don't say, "There must be something on your
mind. Tell me about it" or "You don't seem to be feeling well.
What's the matter?" Under such pressure the youngster will not feel
free to confess for fear of your criticism.

Instead, wait for some further cue. If an unacceptable incident does come to your attention, talk calmly and quietly about it.
Don't hurry or rush the child. Ask for a description of the circumstances under which an act occurred. Don't force children to
admit guilt, for they may resort to denial or fabrication in explaining an incident, thus compounding their problems. If you maintain
your composure and listen quietly, you will probably learn the
details of the situation.

A mere confession will not relieve guilt feelings. Something must undo the guilt-producing act. The child should apologize and you should offer your forgiveness. Provide an opportunity for some form of restitution or penance—perhaps being temporarily grounded, giving up some privilege, possibly earning money to pay for replacement or repair of injured property. Give the young person an opportunity to select his or her penalty and be certain it is one that can be implemented and concluded within a reasonable length of time.

Children with Low Self-Esteem

Children like Teresa, whose self-esteem needs are met by neither their parents nor anyone else, are basically empty, lonely human beings. They tend to reach out to peer groups as a substitute for the lack of affection at home. They may use the group's escape mechanisms—the beer-drinking episodes, the marijuana parties, or illicit sex—as a means of denying their loneliness. In extreme cases such as Teresa's they become delinquents. All this is done partly out of defiance of their parents and partly because they feel they have nothing to lose since they have not had their share of nurturance in the first place.

In such cases it is usually futile for parents or authority figures to confront them. They will deny their actions. No punishment is likely to have more than minimal effect. In such a situation it is recommended that parents seek professional help.

How to Minimize Children's Guilt Feelings

How can you prevent excessive guilt from developing in your children? Here are a few suggestions:

Don't condemn them for minor offenses (spilling a glass of milk, for example).

Teach them the primary importance of their relationships with other people.

Teach them to avoid dishonesty, irresponsibility, disloyalty, drugs, improper use of alcohol, and other undesirable behaviors.

Finally, teach them principles of acceptable and proper sex conduct by telling them how to control and channel their own sex drive in an acceptable manner.

RESPONSIBLE SEX BEHAVIOR AND SELF-ESTEEM

Nearly every parent dreads the prospect of a child's suffering an unhappy marriage or engaging in unethical sexual activities. Yet parents, on the whole, do very little direct teaching of their children in this important emotion-charged area.

Teaching ethical sex behavior is primarily your responsibility for two reasons:

First, in the entire area of social values (in which sex plays a significant part) your own standards are the basic reference point for your young people. They identify with your behavior and in particular your support of principles of upright sexual conduct. You are also the principal source of their self-esteem.

Second, such a wide variety of attitudes about sexual ethics prevails among teachers and other school personnel and, to some extent, even among clergy, that adolescents need to hear your views—clearly, explicitly, supportively, and consistently expressed.

The Current Scene

Nearly 500,000 yearly cases of venereal disease contracted by adolescents under twenty-one. . . . One out of every five births to adolescent girls in the United States today. . . . Total number of teenage pregnancies 1.3 million for girls age fifteen to nineteen resulting in some 560,000 live births every year. . . .[15]

This is alarming evidence that countless parents are either irresponsible or incapable of teaching their children sound principles of sexual ethics. Notwithstanding the availability of birth control, thousands of babies are born annually to young teenage girls in or (more often) out of wedlock and millions of dollars are spent annually on their medical and social care. A high-risk pregnancy group because of their inadequate physical development, these girls—barely more than babies themselves—often produce children doomed to lead crippled lives because of physical and neurological handicaps. Usually uneducated, unskilled, and eventually dependent on welfare, these young parents and their children represent not only a tremendous drain on the tax-paying public but also a gloomy commentary on the health of present-day society. Freud warned us many years ago that any society that fails to help its members to control and channel the sex drive is doomed.

The Preadolescent and Adolescent Years

"Dad, we're so tired of seeing those movies on sex. We want something more. We want to know how to behave."

Most so-called sex education courses in schools give only biological information. They deal neither with essential moral values nor with children's real concerns:

. . . Sex education in schools does not get to the deeper sources of anxiety. . . . It is also naive to believe that simple educational measures can alleviate guilt over acts where fantasies may involve forbidden and guilt-laden themes. [16]

Training in sexual ethics is your responsibility.

The sex drive surfaces rapidly between the ages of 12 and 14, often catching the preadolescent unprepared. Both boys and girls need help. The physiological and hormonal changes occur at a time when many other responsibilities and expectations are being forced on them. They must do well academically. College (or post-high school training) is only a few years away. They are somewhat self-conscious with their rapidly growing and changing bodies. Complexion problems and braces on their teeth may further lower their self-image. They are expected to adopt their own sense of values, to be mature in their relations with teachers and peers, to become increasingly independent and self-reliant.

Many young people are ill-prepared for these new roles. As a result they are often overwhelmed by the numerous expectations and pressures and can become moody, withdrawn, and difficult in the family.

The pubescent period is unquestionably trying. But children at this stage need more support and nurturance from you, not less. Girls as a group seem to survive the period better than boys. The young adolescent boy needs much sympathetic support, especially from his father. Unfortunately, many parents have the mistaken notion that they should lessen nurturance for a son at this time so that he will become more independent. Their neglect only increases his insecurity. As a result he may turn to his own body as an escape.

It is well known that the sex organs can be the focus of much nonsex emotional experiences such as loneliness, low self-esteem, or sense of defeat and rejection. Like drugs and alcohol, secret sexual activity temporarily dulls reality and can become a form of escape.[17] Research also indicates that it can be an expression of displaced hostility and defiance against parental dominance.[18]

Dr. Richard Gardner, a well-known specialist in child development, says that the child who is exploring his body excessively

is essentially communicating to the parent this message: 'I must turn to myself for pleasure because you don't provide me with the love I need.'[19]

Preoccupation with the body is *not* characteristic of all young people. It occurs in a larger percentage of boys than girls. In productive, busy, mentally healthy boys it is relatively uncommon. In both sexes it occurs more frequently in authoritarian, dominant homes that lack affection and warmth. In homes characterized by affectionate parental support it is rare.[20]

Conscientious parents want to help their young people through these years. The best insurance of their healthy and normal sexual development lies in keeping them happy and secure. Your relationship with them should be guided by the same principles that have been discussed in previous chapters:

● Provide them with abundant affection, support, and an atmosphere of easy, open, two-way communication.

● Refrain at all costs from excessive criticism, constant demands, and rejection.

● Help them to broaden their interests. In particular, encourage them to develop a variety of skills and to join skill-centered group activities. At this age they can be busily involved in Scouts, amateur musical or dramatic undertakings, field trips, sports, community or church activities.

● Take continual interest in their involvement in any such groups. Be sure to be on hand to witness their role in planned events, and applaud any recognition they receive, no matter how small. Such activities are not only stimulating and challenging, they also reduce opportunities for youngsters to retreat into loneliness and despair. They need to feel a growing sense of all-round competence and confidence among their peers as they approach the challenges of growing up.

Dating Practices

Properly handled, dating can be a valuable interpersonal experience. It helps young persons to learn more about each other and hence more about themselves. They can compare notes on their basic attitudes toward life. They discover similarities and differences in their individual tastes, preferences, likes, and dislikes. They can discuss a great variety of subjects of mutual and general concern and in so doing clarify their own views. Dating is an important step in preparing an individual for an eventual healthy, happy, and lasting marriage.

Dating situations should be protected with certain safeguards. Dating is enjoyable and instructive socially, but teenagers, especially the young and inexperienced, need some protection. On a date the prolonged privacy and relative physical closeness between a sexually mature boy and girl have the potential for leading to inappropriate sexual involvement. Reasonable safeguards can be said to exist under the following conditions:

• You are confident of your young people's basic maturity and emotional security.

• Your previous relationship with them, especially your interpersonal communication, has been comfortable, open, and honest.

• You have talked together about dating, including its intimate aspects, with some frankness and have made your own views known to them about the value of maintaining high personal standards.

• You have compared notes with them about the confusing prevailing standards of sexual conduct.

• You do not sense in them any suppressed hostility and rebellion that might lead them to wish to hurt you by experimenting with their new social freedom.

In certain cases, you may have to cope with the problem of different maturity timetables.

Thirteen-year-old Judith has already almost reached her full adult height; she is curvaceous, pretty, and (in her own mind at least) quite sophisticated. Across the aisle sits her eighth-grade classmate Ralph; he is a month older, six inches shorter, still slight of stature, and somewhat overpowered by the presence of the self-assured young lady sitting nearby.

Both children face common but different problems. Ralph needs much extra parental encouragement and support to help him live through the painful period in which many of his peers are ahead of him in physical growth. Typically, things will get better by the time he's sixteen or seventeen. Judith's problem causes a different kind of parental concern. In a year or so, on entering senior high school, she may well be sought out by older boys. The implications of the three-year age difference between Judith and a young man who has car keys in his pocket, extra cash from a part-time job, and a determination to "make it" socially with his peers are, speaking plainly, problematical. Before she dates these older boys, Judith and her mom should have a good talk.

Remember the advantages of group activities for younger adolescents. The most rewarding dates involve active participation in mutually enjoyed athletics, games, and cultural events. Much wholesome group social life takes place in after-school programs such as band or orchestra rehearsals, dramatics, debating, work on the school paper, and the like. Well-supervised school- or church-sponsored square dances, cookouts, hikes, or bike trips provide excellent social experiences for younger adolescents like Ralph who may not feel ready for individual dating.

Older boys and girls on good terms with one another enjoy study dates combined with breaks for coffee and snacks. On the other hand, the hazards of casual blind dates between young people who have not previously known one another are generally recognized.

Do provide sensible ground rules and guidelines.

"You don't trust me!"

Dating guidelines for your adolescent are likely to be challenged by such remarks. It is wise not to assume too much. You can always reply, if necessary, "I trust you, but I don't trust the situation."

Currently, young people are given far more freedom and mobility in their social life than ever before. Nevertheless, certain safeguards and ground rules are still appropriate and helpful, especially for high school youngsters still living at home. Don't hesitate to articulate and enforce these rules.

It may be old-fashioned, but it is still reasonable for you to ask certain questions of your high school-aged son or daughter before he or she leaves on a date. At the very least, you can be told of the advance arrangements.

"Where are you going?"

"What kind of function are you planning to attend?" (If movies, what is the title and reputation of the film? If a concert, is it classical, folk, country and western, or rock? If a private party, will the parents be at home?)

"In whose car will you be traveling and who is driving?"

"Will you be alone or with a group?"

"At what hour do you expect to return?"

It helps greatly when the families of the young people know each other or are at least casually acquainted. It also helps if the young man is introduced to the girl's parents if he has not previously met them.

Fathers especially should take responsibility for confidential admonitions to their sons on such elementary matters as the following: treating a girl at all times with respect and courtesy; returning her to her home at the agreed-upon hour; avoiding sex movies, alcohol, drugs, and prolonged privacy.

Mothers should warn their daughters about a young boy's vulnerability to sexually stimulating situations. They should firmly tell her to refuse to ride with any boy who she knows has been drinking and if necessary to call her home, or the police, to be taken home under such circumstances. You can also warn her against the questionable X-rated movie and about attending any function in a private home where the parents are not present.

Old-fashioned advice? Let's not be ashamed to give it! Our children will eventually thank us.

Morality in Productive Adolescents
That productive adolescents as a group live responsible moral lives is illustrated in such reports as the following:

A study in 1969 of 96 McGill University freshmen who had been selected from a population of 1,200 for an in-depth mental health investigation showed that few of the mentally healthy subjects had had sexual relationships. According to personal testimony of the researchers, masturbation was no problem in this group.[21]

In 1977 a significant poll was conducted of 24,000 high school juniors and seniors who were recognized for their leadership and achievement in numerous activities. Eighty percent of these students favored traditional marriage and 70 percent had not had sexual intercourse. Half of the teenagers polled had never had a drink of alcohol and 90 percent used neither tobacco nor other drugs. Sixty percent opposed the legalization of marijuana.[22]

Of the 23,200 highest achievers listed in the 1979–1980 edition of *Who's Who Among American High School Students*, 78 percent had not had sex, only 8 percent used marijuana as often as once a month, and 74 percent opposed legalization of marijuana.[23]

There is no escaping the pervasive presence of sex in today's media—television, cheap movies, advertising, pornographic magazines and books. Many of today's parents are confused about their own role in teaching their adolescents responsible sex behavior. They should not hesitate to take a stand.

Recently Dr. Armand Nicholi, a nationally known psychiatrist specializing in adolescent behavior, stated firmly: "Clinical experience has shown that the new permissiveness has often led to empty relationships, feelings of self-contempt and worthlessness. . . ." He further adds that some young people

find the clear-cut boundaries [imposed by the basic Judeao-Christian morality] less confusing than no boundaries at all and more helpful in relating to members of the opposite sex as "persons rather than sexual objects."[24]

Dr. Nicholi has listened in his office to many troubled students who describe their haunting guilt and concerns about past sexual adventures. In his words, these young people are merely reaffirming the truth of Freud's statement made many years ago: when freedom flourishes unrestrained in a society, "love [becomes] worthless and life empty."[25]

DEALING WITH THE DRUG MENACE

The junior high gang congregates on the playfield nearly every afternoon. Beer is handy, and sometimes a bottle of Scotch has been sneaked out of a parent's liquor chest. . . .

The two sixth-graders light up before they are out of the school yard. They've been smoking for three months. . . .

The college freshman has been on pot for over a year. His grades are dropping badly and he couldn't care less. . . .

No social problem is more alarming to parents than drugs. "Substance abuse," whether of alcohol, tobacco, marijuana, or any of the more dangerous and addictive narcotics, is rampant in all types of communities. There appears to be no effective control over the flood of illegal products being steadily and viciously smuggled into our nation. During the past two decades the frightening explosion in drug usage has involved an ever-growing percentage of our younger and highly vulnerable boys and girls.

Patterns of drug abuse of course vary widely. One thing, however, is certain. Community, ethnic, and socioeconomic factors do not, in themselves, cause an individual to turn to drug use or abuse.

Alcohol

Alcohol is widely available and its abuse is on the increase. The dangers of young persons' drinking are legion.[26] Drinking hinders academic productivity. It is a frequent cause of the serious and often fatal automobile accidents that involve the sixteen- to twenty-year-old drivers whose accident rate is already high. It contributes to most acts of violence in this vulnerable group and certainly loosens all forms of control, sexual and otherwise.

Drinking among school children is not only rapidly increasing, but occurring much more openly than in former years, and among ever-younger boys and girls. These facts suggest at least a degree of tacit acceptance and tolerance from parents and others who are themselves part of the enormous majority (probably at least 80 percent of the population) of adult social drinkers.

Young people's habitual drinking appears to be associated with low self-esteem. Their motives are governed both by peer pressure and by a desire to identify with current adult society. (One study found that 30 percent of the subjects drank to avoid being "different" or left out while 40 percent did so to gain a feeling of being "smart" or grown-up.)

The control of alcohol rests squarely with parents. Almost all adolescents and preadolescents will be exposed to it. When parents drink socially and maintain supplies of liquor in their homes, they may find it more difficult (but nonetheless imperative) to set firm standards for their youngsters. Research indicates that children from abstaining homes have fewer problems with alcohol.

Cigarettes

The nicotine content in cigarettes is known to be addictive and eventually ruinous to health. Yet many young children are habitual smokers. The causes of this alarming trend, similar to those that contribute to the alcohol problem, include the widespread availability and high-powered advertising of smoking materials, the pressures from peers, and the presence of adult smokers in many homes despite the continued efforts of many educational groups to discourage the lethal habit.

Marijuana and Other Drugs

"It is sheer folly for millions of young Americans to indulge in a drug while so little is known about its long-term consequences."[27]

The general public realizes that hard drugs such as heroin are highly addictive and dangerous. Unfortunately, the effects of marijuana have until recently been less clear. Consequently many young persons have remained unconvinced that their use of the weed was, in fact, hazardous to their long-term health. Now there is growing recognition of the dangers of marijuana—particularly the chemically complex and potent "street marijuana" that is now everywhere available.[28] According to Peter Bensinger, former director of the Drug Enforcement Administration, marijuana is our biggest health problem because it is so widely used.[29]

The true extent of possible long-term damage is still not fully known but there is great cause for concern. Studies show that marijuana can adversely affect four aspects of the body: the respiratory tract, the reproductive system, the brain, and the body's immunological defenses. Here is a brief summary of these hazards:

> *Pulmonary effects.* Marijuana is highly irritating to the respiratory tract. It is reported that one year of daily marijuana smoking can produce as much damage to the nasal membranes, pharynx, bronchial tubes, and lungs as would result from twenty years of cigarette smoking.[30]

> *The reproductive system.* Marijuana is fat soluble. Its active psychotropic ingredient (delta-9-THC) accumulates in the fat-laden tissues of the body, lingering for several days before being fully metabolized. The reproductive organs are largely of fatty consistency. Damage to this crucial area is reported as including

> *. . . inhibition of cellular growth, reduction in sperm production, development of abnormal sperm cells, interference of the synthesis of important genetic material in the cell . . . destruction of chromosomes, abnormal embryonic developments and birth defects in experimental animals. . . .*[31]

> *The brain.* The brain is also largely composed of fatty tissue and therefore vulnerable to the effects of marijuana. Psychiatric studies report "impaired judgment, diminished attention and concentration span, slowing of time sense, loss of motivation, loss of thought continuity, loss of learning ability and in numerous instances, psychosis."[32]

> *The immune system.* A number of scientific studies now demonstrate that marijuana use endangers the functioning of the body's immunological defense system.[33]

The Typical Drug Addict

A young person may begin to use drugs such as marijuana primarily out of curiosity. However, if he is drawn into further and habitual use, he will find more and more reasons to justify continued involvement not only with marijuana but with ever-more-dangerous substances or combinations thereof.

We can learn something from studying the characteristic personality of the *confirmed drug addict*. Fundamentally, he is a lonely, insecure person, uncertain of his identity and low in self-esteem. He has turned to drugs in an effort to compensate for some void in his life. He views them as a means of escaping reality. He is seeking reassurance and relief from depression or sadness.[34]

Heavy users of hard drugs are typically immature, passive, dependent, unreliable, and unable to postpone gratification. Their coping skills are usually inadequate. They are bored and dissatisfied. Their relations with authority figures are poor. Sexual activity is rampant in this group.

The home of the confirmed drug addict is deeply insecure in many ways. The father is typically weak, emotionally distant, minimally involved in the family. The mother is inclined to be overprotective, overindulgent, and domineering. The parents are in frequent conflict with one another; the young people are often at odds with either or both parents. Child-rearing standards have been permissive and inconsistent; limits of behavior have been poorly defined. The parents are often social drinkers, suggesting that their own attitudes toward liquor and drugs are easygoing and tolerant. They also tend to be "pill-poppers," to use tranquilizers and pain relievers. Impulsive behavior, inability to control and direct aggressive feelings, a lack of normal intimacy and closeness, sex-role confusion, and lack of achievement orientation have also been noted in these homes.

Imagine any adolescent living in such a home, and you can easily understand some of the reasons why he or she has become involved in drugs.

One investigation studied the behavior and attitudes of children in 101 families. The families were then ranked on a drug-risk scale. The low-risk homes (where children were not drug-involved) were reported as happy and healthy. By contrast, the children of the high-risk homes were evidently being deprived of essential "emotional sustenance" (affection and support). Seeking a substitute for their unmet needs, they were turning to peers and peer influences.[35]

How You Can Deal With the Drug Problem

It is easy to become alarmed over the serious implications of the drug situation. However, if you have established a warm, caring atmosphere in your home you have already developed the strongest defense against your children's involvement. Keep in mind the value of the following suggestions:

Encourage free discussion.

"Daddy, what do you think of marijuana?"

This comment gives you a hint. Your children want to talk about the problem. Let them know of your honest concern. Share with them the known facts about the physical effects of marijuana and other drugs. Listen carefully to what they have to say. Remember that a child may be hearing other comments ("Don't worry." "It won't do you any harm." "It's fun.") from his or her peers.

Get to know your children's friends. Make a point of becoming acquainted with them. If possible, observe them in your home. You can quietly discourage a close relationship with children from families whose values you do not approve of.

Supervise social events. You should always be at home when your child is entertaining a group of friends. He or she should not attend any party in a private home when the parents are absent.

Scrutinize "vulnerable" social situations. Weekend rock festivals are notoriously conducive to drug usage. Any place where teenagers gather to be free of supervision is likely to attract the drug peddler. Explain to your children that you trust them and their friends but you don't trust the situation.

Avoid scare tactics and lecturing. Such techniques will not in themselves discourage a child from experimenting with drugs. Similarly, it is well to refrain from being bossy, over-solicitous, or domineering. Studies show a large number of drug users whose mothers, in particular, display these traits.

Try to be at home as much as possible. The teenage years are a time when parents need to be around. It's easy to become involved with errands, social obligations, and well-intentioned community activities that take us out of the house four or five evenings a week. If we are habitually out, particularly on weekends, we are almost inviting our teenager to drift toward the peer group. There's no better way to keep peer group influence at a minimum than to be there at home, or, better still, to make appealing family-centered plans whenever possible.

If you drink or smoke yourselves, you cannot really expect your children to abstain from using alcohol or tobacco since they are present in the home. But by all means explain why you use them and establish a clear understanding with your children as to how old they must be before they can drink or smoke, and under what conditions.

Most young people who are secure and happy have no difficulty doing without drugs. They cope with the challenges of school and social life. However, it's well to remember that much depends on their having a *sense of commitment and direction*. This basically comes from you. With it they can focus on their principal objective of doing a good job in school. Together with children of other parents who are providing this same kind of direction, they will be busily involved with immediate and well-defined tasks—their day-to-day assignments, homework, teacher conferences, and numerous extracurricular activities.

Your children will, however, observe drug usage around them. Drugs are commonly sold in and around schools—even in classrooms. High achievers are too busy to be vulnerable, but low achievers, marginal students—anyone who appears to be drifting, insecure, or uncertain of where he or she is going—such individuals are fair game for the drug-peddling that exists in virtually all our communities.

There is recent encouraging evidence that adolescents are beginning to be aware of the dangers of marijuana, alcohol, and tobacco and that usage of all three is gradually declining—at least according to surveys of older high school students. Nevertheless the director of the National Institute on Drug Abuse, Dr. William Pollin, reminds us of the grim fact that our teenagers "still show the highest level of drug use of young people anywhere in the industrialized world."[36]

SOCIAL VALUES AND RELIGION

Research on productive persons reveals them as basically concerned, caring, giving individuals. One aspect of their social responsibility that has not been previously mentioned is the role religion plays in their lives. Religion would be expected to enhance their general sense of values and the value they place on other human beings.

Research in the area of religion and ethical behavior is sparse and somewhat poorly designed. Some degree of formal religious commitment undeniably plays an important part in the lives of thousands of productive families.

George Smith is a National Merit Scholarship finalist. He has attained exceptionally high test scores, remained consistently on the honor roll, and received a special recommendation from his high school principal. George has been on the school debating team; he has participated in the Model UN and in varsity track. He is also a lector in the local Catholic church.

Many successful young people like George (whose story was reported in our local paper some months ago) include among their numerous activities some form of involvement in church or temple. There is evidence that their high self-esteem and strong moral convictions have been nurtured by parents whose lives have a religious base or who are sustained by some form of transcendent belief. We have known a number of outstanding young people from families who adhere staunchly to their chosen faith.

There is also occasional reference to such individuals in the research literature. In 1960 a study of 40 mathematically gifted adolescents rigorously selected from a field of 5,000 for special summer training found them to be somewhat anxious and competitive but noted that they appeared to be maturing much more rapidly than their peers and were uniformly well adjusted, concerned with ethical problems, and faithful church attenders.[37]

Other references to religion in the research literature on productive persons are somewhat more vague. Three quarters of the 23,000-odd high achievers listed in the 1979–1980 edition of *Who's Who Among American High School Students* stated that religion plays a "significant role" in their lives.[38] A Texas-based study of unusually healthy, well-functioning families reported in 1976 that these families seemed to be sustained in times of crisis by a "functional transcendent value system."[39]

Other investigators have found in highly productive persons a strong support for the ethical and humanistic principles that characterize most religions. Abraham Maslow, in his study of "self-actualizing" persons including outstanding leaders such as Jefferson, Lincoln, and Eleanor Roosevelt, stressed their

Gemeinschaftsgefühl—their love for humanity.[40] A similar trend is evident in the personality studies of Donald MacKinnon. Exploring the backgrounds of unusually creative and outstanding architects, MacKinnon found that their families had put strong emphasis on personal ethical codes (integrity, forthrightness, honesty, respect for others, and so on) as opposed to mere adherence to formal religious institutions. As mature individuals, these architects repeatedly demonstrated deep personal concern for others, including considerable professional generosity toward their colleagues.[41]

The influence of the religious beliefs and attitudes held by successful people, whether or not accompanied by active involvement in church or temple, is an important area for further research although it is exceedingly difficult to measure in scientific terms.

CONCLUSION

This chapter has summarized some of the current research findings and professional views on various aspects of social responsibility. Regardless of your own specific attitudes and practices in any of these areas, you are obligated as parents to teach your children sound ethical principles in respect to their behavior toward others. In the last analysis you can best accomplish this through your own example, by living a socially responsible life in relation to your own household, your neighbors, customers, professional colleagues, the Internal Revenue Service. Your own loyalty, dependability, honesty, and generosity are the best models for your children to follow. You can also give them explicit instruction and guidance, explaining why we behave in certain ways and not in others.

Ultimately, we must stress the importance of character. Commitment to high ethical principles also gives the individual—child or adult—a sense of identity. People are known by their values. When so committed, they can be at ease with others, functioning effectively in their roles as parents, mates, neighbors, colleagues, or citizens. Living by principle also frees these individuals from the guilt feelings which render a person hostile, defensive, even aggressive, and so interfere with healthy human relationships.

In the lives of productive persons there is evidence of a commitment to such values. In particular, these individuals generally seem to believe in the importance of maintaining high personal standards in the realm of sexual ethics and to be committed to the ideal of the sanctity of the marriage relationship. The attitude of the genuinely productive, morally concerned individual will be reflected in his or her attitude toward and treatment of members of the opposite sex; it will also influence behavior in other aspects of life. For this reason, you are urged to guide your young people in a life that best prepares them for a fulfilling and permanent marriage. Out of a happy marital union will come the productive young people who can give the most to the future of society.

SPECIFIC SUGGESTIONS

Do:

Do remember that your child's concern for others is closely related to his or her own self-esteem.

Do set a good example.

Do praise all acts of generosity, honesty, and maturity.

Do provide wholesome information and share freely with your children your views about ethical sex behavior.

Do give special support to your preadolescent during the trying years between twelve and fifteen.

Do discuss privately with your son or daughter the basic rules concerning dating behavior.

Do caution your adolescent about the great dangers of drinking and driving.

Do discuss drug usage and listen closely to your children's comments about it.

Do make a point of knowing your children's friends.

Do remember that you are responsible for knowing where your child is at all times.

Don't:

Don't frighten a child into confessing an act of wrongdoing.

Don't lecture or use scare tactics in warning your children of the dangers of drugs.

Don't expect your children to abstain from tobacco or alcohol if you smoke or drink yourselves.

SELF-ESTEEM, HEALTH, AND ANXIETY

Mens sana in corpore sano. **"A sound mind in a sound body."**

Juvenal

We are all concerned with good health. No one questions the importance of preventive medicine and its role in reversing or at least slowing today's alarming trends toward obesity, high blood pressure, heart disease, and related ailments. Thanks to the miracles of modern medical technology and public health regulations, we no longer suffer from the worst of the ills that befell our ancestors. There's increasing awareness that maintaining one's health is an individual responsibility, and most parents now realize that they can and should instill good health (particularly good eating) habits early in their children's lives.

There is evidence that productive young people as a group usually enjoy better than average health. Happy and achieving elementary school children are seldom absent with minor illnesses. Studies of high achievers in high school, college, and graduate school show similar trends; there is a low incidence of physical health problems among these groups.[1]

On the other hand, research has found minor ailments to be one characteristic of unproductive persons of various ages. A large percentage of learning-disabled children are thus afflicted. University and secondary school health services find that the largest percentage of their patients are from average or below-average student groups.[2]

Any illness or bodily malfunctioning, however minor, tends to interfere with educational and social development. Children's absences from school interrupt the learning process. Some conditions are more crippling than others; all of them prevent the individual from entering to the fullest extent into normal activities.

Parents who suffer from health problems themselves—particularly chronic ailments—tend to be somewhat preoccupied with their own condition and unable to empathize fully with their children's emotional needs. If their youngsters also suffer from such ailments, there is much additional worry and concern. In any case, anxiety about the health problem tends to be transmitted to and absorbed by the children. Highly contagious, anxiety can also cause a physiological reaction.

THE BODY'S REACTION TO STRESS

All human beings are equipped by Nature to respond physiologically to perceived danger or emergency:

An hour before the big varsity football game Ken has butterflies in his stomach and doesn't feel like eating much lunch. When the game starts, however, he will throw himself into the first offensive.

People also respond to other types of stress:

Janet hangs up the phone, her face scarlet—the good-looking senior boy she had hoped to go out with Saturday night has just called and broken their date.

Ken's nauseated stomach and Janet's flushed face are normal reactions to a situation that is stressful, anxiety-provoking, or threatening to self-esteem. They are a physiological response to perceived danger, crisis, or psychological threat via the functioning of the brain, the autonomic nervous system, and various glands throughout the body. Usually such reactions subside when the threat that has triggered them is past.

All of us have experienced similar reactions at one time or another. The nervous speaker's dry mouth, the palms that grow clammy during a suspenseful movie, the gasp of terror, the grief-stricken sob, and many other reactions are all familiar. Unquestionably, our bodies express and reflect our emotional state.

For reasons that are complex and still not fully understood, there are a variety of physiological complaints that have come to be known as "psychosomatic" conditions. The term *psychosomatic* pertains to the body ("soma") as it is influenced by the individual's state of mind or emotions ("psyche"). Interest in the influence of emotions on the body dates from ancient times. The term psychosomatic was first used by a German psychiatrist in the late 1800's, and Freud's psychoanalytic theory sparked a marked interest in psychosomatic medicine in this country during the 1930's.[3] The label can be applied to a variety of bodily ailments the exact cause of which (such as an infection or organic condition) cannot be specifically identified. The origins of certain disorders of the skin, the breathing apparatus, the digestive tract, and the circulatory system are often baffling and complex. The symptoms of a skin rash or stomach ulcer (as opposed to smallpox or a strep throat) may respond to medical treatment but their cause often goes unexplained.

It is inevitable that every person's past experiences and future expectations determine to some extent his awareness of and reaction to his specific illness or disability. Thus, all diseases are in a very real sense psychosomatic events.[4]

In psychosomatic illness, as in any illness, there is usually a complicated interaction among many factors—genetic, neurological, chemical, emotional, even social or cultural. The precise causative role of any one of these factors is often difficult to determine. For example, there is some discussion among members of the medical profession about the possible influence of a genetic predisposition to certain of these conditions. Some ailments such as allergies appear to run in families.

At the same time it seems fair to state that we cannot rule out the involvement of the emotions in cases where neither a specific infection nor an organic condition can be identified as a cause. Emotions may or may not be involved, and in most cases it may be impossible to do more than theorize as to how a chronic disorder originated many years earlier. Some schools of psychiatry have explanations for the onset of specific disabilities including asthma, colitis, and obesity which are documented by reports of successful treatments of certain cases. It is beyond the scope of this discussion to detail these theories. What we do know is that most psychosomatic complaints appear to be accompanied by some unresolved emotional conflict based on temporary or chronic anxiety.

When a young child suffers from a chronic ailment, his parents are typically much concerned, often frantic. Their anxiety is at best unproductive; usually it only serves to aggravate the child's problem and even to trigger chronic flareups of the symptoms.

In this chapter we offer a few suggestions to parents whose children are thus afflicted. Because the subject is vast and complex, we will limit ourselves to a brief discussion of three typical problems that may occur in young children. Each problem is illuminated by an actual case in which the intervention of parent education proved helpful.

Discussion of these cases doesn't prove that such educational intervention on a large scale would alleviate *all* physiological disorders in children. It merely suggests that parents can try to develop calmer, more rational, and more philosophical attitudes about their youngsters' minor health problems, at the same time focusing their efforts on increased nurturance and expressed affection and support.

We hope to help parents understand that in certain circumstances physiological ailments can suggest the presence of low self-esteem in the young sufferer. We have found that once parents understand the importance of improving their children's emotional security, they are willing to increase their caring, empathy, and nurturance. When this happens, parents find themselves better able to cope calmly with the problem at hand since their own self-esteem and confidence are enhanced. The physical results of these changes of parental attitude have often been very gratifying.

On the other hand, parents should never go to the extreme of assuming that every complaint in a child is emotional in origin. The diagnosis and treatment of such ailments as eczema, asthma, hay fever, or mysterious skin rashes is the province of the allergist or dermatologist. If a child has a bad stomachache or severe nausea for any length of time, the parents should by all means call a physician who will determine, if necessary by suitable tests, whether the child has appendicitis or a similarly critical disorder.

THREE CASE STUDIES

The three cases that follow are drawn from our records or from those of colleagues in our educational program. Names of all individuals have been changed.

Weight Problems

Mr. and Mrs. Jones, parents of four children, sought counseling several years ago. They were particularly concerned with the school perform-

ance of their third child, Tom, who was doing very poorly in the seventh grade.

For several weeks the Joneses met with the counselor, Mr. B., who provided them with guidance and suggestions concerning Tom (more affection, empathy, and encouragement; more interest in and support of his schoolwork; less criticism; higher expectations, and so on). The parents put forth considerable effort to improve Tom's situation. Although the siblings were not discussed in the interviews, Mr. and Mrs. Jones evidently also saw the application of the counselor's suggestions to their other children. In particular, they apparently made some changes in their attitudes toward Tom's older sister, Marie, who at that time was fifteen and considerably overweight.

At the end of six months, when Tom's third-quarter grades were compared with his average at the end of the preceding year, they showed marked improvement. Even more dramatic, however, was what had happened to Marie's weight. She had lost twenty-five pounds.[5]

An individual's weight is inescapably associated with his or her habits of food intake, which in turn are influenced by numerous internal and external factors such as body chemistry and lifestyle. The physical problem basically resolves down to calories.

Cultural and social factors are, of course, a potent influence on attitudes toward weight. Ethnically related nutritional habits can affect weight patterns; cooking popular in some cultures is often high in carbohydrates. Rural populations tend toward a heavier diet than residents of urban areas; thinness is sometimes associated with a state of poor health. In recent years the trend toward extreme underweight in teenage girls is at least partly a result of the current vogue of slimness that is heavily promoted by the advertising media as well as by the pressures of peers.

There is also a close association between food and the emotions. The theory of Otto Fenichel outlined briefly in Chapter Four describes the infant's first experiences of simultaneously being given both physical and psychological nourishment. Whatever else we accept as factors influencing a weight problem in a given individual, we must recognize that emotions play some role.

Most feeding problems in children begin at some point in the family environment. When food becomes an overriding issue in any home, one of two problems can result: either overweight or underweight. We all want to protect our children from becoming adults who are seriously afflicted with weight problems. Let us briefly examine the predicament of both gross adult obesity and severe malnutrition.

190 • Self-Esteem, Health, and Anxiety

Extreme overweight (obesity).[6] Weight and height in growing children normally increase by regular increments. During puberty, boys and girls experience a temporary growth spurt usually featuring sudden gains that subsequently stabilize at physical maturity. Allowing for the marked changes of these years, however, it is safe to say that whenever a child's weight has increased so as to be 20 percent or more above the average for his or her height and age, there is some tendency toward overweight. Roughly 10 percent of grade-school youngsters and up to 15 percent of adolescents are probably in this category. If not controlled, their problems can become serious.

Grossly overweight adults are handicapped people. Psychologically, they are characterized by dependency, insecurity, a sense of emptiness which impels them to continual eating, and a basic sense of bitterness and depression. They really have two "selves," the fat self of reality and the idealized thin self (they fantasize that they would be loved more if they were less heavy).

Many obese persons utilize the defense mechanism known as denial; they may joke about matters that other people fail to find humorous. Despite their surface jocularity, these persons are somewhat hostile and anxious, and have a limited capacity for empathy.

Continual talk about diets and continual relapses from dietary regimes are characteristic of many obese persons. The current emphasis on diet that is so intensively advertised by publishers and weight-reducing organizations does little to contribute to their basic self-esteem needs. It deals with symptoms, not causes.

The story of Marie shows that a child's overweight problem can sometimes be helped once parents have been taught how to show more support and affection toward an afflicted youngster. This particular case is even more dramatic inasmuch as the educational intervention was originally focused on another child in the family. Its success with Marie verifies the fact that obese persons, children included, usually lack sufficient affection and nurturance. When parents replace critical and negative attitudes with warm, caring concern, an overweight child can lose pounds, sometimes quite miraculously, without the mention of calories by anyone.

You should make every effort to help your children maintain a normal weight for at least three reasons. First, maintenance of normal weight helps any child's self-image. In the second place, obese persons of all ages are vulnerable to a variety of life-threatening physical health problems. Finally, such persons are at a distinct disadvantage from the viewpoint of college admissions and future employment.

In addition to providing more adequate nurturance and affection to a youngster with a weight problem like Marie's, you can also help her by banishing rich, calorie-laden foods from the house and providing attractive substitutes; by keeping mealtime pleasant, serving small portions, and not insisting that she "clean her plate"; by not making an issue out of food; and by avoiding direct or tactless references to the extra pounds of which the child is already uncomfortably aware.

Extreme underweight (anorexia nervosa). Anorexia nervosa is the clinical name of an extremely underweight condition that occurs almost exclusively in girls, usually between eleven and fifteen. The underweight that is typical of many girls in this age group is not necessarily synonymous with anorexia. Nevertheless, the condition—which can develop at both younger and older ages—is currently on the increase, especially among middle-class high school and college girls.[7]

The cause of this affliction appears to be almost entirely psychological, dating to early infancy, when a domineering parent may have overemphasized the importance of food. In such circumstances the child may have refused to eat normally. As she grows older the situation may worsen; there is not only excessive weight loss but also severe malnutrition.

Young girls with anorexia nervosa are often extremely stubborn, quite hostile, and inclined to use denial as a defense. Associated with their abnormal thinness is often a somewhat desexualized body image; some girls are given to unusual sexual fantasies such as associating food intake with becoming pregnant.

Anorexia nervosa is difficult to treat medically and psychologically. In less serious cases girls may carry on a semblance of normal activities while subjecting themselves to rigid dieting. In more serious cases, hospitalization may become necessary, and in some instances death has occurred. Along with medical treatment both parents and daughter should receive psychological help. This approach has sometimes succeeded in treating the basic cause of the condition and terminating its behavioral and physical manifestations.

Enuresis (Inadequate Bladder Control)

In 1970 a Boston University doctoral candidate conducted a carefully designed research project comparing various methods of treating learning-disability problems in 104 elementary school children from the first to the fifth grades. Both the children and their mothers participated in the study. Dividing the subjects into numerous subgroups, the investigators evaluated the relative effectiveness of "primary" intervention (private tutoring or special class instruction for the children), "secondary" intervention (special counseling for the mother or play therapy for the children), and various combinations of these. Nearly all the children were described as enuretic, and many were under the care of a physician for other ailments.

The researchers found that the most effective means of improving the children's school performance was a combination of both primary and secondary treatments. Specifically, counseling for the mothers either with or without additional play therapy for the youngsters, in conjunction with the work done in the special classes, resulted in more academic improvement than that produced by either tutoring or classwork alone.[8]

Although enuresis was not one of the hypotheses to be tested in this project and hence was not discussed in the report, the investigators' observations concerning the subjects' bladder problems became an interesting by-product of their findings. As the project continued, mothers began to comment that the enuresis was becoming less frequent. In about two thirds of the cases it had completely stopped before the project ended.

Numerous clinicians who have worked with parents of enuretic children report similar experiences.

Enuresis is generally defined as a child's habitual wetting of clothes or bed past age five. It is associated with more parental anxiety, misunderstanding, and ineffectual treatment than almost any other childhood problem. At least one cause is tension between parents and child. By the time a youngster is eight or nine, cause and effect have become thoroughly entangled; the parents are mortified and annoyed that the child (usually a boy) has not yet gained control of his bladder and the boy indubitably feels the parents' anxiety and disapproval. The result for the youngster is an ongoing sense of low self-esteem and continued problems of incontinence.

In this situation the parents have to break the deadlock.

Other possible causes of an enuretic problem (diabetes, kidney disorder or infection, abnormal neurological functioning, and others) must first be explored through proper medical procedures. If these are ruled out, attention must be shifted to the psychological components. A child who is enuretic well beyond the preschool years is usually basically anxious and uncertain about his identity, and this situation suggests that support and affection from one or both parents is lacking.[9] He needs much more empathy, affection, and genuine concern than he is receiving. His incontinence results partly from his fear of expressing his insecurities verbally to his parents. His father and mother must become more relaxed about his problem and must concentrate their efforts on more empathic support—particularly freer communication with their son. The fact that enuresis occurs more often in boys than in girls is consistent with the finding that boys generally receive less support and nurturance than girls.

A Respiratory Problem

Young Mr. and Mrs. S. were proud parents of little Ben, but early in his life he had one problem. Each spring during his first three years he suffered acute nasal congestion: stuffy nose and constant sneezing made him restless and fidgety during the day and kept him and his parents awake at night. The S.'s were beside themselves during the spring months although the problem was less troublesome at other times of the year. It had all the earmarks of a seasonal upper-respiratory inflammation.

Ben's father first learned of our program when Ben was four years old. At the time Mr. S. was becoming acquainted with a new approach to parenting, he noted that Ben's respiratory ailment began to show signs of improvement. As the young father found himself beginning to relate to his small son with more empathy and affection, and less anxiety and annoyance, the symptoms began to subside despite the fact that during the spring months they had normally been acutely troublesome.

Ben's respiratory condition improved markedly that spring. It has not reappeared. No medication has been given. He is now an alert, creative 9-year-old functioning well ahead of grade level and pursuing numerous outside activities.[10]

It has been observed for many years that our breathing apparatus—the upper respiratory tract, windpipe, bronchial tubes and lungs, and even the skin (also an organ of breathing)—is influenced by the emotions. No one doubts that breathing is under both voluntary and involuntary control and is hence the means through which we express all sorts of feelings. Breathing is involved in laughing, weeping, gasping in fear or surprise, expressing intense anger. (Breath-holding during a child's temper tantrum is an example.) It is also known that emotions can affect the tissue lining of the nose and throat. The throat becomes dry when we become anxious; hence the speaker's stand is provided with a glass of water. Some persons experience runny noses in temporarily stressful situations as well as during the course of a common cold.

Seasonal upper respiratory infections of the nose, sinuses, and throat are commonly referred to as hay fever or rose fever. It is more accurate to say that such infections occur in certain persons who appear to be sensitive to the antigens in the air at certain times of the spring and summer and in certain geographic locations. The reason for a predisposition to these sensitivities to the surrounding atmosphere has not been fully established, although persons so afflicted often point to another family member who has previously suffered a similar condition. The ailment can be treated medically but the actual cause, other than the environmental irritant, is more obscure. There is, however, general agreement that there is some emotional component.[11]

In our work with parents over the years we have found that our emphasis on increased self-esteem and improved academic achievement has produced another benefit: numerous parents have reported improvement in respiratory ailments similar to those of little Ben in the case cited above.

In addition to weight problems, enuresis, and respiratory ailments (only three of the many possible childhood health issues), there are certain problems peculiar to the adolescent period. Probably the most vexatious of these are the skin conditions usually identified as acne.

THE PROBLEM OF ADOLESCENT ACNE

Acne in young persons between the ages of thirteen and eighteen is so prevalent that many parents regard some degree of it as a normal adolescent affliction. However, it should be noted that not all teen-agers suffer from acne. In recent decades the condition appears to be decreasing.

There is little doubt that the body's hormonal and chemical changes during the teenage years affect the skin of the average girl or boy. The interrelationship between acne, emotional tension, and endocrine factors can be observed in young people before an important athletic contest, a Scholastic Aptitude Test, or the onset of a girl's menstrual period. Like other stress-related conditions, acne occurs more frequently and with greater severity in boys than in girls.

Adolescence is a time of stress. As pointed out in Chapter Five, it is a time when many parents, feeling that it is wise to put young sons or daughters increasingly on their own, may unwittingly reduce the expressed affection, support, and nurturance with which they surrounded their child during younger years. The tendency is particularly evident with respect to boys. At the same time, the adolescent's life is becoming increasingly challenging and often threatening; society expects more and more of the young person at the very time in life when rapid bodily changes are occurring. Academic records, test scores, decisions made during these years are irrevocable. Pressures are terrific.

When societal expectations increase and emotional support lessens, these young people normally experience greater anxiety to which their bodies must respond in some manner. In the interaction between certain portions of the brain (particularly the hypothalamus) and the endocrine system, a hormone imbalance can occur in the young individual to help him or her meet a real or imagined threat. Research has indicated that persons of both sexes who suffer from severe acne tend to exhibit such endocrine activity in the form of skin eruptions caused by excessive secretions of sebaceous glands. The resulting skin problems, no matter how minor, are acutely distressing to the young sufferer although modern treatment methods plus scrupulous care of the skin's cleanliness are usually helpful.[12]

If a teenager's family life is one of continual tension and conflict, severe acne can become an ongoing problem. Adolescents so afflicted are, like the youngsters described in the previous cases, usually unable to express their feelings freely and directly. They are often somewhat immature, dependent, and generally insecure. Most cases of severe acne result from a combination of physical, social, family, and educational factors.

What Parents Can Do

Most cases of adolescent acne are fairly minor though usually distressing to the young person. You should be sympathetic to the fact that both boys and girls react to even minor blemishes with excessive concern. There are several things you can do if you have a teenage sufferer in your home.

• See that he or she is treated by a competent dermatologist. New medical treatments are encouraging.

● Recognize that the problem can be aggravated by emotional tension.

● Encourage a close relationship between an afflicted boy and his father.

● Try to be sympathetic with the problem but do not dwell on it openly, thus causing further embarrassment and humiliation.

● Provide and encourage the consumption of a healthful diet low in rich and fatty foods, but don't make an issue of food.

● Above all, refrain from excessive and continual criticism. It also helps to remember—and to reassure your young people—that acne is not "forever."

CONCLUSION

In the foregoing discussion we have barely scratched the surface of a vast area of parental concern: how to deal with children's chronic health problems. Many conditions not mentioned here, such as bronchial asthma, can be severe and even life-threatening, requiring continual monitoring and medical care. There are no easy answers for parents whose youngster is so afflicted.

We still don't understand all the causes of certain chronic physical ailments, particularly the possible role of inheritance. In addition, environmental factors (air pollution, for example) must sometimes be considered, and families living in severely disadvantaged circumstances often suffer health problems caused by conditions well beyond their control. For most of us with less acute problems, however, a few common-sense guidelines may be helpful.

Regardless of cause, what should be the parental role toward a child who suffers from a chronic ailment?

● You should seek competent medical help for the condition and try to carry out the physician's instructions calmly, quietly, and reassuringly.

● Beyond this, pay attention to the home and family situation. Ask certain questions. Are there any cues in the child's behavior suggesting that he is bothered by something? How does he feel about the persons close to him—his mother, his father, his big brother, his baby sister? Does he talk freely about what is on his mind or is he morose, silent, and preoccupied? How often do you sit down with him and encourage him to express his feelings freely while you listen attentively and sympathetically? Does he share his anxieties and misgivings about school, playmates, and events away from home?

• Also examine your own emotions. How do you really feel about your child? What is your reaction when you see that runny nose or view the wet bed in the morning? When you find that your plump teenage daughter has emptied the cookie jar or observe the newest devastation in your 16-year-old son's complexion? Are you willing to face up to yourselves as a possible part of the cause?

• Recognize your responsibility to instill healthful eating habits early in your child's life; make use of the abundant suggestions in newspaper columns, magazines, and books that reflect new awareness of important facts about nutrition and its influence on health.

• Encourage the enjoyment of informal physical exercise for all members of your family. Softball, jogging, hiking, or (if a safe route is available) bicycling are both inexpensive and a lot of family fun. None of us needs to be an outstanding athlete to participate in such pastimes.

• Finally, accept the fact that stress is an inevitable part of modern living and we and our children must learn how to cope with it with some degree of composure. If we view life as a problem to be solved rather than as a source of anxiety, we can gain much. When illness strikes, deal with it as calmly as possible, and regard chronic complaints with a bit of philosophical resignation.

Above all, don't lose sight of the principles of the "magic triad"—the hug, the smile, and the kind and understanding communication—that can keep your child free of unnecessary anxiety.

SPECIFIC SUGGESTIONS

Do:

Do encourage your child to express his or her feelings freely to you at all times.

Do encourage good general health habits, particularly good eating habits.

Do keep mealtime pleasant and (at least at dinner) as leisurely as possible.

Do encourage your child's early enjoyment of relaxed physical and athletic activities.

Do be sympathetic with your teenagers' minor overweight or complexion problems.

Don't:

Don't make an issue out of food.

Don't ever assume that a physical complaint is entirely emotion-caused. If in doubt, always seek a medical opinion.

12

THE ROLE OF HIGH ASPIRATIONS

"You know, Daddy, I've been doing a lot of thinking. I want to go to college when I'm through high school. Then I want to be head of some health organization and help a lot of people."

The words are those of young Jill, whom we met as a 10-year-old in Chapters Two and Three. While walking with her father one Sunday afternoon, she was already beginning to dream about a career in public health.

The sequel to this story (and it is a true one) shows that childhood aspirations voiced within a devoted and supportive family are often realized in later life. A dozen years later, soon after graduation from college, Jill became an intern in a federally funded community clinic serving a poor rural population in the Southwest. Within a few months she was assigned the responsible task of developing, in an isolated mountain area, a small clinic to operate as a satellite of the larger public health unit. Under her direction the mountain clinic became a reality. After two years' experience, Jill entered the graduate school of business in a large university for further training in health care administration to increase her skill and competence in a demanding profession.

The other productive young people we met in Chapter Two—Adam, Mary, Steve, and Dan—all had a clear idea of what they would like to do when they grew up.

THE YOUNG CHILD'S VIEW OF THE FUTURE

It is not unusual for children in the primary grades to begin thinking about their future. The early dreams may be a little ambitious (driving the space shuttle, being a prima ballerina). In general, however, happy children gradually revise their plans and, as the years go on, begin to focus on more attainable goals. The important aspect of Jill's comments is that they show a little girl feeling sufficiently secure with her parents to express her dreams freely to her father.

The process of projecting themselves into the unknown world of the future is a new experience for children. To envision themselves thus, they need two personality strengths:[1]

> *The capacity to adopt a long-range view of time.* In the first place youngsters must deal with the concept of time in a manner not ordinarily required in their routine school and social activities. During the preschool and early elementary grades, their sense of time is still somewhat limited. They can conceptualize next week or month, next summer vacation, their next birthday—all of which occur within a familiar context. But to imagine themselves at age 25 or 30, encumbered with numerous adult responsibilities and without the protection and support of parents and familiar childhood surroundings, can be frightening for them, especially if they are emotionally insecure.

> *The ability to tolerate delay.* Children must also have the security to wait, possibly many years, before their wishes for the future are realized or their plans fulfilled. They cannot, for example, have the status, money, and other advantages that accompany establishment in a profession without prolonged effort, self-discipline, and sacrifice over a period of several years. They must renounce some immediate pleasures for the sake of eventually attaining worthwhile future objectives. They may have to save job earnings in high school instead of buying a car, forgo social activities during exam periods in order to maintain the high academic record needed for admission to college and professional school. Other sacrifices may be necessary.

CAREER CHOICE, SELF-ESTEEM, AND HOPE

Discussing your children's vocational and other ambitions with them will be of no value unless they first feel secure and happy. They can project themselves imaginatively two decades hence into the unknown only if they have complete trust in the present. In a word, they must have hope.

A child's sense of hope is the assurance that no matter what happens, his or her parents will always be there. Happy, productive youngsters are confident that they can cope with the future because they are guaranteed their parents' continuing and unqualified affection, encouragement, and support. Because their current self-esteem needs are fully met, they can wait many years if necessary to see the results of long-range efforts.

Children who refuse to give any thought to their future are usually in quite a different situation. Such children tend to be retiring and withdrawn. They lack confidence. Sometimes they are impulsive, shortsighted, and lacking in judgment. They are preoccupied with the pursuit of immediate pleasures. Most of all, they seem to lack a sense of direction and purpose.

Young Ned, whom we met in Chapters Two and Three, is a typical example. When asked what he would like to do as an adult, he would shrug his shoulders and reply, "I dunno." His parents have told Ned that he can be anything he wants to be; it's up to him. Such comments do absolutely nothing to encourage a boy like Ned's serious contemplation of his future. They also tell us that his parents have so little concern for Ned that they won't even take the trouble to talk with him about his present problems, to say nothing of his future concerns. Ned is consequently so preoccupied with his current need for nurturance and support that he can't visualize anything beyond the here and now.

The Importance of Fathers
Fathers in such homes as Ned's are often cold, detached, and almost totally uninvolved with their families. Sometimes, for one reason or another, they are absent from home for long periods. The children are almost always injured in some way. In particular, their attitudes about the future may suffer.

Father absence or neglect affects children of all ages. One study of fourth-, fifth-, and sixth-grade boys whose fathers were frequently away from home reported that these youngsters showed less "future time perspective" than boys whose fathers were present in the home. A survey of college students whose fathers were physically present but psychologically distant found these students less able to extend themselves into the future and less able to anticipate later events than students who had enjoyed close and supportive relations with their fathers.[2]

On the other hand, many benefits result from close, compatible bonds between fathers and children. In certain professions fathers seem to exert a direct influence upon their sons' career choice. One study found that nearly half of the sons of doctors (43.6 percent) chose to enter medicine while a survey of lawyers revealed a similar trend (27.7 percent choosing their father's field).[3]

Fathers can also be a profound influence on the future achievement of their daughters. The woman president of one of our top-ranking women's colleges has been quoted as saying:

This position means the world to my father. I am his oldest child. To have the respect of the academic community is everything to him. . . . My father always told me that what I had in my head, no one could take away.[4]

The Basis of Future Job-Related Skills

The basis of competence in all jobs, professions, or careers lies in well-developed cognitive skills, especially verbal skills. An especially high degree of verbal (and, increasingly, mathematical) competence is indispensable for all persons who wish to qualify for any of the more advanced professions such as law, medicine, business, or engineering. The foundations are already being laid in a youngster's grade-school years.

Today, moreover, almost all semiprofessional or service-oriented occupations, and even some skilled trades, require above-average verbal and numerical skills. *All* intellectual skills are stifled in a critical and negative home atmosphere.

Object-Related and People-Related Careers

It has been found that children raised in critical and noncaring homes tend in the job world to turn to object-related occupations requiring manual or motor dexterity rather than a high degree of intellectual competence:[5]

Simon goofed off in school. He graduated by the skin of his teeth. Now he's pumping gas for a living. His parents say that he "works better with his hands."

It is more accurate to say that Simon has turned to a job at the gas pump because his parents have denied him the emotional security that would have enhanced his verbal development.

There is a difference between persons who gravitate toward object-related work and those who are more people-oriented. It is the more emotionally secure person who feels able to work with people. There is general agreement that girls receive more warmth and affection than boys, and we also know that they traditionally like to work with people. (An interesting study has found that girls who have had somewhat negative relationships with either parent, particularly the father, tend to avoid work that brings them into contact with people.)

The Phenomenon of Upward Mobility

Upward mobility has been defined as the tendency of children to choose a vocation that is higher on the socioeconomic scale than their father's. Sociologists usually determine levels on this scale according to such factors as the amount of education and training required for various occupations. For example, a highway maintenance man requires a minimum of education and job training; a cardiac surgeon needs years of both. Advanced education has traditionally enabled many young men and women from modest home backgrounds to move upward in the occupational world to a status higher than their family's:

The U.S. congressman from South Dakota got his start in the small midwestern village where his parents still work the family farm.

Upward mobility is a well-known phenomenon of the Western world.

Investigators have found marked personality contrasts between upwardly and downwardly mobile groups; these differences are related to their self-esteem.[6] Upward aspiration seems to be associated with close parent–child relationships, especially with the father. In the above example, the farmer without advanced formal education himself takes enormous pride in the son who successfully surmounts educational, professional, and political hurdles to become an active member of the highest lawmaking body in the land. It is certain that this father has always encouraged his son's aspirations through faith and consistently high educational expectations.

Sometimes we see differences in social mobility within the same family:

Martin, now thirty, has just passed his bar exams and is getting started in the downtown law office. His brother, Frank, three years younger, quit school halfway through his freshman year and now gets along by doing odd carpentry jobs.

What do these differences between Martin and Frank mean? Conceivably, that the two young men have been treated differently in the past. Martin may have received a larger share of genuine parental attention, affection, stimulation, and encouragement to achieve than his younger brother.

Parents who do not have high aspirations for their children's futures tend to question the importance of advanced education. It is easy for them to compare teachers' salaries with the earnings of skilled tradespeople or to reflect on the six-figure contracts of certain professional athletes. Nonetheless they, and we, must retain faith in the long-term value of education for making possible a life of genuine productivity and richness in the broadest sense of the word. All fathers and mothers, particularly those who have been vocationally successful themselves, owe their children the same encouragement and sense of expectation they received from their own parents.

Common Parental Misconceptions

"You can be anything you want to be. Choose your own career. We'll back you up." With such a statement many parents assume that they are doing a good (i.e., hands-off) job. But by itself the remark is little more than a cop-out. In not discussing their children's futures with them and lending active support and encouragement, the parents are really abandoning responsibility for helping their youngster face an area that is full of uncertainty and anxiety. A child is likely to view this attitude as both uncaring and rejecting.

"He doesn't know what he wants to be. When he 'finds' himself, he'll do better [presumably, in school]." A child's lack of career choice does not explain poor school performance. If parents rationalize poor grades on this basis, the child is all too prone to seize upon the same excuse. Children who are doing poor academic work will not automatically improve merely by choosing a specific career. Neither academic achievement nor intelligent career choice is possible without steadfast parental support.

"You're 'good at' [mechanical, musical, artistic, outdoor, or other] things, so you should be able to get a good job." It is not necessary to limit choice of a vocation to an area or areas in which there is some evidence of potential skill. Many such skills have grown out of our early experiences with parents or friends and may not be related to a life career. Some of these

can and should be kept as hobbies if the individual has a marked interest in a different area. (Medicine can be chosen as one's profession rather than music, for example.) Normally endowed and emotionally secure children can profit from training in the areas in which they are interested.

"Let him/her take an interest test." Occasionally parents and their adolescent may benefit from the child's taking an interest test. In general, however, they will not be surprised by the results; the tests often merely reflect prevailing family interests and tastes. It is possible that the test answers are reflecting the parents' rather than the child's interests. They often confirm the young person's lack of career choice by not revealing any specific vocational preferences. Such tests have been constructed for a post-high school population and are therefore of limited usefulness for the adolescent group.

"Maybe he should take a course in vocations." Any discussion of the vast number of specialties in today's occupational world is of little value to the student who refuses to give any thought to the future and whose basic problem is one of low self-esteem and uncertain identity. Furthermore, parents of such a child are not likely to be supportive of a vocational choice in an area that is still regarded by the general public as somewhat new, unusual, and not yet fully established.

HOW YOU CAN FOSTER INTEREST IN THE FUTURE

Parents can play an active and sympathetic role in encouraging their children to think about their futures. Keep in mind the value of the following:

Your *daily, ongoing interest* in all that they are currently doing provides meaning and encourages them to continue their efforts.

Occasional *exploratory discussions* like those between Jill and her father provide a sense of remote goals and give direction and purpose to schoolwork. These discussions, which can be started in the primary grades, are also intellectually stimulating; they spark imaginative and curious inquiries: "What do I have to do to become a lawyer? An engineer? A nurse? A doctor? A banker?" Furthermore, they contribute to a child's sense of identity and security.

It is also helpful to take a *sympathetic and enthusiastic interest in hobbies.* Young Mary, described in Chapters Two and Three, spent leisure time during grade school at work on many small scientific projects in her parents' basement. Out of these experiences has evolved her orientation toward a scientific—specifically, a medical—career. Anne Roe made extensive studies of the childhood backgrounds of outstanding scientists. A physicist reminiscing about his own childhood hobbies had this to say:

Father never helped me make anything. On the other hand if I asked him how to do something he always knew and he had tools around. . . . He never gave me any formal instruction but I learned a lot.[7]

Always there was sympathetic interest and support from parents. At the same time, there was no attempt to force the child into an adult mold.

As far as possible, *let children use some of their leisure time to explore and experiment freely on their own.* Don't pressure them with continuous planned activity. Encourage them to "keep their options open" regarding their final choice of a profession or life work.

Recently we read of a young man who is doing such exploring:[8]

Steven Gordon has his eyes on the frontier. The kind of exploring he wants to do is medical.

Steven will enter Tufts University, which he has chosen because of its offerings in medicine. During high school he has in his spare time had contact with at least three professional areas. His prime interest in medicine grew out of work in a laboratory at the Harvard School of Public Health; he has taught Hebrew to young pupils at the temple school in his home town of Brookline; and he has been an enthusiastic, dedicated worker for various political causes and candidates from age nine (when he helped distribute political endorsements). However, medicine has always been uppermost in his mind for a life's work.

THE JOB WORLD OF THE FUTURE

"What will life be like when my third-grader looks for a job fifteen years from now?"

It is difficult to imagine. Fifteen years hence the world is likely to have a very different look. Some trends are becoming dimly evident:[9]

● Future workers will be more sophisticated, better educated, and unwilling to settle for dull, routine, menial, repetitive jobs (which will be wholly taken over by technology).

● Competition for jobs will be intense, with women and minority groups vying with men for the most attractive positions. (More mothers will be in the labor force. In 1979 the percentage was close to two thirds; within ten years it is expected to climb to three quarters.)

● Judging from the trends of the past thirty years, there will be an increasing number of jobs at the professional-managerial level. (In 1950 such positions constituted only one out of twelve jobs; by 1979 the proportion had increased to one out of four!)

● Mathematical expertise will be in demand in perhaps two out of every three jobs.[10] Already we are dealing in ever-larger amounts of data and information and one must be familiar and comfortable with quantitative terminology—"cost-benefit analyses," "margins," "bases," "indices," a growing host of words with which one must deal merely to keep pace with present business, industrial, and economic activities. The trend can only be intensified in coming decades.

● In numerous areas—engineering and health, for example—many new professional specialties will continue to emerge.

● There will be demands, particularly from women who are simultaneously rearing families, for more flexible working hours as well as child-care facilities at or near places of employment.

● A shorter work week is possible.

● There is likely to be heavy emphasis on service-oriented industries: health care, information processing, communications, insurance, and others.

● Traditional professions such as law and medicine will be even more competitive and demanding.

THE FAMILY OF THE FUTURE

At present we are witnessing a fundamental change in the job world due to the growing equality between the sexes. Women are now selecting some vocations (engineering, for example) that were formerly a man's domain. Many young women are planning to raise a family as well. In becoming mothers they are assuming the burdens of what should properly be regarded as a second, and very demanding profession. Unfortunately, young men as a group are not yet fully convinced that their role as fathers is likewise tantamount to a second profession. Among the more educated, the attitude is beginning to change and we hope it will continue to change.

One thing is certain. Society is making heavy demands on all professions, including parenthood. As more and more young women secure advanced education and training, at the same time wishing to become mothers, many attitudes concerning family life must be revised. Young husbands will have to share household and child-care responsibilities with their wives. Married couples will need flexibility in hours and schedules, ingenuity in meeting unforeseen situations that inevitably arise (illness and other emergencies), and continuous and intelligent division of labor between the partners. In all of this the children must not suffer.

There is much challenge, but also much promise in today's families in which both parents work at chosen careers. Children in such homes have an opportunity to observe the commitment of both father and mother to their work. If secure and happy, they will eventually become a part of their parents' professional worlds. Each parent's work will contribute to the children's sense of identity. The parents are also models for the youngsters' future development.

In encouraging your children to be productive, stress the importance of a goal, a purpose for this effort. Help them to keep their sights high and to prepare for service to society by obtaining the best possible training.

The basic reason each of us chooses a certain career is that it contributes to our self-esteem. Our choice gains us the approval and support of others—first, from our parents; later from others. Sometimes a teacher, a coach, or a favorite relative functioning as a parental surrogate can influence a young person's career choice but this situation is rare. And the peer group exercises practically no influence.

One thing is certain: to be truly successful in any occupation—regardless of whether we are professionals, semi-professionals, business people, members of service-oriented occupations, or even skilled tradespeople—we must sense that someone believes in us.

CONCLUSION

Each time we become parents we enter into a permanent relationship with another human being. We are always parents to our children even if we divorce our mates, just as we remain the children of our own parents after they are gone.

But parenthood is more than a lifelong bond. Because it is a highly rewarding, but often puzzling and challenging experience, "parenting," as it is coming to be called, should be regarded as a profession. Unfortunately, it is still far from being such.

To be worthy of the name, any professional training should involve three prerequisites:

● Academic preparation
● Training in specific skills
● Supervised work experience

Currently, none of these is formally required of any father or mother. We marry, eventually the woman becomes pregnant, we wait nine months, we go through the exciting birth experience, and then we find that we are parents.

What resources are available to help us raise the tiny individual who lies kicking and squirming before us? The most important medical assistance from our pediatrician. Temporary help from a mother, mother-in-law, sister, or some compassionate relative. Perhaps much free advice from our neighbors. And volume after volume of books. That is all.

Most of us, however well-intentioned, are plagued with uncertainties along the long parenting road because we usually lack agreed-upon guidelines and a solid academic background for the most important job we will ever undertake, raising a productive human being.

As conscientious parents we are tormented with doubts, ask legions of questions. Are we doing the *right* thing? Are we being too strict? Too easygoing? Which books should we be reading? Which suggestions are the most useful? Which school of psychology has the best answers? Will behavior modification work? Logical consequences? Active listening? No wonder people become confused, guilt-ridden, prone to vacillation and inconsistency in dealing with their children!

In this book we have tried to outline a simple approach to parenting. We hope it will dispel some of the confusion evident in the foregoing questions.

All these questions can be reduced to two simple queries that parents can and should ask themselves again and again over the years:

How will my present actions (words, gestures, even thoughts) in this particular situation affect my child's self-image?

How would I feel if I were in my child's shoes at this moment?

All of the guidelines (the specific Do's and Don't's at the chapters' endings) are simply suggestions to help parents respond to these two basic questions. They can be adopted by parents in all sorts of circumstances regardless of their religion, race, education, or income level. There is nothing to buy; there are no schedules to make or records to maintain. The only requirement is parental affection for each and every child in the family, a deep concern for meeting that child's self-esteem needs, and an ongoing commitment to help the child acquire the skills that will make it possible to develop into a successful adult.

Even though the theory of productivity is valid and its application simple and clear, the improvement in your children's academic and other accomplishments will depend on your own values as well as your goals for your young people. These recommendations, faithfully carried out, can increase their general productivity, but regardless of your efforts or your children's abilities, their achievements will be no more than average unless you yourselves are committed to the best in their performance. Children's achievement will be no higher than their parents' dreams for them.

If parents really want excellence for their children, they will be conscientious in applying these suggestions. They will set higher goals for their family and will give more direction to its organization. They will pay more attention daily to their children's schoolwork and give more recognition to each small accomplishment. The level of their children's achievement will then reflect their concern, their devotion, and above all, their expectations. Parents who are merely satisfied with "good" work will be rewarded with mediocrity; by accepting the good they destroy the best.

The issue of productivity should be viewed not only in terms of the individual family but also in a broader social context. We in the United States are not as productive in proportion to our assets as are a number of other countries. Like the C student with a high IQ, we could probably be doing better. Our achievements as a country will be no greater than the sum of our individual accomplishments. Each person, each family has a stake in our performance as a whole.

We all need to commit ourselves to hard work to make this world a better place. The burden of meeting and solving the problems of future decades will be our children's. Being productive means giving one's skills, time, and energy to the welfare of others. We must see that our children are equipped with all that is necessary for this task.

NOTES

CHAPTER 1

1. B. L. White, *The First Three Years of Life* (Englewood Cliffs, N.J.: Prentice-Hall, 1975), pp. 222–226. See also R. Miller, "Development from One to Two Years: Language Acquisition," in J.D. Noshpitz (Ed.), *Basic Handbook of Child Psychiatry*, Vol. 1 (New York: Basic Books, 1979), pp. 127–144, with an extensive bibliography of references to other articles on the subject.

    2. J. V. Gilmore, *The Productive Personality* (San Francisco: Albion Publishing Co., 1974), pp. 7–8.

    3. J. V. Gilmore, *The Productive Personality*, pp. 16, 21, 22.

    4. P. W. Pruyser, "Phenomenology and Dynamics of Hoping," *Journal for the Scientific Study of Religion*, 3 (1963), 94–95. E. Stotland, *The Psychology of Hope* (San Francisco: Jossey-Bass, 1969), pp. 151–176.

    5. J. A. Clausen, "Family Structure, Socialization, and Personality," in M. L. Hoffman and L. W. Hoffman (Eds.), *Review of Child Development Research*, Vol. 2 (New York: Russell Sage Foundation, 1966), pp. 1–53. S. Coopersmith, *The Antecedents of Self-esteem* (San Francisco: Freeman, 1967). F. Barron, *Creativity and Personal Freedom* (Princeton, N.J.: Van Nostrand, 1968), pp. 37–65. W. A. Westley and N. B. Epstein, *The Silent Majority* (San Francisco: Jossey-Bass, 1969). M. Rosenberg, *Society and the Adolescent Self-Image* (Princeton, N.J.: Princeton University Press, 1965). J. Lewis, W. R. Beavers, J. T. Gossett, and V. A. Phillips, *No Single Thread* (New York: Brunner/Mazel, 1976).

    6. J. R. Hurley, "Parental Acceptance-Rejection and Children's Intelligence," in G. R. Medinnus (Ed.), *Reading in the Psychology of Parent–Child Relations* (New York: Wiley, 1967), pp. 106–116. E. Douvan and J. Adelson, *The Adolescent Experience* (New York: Wiley, 1966). Coopersmith, *The Antecedents of Self-esteem*, pp. 100, 196–197.

7. E. Bing, "Effect of Child-Rearing Practices on Development of Differential Cognitive Abilities," in Medinnus, *Readings in the Psychology of Parent–Child Relations*, pp. 205–222. See also Miller, "Development from One to Two Years," for extensive bibliographical references to the subject.

8. L. Carlsmith, "Effect of Early Father Absence on Scholastic Aptitude," *Harvard Educational Review*, 34:1 (1964), 3–21. M. E. Lamb, "The Role of the Father: An Overview," in M. E. Lamb (Ed.), *The Role of the Father in Child Development* (New York: Wiley, 1976), pp. 13–21. H. B. Biller, "The Father and Personality Development: Paternal Deprivation and Sex-Role Development," in Lamb, *The Role of the Father*, pp. 89–156. R. A. Knox, "Fathers, Babies Together," *Boston Globe, Living* section, June 21, 1981.

9. J. Foreman, "Working Parents Do Better in Boston," *Boston Globe*, April 8, 1981. J. S. Lublin, "The New Interest in Corporate Day-Care," *Wall Street Journal*, April 20, 1981. M. Bralove, "Problems of Two-Career Families Start Forcing Businesses to Adapt," *Wall Street Journal*, July 15, 1981.

CHAPTER 2

1. J. V. Gilmore, "A New Venture in the Testing of Motivation," *College Board Review*, November 1951. See also the author's unpublished paper, "Summary of Findings of a Study of Noncognitive Factors in the Academic Achievement of M.I.T. Freshmen in 1951" (on file at the Gilmore Institute, Boston, 1977).

CHAPTER 4

1. O. Fenichel, *The Psychoanalytic Theory of Neurosis* (New York: Norton, 1945), p. 41.

2. J. Aronfreed, *Conduct and Conscience* (New York: Academic Press, 1968), pp. 143–145.

3. H. Ginott, *Between Parent and Child* (New York: Macmillan, 1965, 1971), Chap. 2.

4. J. D. Scott, "Count Your Compliments," *Reader's Digest*, December 1976.

5. S. B. Simon, *Negative Criticism* (Niles, Ill.: Argus Communications, 1978).

6. See also T. Gordon, *Parent Effectiveness Training* (New York: Peter H. Wyden, 1970), and V. Satir, *Peoplemaking* (Palo Alto, Cal.: Science and Behavior Books, 1972).

7. See also Simon, *Negative Criticism*, pp. 109–116.

CHAPTER 5

1. J. V. Gilmore, *The Productive Personality*, (San Francisco: Albion Publishing Co., 1974), pp. 44–45.

2. E. H. Erikson, "The Problem of Ego Identity," *Journal of the American Psychoanalytic Association, IV:*1 (1956), p. 74.

3. R. Schafer, *Aspects of Internalization* (New York: International Universities Press, 1968), p. 151.

4. *Ibid.*, p. 142.

5. *Ibid.*, pp. 151–152.

6. Erikson, "The Problem of Ego Identity," p. 53.

7. P. H. Mussen and N. Eisenberg-Berg, *Roots of Caring, Sharing, and Helping: The Development of Prosocial Behavior in Children* (San Francisco: Freeman, 1977), p. 87.

8. A. P. Peterson and D. Offer, "Adolescent Development: Sixteen to Nineteen Years," in J. D. Noshpitz (Ed.), *Basic Handbook of Child Psychiatry, Vol. 1* (New York: Basic Books, 1979), p. 224.

9. M. E. Lamb, "The Role of the Father: An Overview," in M. E. Lamb (Ed.), *The Role of the Father in Child Development* (New York: Wiley, 1976), p. 8.

10. P. H. Mussen, J. J. Conger, and J. Kagan, *Child Development and Personality*, 3rd ed. (New York: Harper, 1969), p. 359. P. Wyden and B. Wyden, *Growing Up Straight* (New York: Stein and Day, 1968), p. 61.

11. H. B. Biller, "The Father and Personality Development: Paternal Deprivation and Sex-Role Development," in Lamb, *The Role of the Father*, pp. 89–156. E. M. Hetherington, "Effects of Father Absence on Personality Development in Adolescent Daughters," *Developmental Psychology*, 7 (1972), 313–316.

12. See "Three Developmental Routes through Normal Male Adolescence," in Peterson and Offer, "Adolescent Development," pp. 224–229.

13. "Three Developmental Routes," pp. 226–228.

14. A. R. Lucas, "Muscular Control and Coordination in Minimal Brain Dysfunctions," chap. 10 in H. E. Rie and E. D. Rie (Eds.), *Handbook of Minimal Brain Dysfunctions: A Critical View* (New York: Wiley–Interscience, 1980), pp. 235–252, esp. pp. 246–247.

15. C. A. Palmer, "Little Evidence to Link Diet, Hyperactivity," *Boston Herald-American*, February 13, 1980.

16. D. K. Routh and G. B. Mesibov, "Psychological and Environmental Intervention: Toward Social Competence," chap. 25 in Rie and Rie, *Handbook*, pp. 618–644.

17. W. M. Cruickshank, "Myths and Realities in Learning Disabilities," *Journal of Learning Disabilities*, 10:1 (January 1977), 54. See also discussion of learning disabilities in Chapter IX.

18. C. P. Malmquist, "Development from Thirteen to Sixteen Years," in Noshpitz, *Basic Handbook of Child Psychiatry*, Vol. 1, pp. 205–213, esp. p. 209.

19. D. Weatherley, "Self-Perceived Rate of Physical Maturation and Personality in Late Adolescence," in J. F. Rosenblith and W. Allinsmith (Eds.), *The Causes of Behavior II: Readings in Child Development and Educational Psychology*, 2nd ed. (Boston: Allyn and Bacon, 1966), pp. 71–79, esp. p. 78.

20. S. Coopersmith, *The Antecedents of Self-esteem* (San Francisco: Freeman, 1967), p. 122.

21. "The Pinks and the Blues," television program produced in September 1980 by the WGBH Educational Foundation as part of the Nova series. Transcripts available from WGBH, 125 Western Avenue, Boston, Mass. 02134.

CHAPTER 6

1. During the decade of the 1960's the topic of birth order received much attention from research workers. Particularly interesting are the survey by W. D. Altus, "Birth Order and Its Sequelae," *Science*, 151 (January 7), 1966, 44 ff.; E. J. Sampson, "The Study of Ordinal Position," in B. A. Maher (Ed.), *Progress in Experimental Personality Research*, Vol. 2 (New York: Academic Press, 1965), pp. 174 ff; and J. A. Clausen, "Family Structure, Socialization, and Personality," in M. L. Hoffman and L. W. Hoffman (Eds.), *Review of Child Development Research*, Vol. 2 (New York: Russell Sage Foundation, 1966), pp. 1–53.

2. B. L. White, *The First Three Years of Life* (Englewood Cliffs, N.J.: Prentice-Hall, 1975), p. 235.

3. N. Newbert, "A Study of Certain Personality Correlates of the Middle Child in a Three-Child Family" (unpublished doctoral thesis, Boston University, 1967).

4. M. Rosenberg, *Society and the Adolescent Self-Image* (Princeton, N.J.: Princeton University Press, 1965). Chapter 6, "Birth Order and Self-esteem," discusses the influence of sex and birth order on the self-esteem of individual children, with interesting references to cultural and religious factors (Jewish influences, in particular).

5. R. E. Grinder (Ed.), *Studies in Adolescence* (New York: Macmillan, 1963), p. 175. B. M. Moore and W. H. Holtzman, *Tomorrow's Parents* (Austin, Tex.: University of Texas Press, 1965), p. 201.

6. "Are Only Children Happier?" Editorial comment in *Harper's Bazaar*, July 1979, p. 73. M. Pines, "Only Isn't Lonely (or Spoiled or Selfish)," *Psychology Today*, 15:3, 15–19.

7. Pines, "Only Isn't Lonely," p. 18.

8. *Ibid.*, p. 18.

9. *Ibid.*, p. 19.

10. *Ibid.*, p. 16. See also M. Pave, "One-Parent Pupils: A Troubled and Growing Minority," *Boston Globe*, July 29, 1980.

CHAPTER 7

1. Representative research on discipline, largely conducted during the 1960's, is summarized in such works as W. C. Becker, "Consequences of Different Kinds of Parental Discipline," in M. L. Hoffman and L. W. Hoffman (Eds.), *Review of Child Development Research*, Vol. 1 (New York: Russell Sage Foundation, 1964), pp. 169–208; M. L. Hoffman, "Childrearing Practices and Moral Development: Generalizations from Empirical Research," in D. Rogers (Ed.), *Readings in Child Psychology* (Belmont, Cal.: Brooks/Cole, 1969), pp. 174–184, and other writings.

    2. D. Baumrind, "Current Patterns of Parental Authority," *Developmental Psychology Monograph*, Part 2, 4:1 (1971). Baumrind identifies three attitudes toward discipline: the authoritarian, the authoritative, and the permissive; the advantages of the authoritative approach (democratic but structured by good adult leadership) are pointed out.

CHAPTER 8

1. R. Dreikurs, *Logical Consequences* (New York: Hawthorne Books, 1964) and other writings. For further useful comments on the family council and its uses, see Chapter 8, "The Family Meeting," in D. Dinkmeyer and G. D. McKay, *Systematic Training for Effective Parenting* (Circle Pines, Minn.: American Guidance Service, 1976), pp. 97–105.

    2. For an excellent and comprehensive discussion of all aspects of the subject, parents are referred to G. W. Weinstein, *Children and Money* (New York: Schocken Books, 1976), esp. pp. 14–15.

    3. S. Cole, "Send Our Children to Work?" *Psychology Today*, July 1980. Available as Reprint No. 50163. The article raises important questions.

    4. *The New York Times*, May 7, 1977, *Letters*.

    5. P. H. Mussen and N. Eisenberg-Berg, *Roots of Caring, Sharing, and Helping: The Development of Prosocial Behavior in Children* (San Francisco: Freeman, 1977), p. 103.

    6. *Ibid.*, p. 104.

    7. "TV's 'Disastrous' Impact on Children," *U.S. News and World Report*, January 19, 1981, pp. 43–45, esp. p. 45 (an interview with Neil Postman, Professor of Communication Arts and Sciences, New York University.)

    8. P. Mancusi, "Tuning in to TV's Effect on Studies," *Boston Globe*, November 10, 1980.

    9. "TV's 'Disastrous' Impact," p. 43.

CHAPTER 9

1. B. L. White, *The First Three Years of Life* (Englewood Cliffs, N.J.: Prentice-Hall, 1975), pp. 222–226.
2. See also J. W. Atkinson and J. O. Raynor, *Personality, Motivation and Achievement* (New York: Halstead Press/John Wiley, 1974, 1978).
3. A. H. Maslow, *Motivation and Personality* (New York: Harper, 1954), p. 207. A. Roe, "The Psychology of the Scientist," in H. Chiang and A. H. Maslow (Eds.), *The Healthy Personality: Readings* (New York: Van Nostrand-Reinhold, 1969), p. 98. D. E. Lavin, *The Prediction of Academic Performance* (New York: Russell Sage Foundation, 1965), p. 107.
4. J. V. Gilmore, "The Factor of Attention in Underachievement," *Journal of Education*, 150:3 (1968), 41–66.
5. J. M. Stalnaker, "Recognizing and Encouraging Talent," *American Psychologist*, 16 (1961), 518.
6. S. Coopersmith, *The Antecedents of Self-esteem* (San Francisco: Freeman, 1967), p. 55. J. V. Gilmore, *The Productive Personality* (San Francisco: Albion Publishing Co., 1974), pp. 65, 144.
7. D. Kipnis, *Character Structure and Impulsiveness* (New York: Academic Press, 1971). Gilmore, *The Productive Personality*, pp. 161–167.
8. J. P. Lynch, "Possible Relationships Between Father Absence and Impulsivity" (unpublished paper, Boston University School of Education, 1971).
9. J. V. Gilmore, *The Productive Personality*, p. 151.
10. E. D. Joseph, "Memory and Conflict," *Psychoanalytic Quarterly*, 35 (1966), 1–17.
11. D. E. Lavin, *The Prediction of Academic Performance*, p. 106.
12. J. V. Gilmore, *The Productive Personality*, pp. 150–151.
13. *Ibid.*, pp. 171 ff. Persistence is a well-known characteristic of high achievers.
14. *Ibid.*, p. 175, citing Knapp (1956) and MacKinnon (1962). Knapp found among college science majors a tendency to be clear and decisive; MacKinnon, who studied highly creative architects, found them demanding not only that problems be solved but that the solutions be "elegant."
15. *Ibid.*, pp. 144–149.
16. Personal communication from Professor John Papageorgiou, University of Massachusetts, Boston.
17. "Are Boys Better at Math?" *The New York Times*, December 7, 1980.
18. F. M. Hechinger, "What's Wrong with Math Textbooks?" *The New York Times, About Education*, April 21, 1981.
19. *Ibid.*
20. *Ibid.* See also S. S. Willoughby, *Teaching Mathematics: What Is Basic?* (Washington, D.C.: Council for Basic Education, 1981).
21. S. Tobias, "Beyond Math, a World is Waiting," *Boston Sunday Globe, Learning*, January 6, 1980.
22. *Ibid.* See also "Women in Math Findings Released," *Guidepost*, American Personnel and Guidance Association, 23: 1 (July 17, 1980), 12.

23. See also "The IQ Myth," broadcast over the CBS television network Tuesday, April 22, 1975. Available in transcript form from CBS.

24. C. Rose, "Why Gifted Children Need Your Help," *Parade*, January 25, 1981.

25. L. M. Terman, "The Discovery and Encouragement of Exceptional Talent," *American Psychologist*, 9: 6 (June 1954), 221–230, esp. p. 229. There are several follow-up studies of this important study, including M. H. Oden, "The Fulfillment of Promise: 40-Year Follow-up of the Terman Gifted Group," *Genetic Psychology Monographs*, 77: 1 (1968) 5–93.

26. W. B. Barbe, "A Study of the Family Background of the Gifted," in W. B. Barbe and J. S. Renzulli (Eds.), *Psychology and Education of the Gifted*, 2nd ed. (New York: Halsted Press/John Wiley, 1975), pp. 111–118.

27. C. Pincus, L. Elliott, and T. Schlachter, *The Roots of Success* (Englewood Cliffs, N.J.: Prentice-Hall, 1980), pp. 32–38. Among numerous other studies of talent and giftedness are J. W. Getzels and D. W. Jackson, *Creativity and Intelligence: Explorations with Gifted Students* (New York: John Wiley, 1962) and J. C. Stanley, W. C. George, and C. H. Solano (Eds.), *The Gifted and the Creative: A Fifty-Year Perspective* (Baltimore and London: Johns Hopkins University Press, 1977).

28. The following works, constituting a background for the present discussion, are representative current contributions to the complex field of learning disability: P. Schrag and D. Divoky, *The Myth of the Hyperactive Child* (New York: Pantheon Books, 1975); J. W. Lerner, *Children with Learning Disabilities: Theories, Diagnosis and Teaching Strategies* (Boston: Houghton Mifflin, 1971); S. Farnham-Diggory, *Learning Disabilities: A Psychological Perspective* (Cambridge, Mass.: Harvard University Press, 1978); H. E. Rie and E. D. Rie (Eds.), *Handbook of Minimal Brain Dysfunctions: A Critical View* (New York: Wiley–Interscience, 1980); H. R. Myklebust (Ed.), *Progress in Learning Disabilities*, Vol. 1 (New York and London: Grune and Stratton, 1968); W. M. Cruickshank, "Myths and Realities in Learning Disabilities," *Journal of Learning Disabilities*, 10: 1 (January 1977), pp. 51–54.

29. A. J. Harris, "A Reaction to Valtin's 'Dyslexia: Deficit in Reading or Deficit in Research?'" *Reading Research Quarterly*, XIV: 2(1978–1979), 223.

30. L. A. Sroufe and M. A. Stewart, "Treating Problem Children with Stimulant Drugs," *New England Journal of Medicine*, 289: 8 (1973), 408.

31. S. Hirsch and R. P. Anderson, "The Effects of Perceptual and Motor Training on Reading Achievement," *Learning Disability Quarterly*, 1: 1, Winter (1978), 178.

32. F. W. Owen et al (1971) as cited in Farnham-Diggory, *Learning Disabilities*, p. 36.

33. D. D. Deshler, "Issues Related to the Education of Learning-Disabled Adolescents," *Learning Disability Quarterly*, 1: 4 Fall (1978), 2.

34. L. Eisenberg, "Hyperkinetic Reactions," in J. D. Noshpitz (Ed.), *Basic Handbook of Child Psychiatry*, Vol. 2 (New York: Basic Books, 1979), p. 442. D. C. Renshaw, *The Hyperactive Child* (Chicago: Nelson-Hall, 1974), p. 80.

218 • Notes

CHAPTER 10

1. M. Hoffman, "Empathy, Its Development and Prosocial Implications,"
in H. E. Howe, Jr. (Ed.), *1977 Nebraska Symposium on Motivation*, Vol. 25
(Lincoln, Neb.: University of Nebraska Press, 1977), p. 202.

2. P. H. Mussen and N. Eisenberg-Berg, *Roots of Caring, Sharing,
and Helping: The Development of Prosocial Behavior in Children* (San Francisco: Freeman, 1977), pp. 71, 169.

3. Hoffman, "Empathy," p. 198.

4. *Ibid.*, p. 205.

5. J. M. Stalnaker, "Recognizing and Encouraging Talent," *American Psychologist*, 16 (1961), 513–522.

6. M. A. Lynch, "Use of the Gilmore Sentence Completion Test as a
Predictive Instrument in Relation to Academic Achievement in Certain
High School Students" (Master's thesis, Boston University School of Edu-
cation, 1960).

7. J. V. Gilmore, "A Study of the Noncognitive Factors in the
Academic Achievement of M.I.T. Freshmen in 1951" (unpublished paper,
1978).

8. J. V. Gilmore, *The Productive Personality* (San Francisco: Albion
Publishing Co., 1974), p. 95.

9. D. W. MacKinnon, "Creativity and Images of the Self," in R. W.
White (Ed.), *The Study of Lives* (New York: Atherton, 1963), pp. 262–278.

10. R. D. Cox, *Youth into Maturity: A Study of Men and Women in the
First Ten Years After College* (New York: Mental Health Materials Center,
1970), pp. 280–281.

11. A. Maslow, *Motivation and Personality* (New York: Harper,
1954), pp. 217–218.

12. J. Aronfreed, *Conduct and Conscience* (New York: Academic
Press, 1968).

13. F. Barron, *Creativity and Personal Freedom* (Princeton, N.J.: Van
Nostrand, 1968), p. 145.

14. Sometimes termed "logical consequences." See R. Dreikurs,
Logical Consequences (New York: Hawthorne Books, 1964) and other writings of Dr. Dreikurs.

15. A. Kirchheimer, "Boys Are Still Confused about Sex," *Boston
Globe, Living* section, February 20, 1980.

16. C. P. Maimquist, "Development from Thirteen to Sixteen
Years," in J. D. Noshpitz (Ed.), *Basic Handbook of Child Psychiatry*, Vol. 1
(New York: Basic Books, 1979), p. 211.

17. W. Bonime, "Masturbatory Fantasies and Personality Functioning," in J. H. Masserman (Ed.), *Dynamics of Deviant Sexuality* (New York:
Grune and Stratton, 1969), pp. 44–45.

18. A. Bandura and R. H. Walters, *Adolescent Aggression* (New York:
Ronald, 1959), p. 301.

19. R. A. Gardner, *Understanding Children* (New York: Jason Aron-
son, 1973), p. 117.

20. Bandura and Walters, *Adolescent Aggression*, pp. 85 ff.

21. W. A. Westley and N. B. Epstein, *The Silent Majority* (San Fran-

cisco: Jossey-Bass, 1969), pp. 6–7, 19, 54. In addition, a personal communication from Dr. Epstein.

22. *Phi Delta Kappan*, 59: 8 (April 1978), 577.

23. "Study Finds Top High-schoolers Are Conservative," *Boston Globe*, December 6, 1979. Reprinted from the Chicago *Sun-Times*.

24. A. M. Nicholi, Jr., "The Adolescent," in A. M. Nicholi, Jr. (Ed.), *The Harvard Guide to Modern Psychiatry* (Cambridge, Mass.: Belknap Press of Harvard University Press, 1978), p. 530.

25. *Ibid*. Dr. Nicholi is citing from Freud's paper, "On the Universal Tendency to Debasement in the Sphere of Love" (1912).

26. L. Johnston, *Drugs and American Youth: A Report from the Youth in Transition Project* (Ann Arbor, Mich.: Institute for Social Research, 1973), especially pp. 9–14.

27. "Pot Use Rising, Report Says," *Boston Herald-American*, April 19, 1979, citing HEW Secretary Joseph Califano (United Press International).

28. "THC vs. Marijuana," *Harvard Medical School Health Letter*, VI: 6 (1981), 5.

29. Statement made on the MacNeil-Lehrer Report television program, July 2, 1981, by the former director of the Drug Enforcement Administration. See also "Cocaine: Middle Class High," *Time*, 118: 1 (1981), 56–63.

30. "Marijuana Damaging to Lungs," *Boston Globe*, June 22, 1981. P. Mann, "Marijuana Alert II: More of the Grim Story," reprinted from the *Reader's Digest*, November 1980.

31. N. A. Pace, "About the Damage Marijuana Can Do," letter to *The New York Times*, May 16, 1977.

32. Pace, "About the Damage Marijuana Can Do." See also "Is Marijuana Really Harmless?" *Private Practice*, July 1977, pp. 41–42; A. Quindlen, "Teen-agers Call Illicit Drugs One of Life's Commonplaces," *The New York Times*, July 19, 1981; its sequel by R. Sullivan, "Surveys Find Youths Regard Illicit Drugs as Harmful," *The New York Times*, July 20, 1981; and P. Mann, "Marijuana Alert I: Brain and Sex Damage," reprinted from the *Reader's Digest*, December 1979.

33. Mann, "Marijuana Alert II." For a comprehensive survey of the entire marijuana problem, see M. Manatt, *Parents, Peers and Pot* (Washington, D.C.: U.S. Department of Health and Human Services, Public Health Service, Alcohol, Drug Abuse, and Mental Health Administration, 1979, 1980).

34. *Drug-taking in Youth* (Washington, D.C.: Bureau of Narcotics and Dangerous Drugs, U.S. Department of Justice, June 1969); "Dopers and Straights on Campus," *Human Behavior* 1:3 (May/June 1972), 50–51.

35. M. Klagsbrun, and D. I. Davis, "Substance Abuse and Family Interaction," *Family Process*, 16: 2 (June 1977), 151–154. See also *Drugs and American Youth*, pp. 88–122.

36. Sullivan, "Surveys Find Youths Regard Illicit Drugs as Harmful"; see also J. H. Rubin, "Teens' Use of Drugs Declining—U.S. Official," *Boston Globe*, July 28, 1981.

37. W. A. Kennedy, "A Multidimensional Study of Mathematically Gifted Adolescents," *Child Development*, 31 (1960), 655–666.

38. "Study Finds Top High-Schoolers Are Conservative."

39. J. Lewis, W. R. Beavers, J. T. Gossett, and V. A. Phillips, *No Single Thread*, (New York: Brunner/Mazel, 1976), p. 70.

40. Maslow, *Motivation and Personality*, p. 217.

41. D. W. MacKinnon, "The Nature and Nurture of Creative Talent," *American Psychologist*, 17 (1962), 484–495.

CHAPTER 11

1. F. Barron, *Creativity and Personal Freedom* (Princeton, N.J.: Van Nostrand, 1968), pp. 59–61. M. H. Oden, "The Fulfillment of Promise: 40-Year Follow-up of the Terman Gifted Group, *Genetic Psychology Monographs*, 77: 1 (1968), pp. 63, 70, 81, 91. M. Rosenberg, *Society and the Adolescent Self-image* (Princeton, N.J.: Princeton University Press, 1965), pp. 22 ff. S. Coopersmith, *The Antecedents of Self-esteem* (San Francisco: Freeman, 1967), pp. 132 ff.

2. The Landmark School, a private school in Massachusetts for learning-disabled children aged nine to eighteen, reports that 90 percent of their students (of whom 90 percent are boys) suffer from allergies. (Personal communication from the director, Dr. Drake.)

3. Early writings of this period include W. B. Cannon, *The Wisdom of the Body* (1932) and Flanders Dunbar, *Emotions and Bodily Changes* (1935). F. Alexander, *Psychosomatic Medicine* (New York: Norton, 1950); R. R. Grinker and F. P. Robbins, *Psychosomatic Case Book* (New York: Blakiston Co., 1954); T. Lidz, "General Concepts of Psychosomatic Medicine," in S. Arieti (Ed.), *American Handbook of Psychiatry*, Vol. 1 (New York: Basic Books, 1959), pp. 649–653; and W. W. Meissner, "Family Dynamics and Psychosomatic Process," *Family Process*, 5: 2 (September 1966), 150–152 are representative of the point of view toward psychosomatic ailments during the 1950's and 1960's. J. Arehart-Treichel, *Biotypes* (New York: Times Books, 1980) is a comprehensive and readable contemporary survey of the subject.

4. J. G. Kavanaugh, Jr., and A. Mattsson, "Psychophysiologic Disorders," in J. D. Noshpitz (Ed.), *Basic Handbook of Child Psychiatry*, Vol. 2 (New York: Basic Books, 1979), p. 349.

5. As reported by James Blackburn, a member of Clinical Practicum III, a graduate training course for parent educators conducted by Dr. Gilmore during the 1960's at Boston University School of Education.

6. Grinker and Robbins, *Psychosomatic Case Book*, pp. 191–196; J. Mayer, *Overweight* (Englewood Cliffs, N.J.: Prentice-Hall, 1968), pp. 84–99; and Kavanaugh and Mattsson, "Psychophysiologic Disorders," p. 373.

7. Arehart-Treichel, *Biotypes*, pp. 55–58; H. Tomä, *Anorexia Nervosa* (New York: International Universities Press, 1967), pp. 21–33, 235–277.

8. B. E. Baker, "The Effectiveness of Parent Counseling with Other Modalities in the Treatment of Children with Learning Disabilities" (doctoral dissertation, Boston University School of Education, 1970); J. V.

Gilmore, "The Effectiveness of Parent Counseling with Other Modalities in the Treatment of Children with Learning Disabilities (Baker's study)," *Journal of Education,* Boston University School of Education, 154: 1 (October 1971), 74–82.

9. T. F. Anders and E. D. Freeman, "Enuresis," in Noshpitz, *Basic Handbook,* Vol. 2, pp. 546–555.

10. The story of Ben was offered by our colleague, David H. Long, as an excellent illustration of the value of the Gilmore program in a specific instance. "Ben" is one of David's children and the story, as his father told it, is presented here with David Long's explicit permission.

11. Arehart-Treichel, *Biotypes,* pp. 63–72; H. J. Schneer, *The Asthmatic Child* (New York: Evanston and London: Harper & Row, 1963), pp. 39–57, 103–117; E. D. Wittkower and K. L. White, "Psychophysiologic Aspects of Respiratory Disorders," in Arieti, *American Handbook of Psychiatry,* Vol. 1, pp. 698–699.

12. Grinker and Robbins, *Psychosomatic Case Book,* pp. 267–272; E. D. Wittkower and B. Russell, *Emotional Factors in Skin Disease* (New York: Hoeber, 1953), pp. 164–176.

CHAPTER 12

1. E. H. Erikson, "The Problem of Ego Identity," *Journal of the American Psychoanalytic Association,* IV: 1 (1956), p. 74.

2. D. B. Lynn, *The Father: His Role in Child Development* (Monterey, Cal.: Brooks/Cole, 1974), p. 267.

3. *Ibid.,* p. 183.

4. M. Christy, "The Presidential Perspective at Radcliffe," *Boston Globe,* June 26, 1979, *Living* section, quoting Matina Horner.

5. Lynn, *The Father,* pp. 182–184.

6. E. Douvan and J. Adelson, *The Adolescent Experience* (New York: Wiley, 1966), pp. 72 ff.

7. A. Roe, "Crucial Life Experiences in the Development of Scientists," in E. P. Torrance (Ed.), *Talent and Education; Present Status and Future Directions* (Minneapolis: University of Minnesota Press, 1960), p. 71. (Papers presented at the 1958 Institute on Gifted Children.)

8. P. Coons, "Brookline Senior Takes Look at Three Careers," *Boston Globe, Extra Credit,* April 29, 1981. Steven Gordon has graciously permitted us to use his name and the facts in the *Globe* column.

9. NBC Nightly News, December 26, 1979, with John Chancellor summarizing job trends in the 1980's. "Careers in the 80's," *New York Times National Recruitment Survey,* Section 12, Sunday, October 14, 1979: Articles by T. C. Hayes, A. L. Goldman, and others.

10. S. Tobias, "Beyond Math, a World is Waiting," *Boston Sunday Globe, Learning,* January 6, 1980.

INDEX

Accident-proneness, 62
Acne, 194–196, 197
"Adam," 18, 21–23, 27, 28, 30, 121, 199
Adolescence, 57–59
  acne in, 194–96, 197
  confused identity in, 59–66
  Continuous, Surgent, and Tumultuous growth groups in, 58–60
  late maturity in, 58, 64
  physical contact of parents with children in, 35
  preoccupation with personal appearance in, 61
  sexual development in, 171–72
Affection, *see* Love
"Age of autonomy," 51
Age spacing and children's development, 73
Agenda for family councils, 100
Alcohol (*including* beer), 27, 65, 169, 176, 177, 181
Allowances, 97, 105, 106
Altruism, 161–63
Anorexia nervosa, 191
Anxiety
  confused identity and, 61–63
  discipline and, 95
  learning disability and, 151
  problem solving and, 123–27
Arithmetic, *see* Mathematics
Athletics, *see* Sports

Attention-getting devices of children, 114
Attention span, short, 124
Automobiles
  boring rides for children in, 91–92
  See also Family car

Babies
  empathic relationship with, 33–34
  identification process in, 50–51
  motivation to learn by, 121
  physical closeness essential for, 34–35
  problem solving by, 122
  tickling of, 40
Baby-sitting by eldest child, 75
Backpacking, 21
Bank accounts, 107, 136
Barbe, W. B., 146
Barrett, Elizabeth, 42
Barron, Frank, 163
Basic trust, 51, 54
Bedtime, individual attention to child at, 67–68
Beck, Joan, 1
Behavioral problems, *see* Discipline
Bensinger, Peter, 178
"Bert," 16, 21–29, 31
"Best Thing That I Did Today, The" (game), 44